A FORESTER IN THE SOLOMON ISLANDS

Diary and Letters – 1953 to 1958

A FORESTER IN THE SOLOMON ISLANDS

Diary and Letters – 1953 to 1958

Chris Hadley

The Book Guild Ltd
Sussex, England

To the Memory of all my friends,
foresters and mountaineers,
who died young.

The Book Guild Ltd.
25 High Street,
Lewes, Sussex.
First published 1991

Set in Baskerville
Typesetting by Kudos Graphics
Slinfold, West Sussex
Printed in Great Britain by
Antony Rowe Ltd.,
Chippenham, Wiltshire.

British Library Cataloguing in Publication Data
Hadley, Chris
A forester in the Solomon Islands: diary and letters 1953–1958
1. Solomon Islands. Social life – Biographies
I. Title
995. 930099

ISBN 0 86332 572 6

CONTENTS

The beginning, 19th September 1953.
Acknowledgement – this photo taken by my Uncle, Edgar Hadley, (died 1990).

INTRODUCTION

'Might suit someone interested in small boats and botany' said the letter from the Chief (and only) Forest Officer of the Solomon Islands, pinned to the notice board in the Oxford School of Forestry, advertising for an assistant.

It was my penultimate term and I had just been reading *Pattern of Islands*. Was it possible that I might go and live on a Pacific Island, like Grimble? Just one thing, though. My love for mountains. I wasn't going where there weren't any. So I read about the Solomons in an article by F. S. Walker, who had done a survey of their forests in 1945 and, yes, they were exceedingly mountainous; very different, therefore, from the Gilbert and Ellice Islands.

Only one more ingredient was needed, and on 1 May at the beginning of my final term I met her, at reel-club, where they do Scottish dancing on Friday night. This beautiful girl actually put up with me for well over twenty years, not only in the Solomons, but also in Africa and later in darkest England. Nothing lasts forever, though. Yes, the mixture seemed complete and I thought the job might indeed suit me. Sorry, us.

* * *

Darwin mentions Vanikoro (in the Solomon Islands) in *The voyage of the Beagle* as an example of an island with a barrier reef. It is fourteen miles long and its highest point, 3,000 feet above sea level, overlooks the rugged sister island of Tevai. The vegetation is forest, from the coastal mangroves, through montane tropical rain forest on the ridges to mossy forest on the mountain tops. Rainfall is twenty feet per annum at the coast, probably more inland, and there is no dry season. Santa Cruz Island, also known as Ndeni, is twenty-nine miles long and rises to 2,000 feet. It has no barrier reef.

Vanikoro has other music than the diapason of the reef: as we waken at dawn, the sweet liquid notes of golden whistlers singing a duet of many themes; at a midday halt by some rocky stream deep in the mountain forest, the shrill song of a cicada hidden in a tree overhead; at any time the low roar as a white wall of obliterating rain sweeps across the valley, turning babbling brooks to thunderous torrents and creating cascades in the gullies; and at night in our house when the moon is full, the orchestra of frogs, thousands of them, in the valley half a mile away, slowly building up to a crescendo, diminishing to almost nothing, then growing again, on, and on, and on. And the rich, organic smell of the reef at low tide; the aromatic distillation from sun-warmed jungle trees; the resin of fresh-cut wood; the sour smell of the red lateritic subsoil bared by diesel fuming bulldozers.

* * *

Minor alterations in the text were made where it seemed desirable, and a few additions were made from memory; otherwise the text substantially follows the original diary and letters. Since there are often several versions of each description or incident, I have had to strike a balance between omitting some or having a degree of repetition. This makes it less readable than it would be if written as a continuous narrative, but I have kept this form here in the interest of authenticity.

NOTE TO READERS

Letters are preceded by the date. The appendix where the letters are listed also show the letter serial number. Diary entries are preceded by the date only.

The main recipient of the letters was Aunt Erica, who brought me up as a child, since my mother had died and my father had gone to South Africa. I also sent letters to her sisters Muriel (Mu) and Phyl, and mentioned their brother, Ted, my uncle. Their other brothers were Harold, Edgar, Walter and Cyril, who was killed in the battle of the Somme.

When I was five my father (Geoff) returned and later married my stepmother, Tiggie. She and her sister Vera were born in South Africa and their father Dr Henry Taylor wrote *Doctor to Basuto, Boer and Briton,* describing their life in Basutoland and Orange Free State between 1877 and 1906.

Tiggie also wrote and illustrated a children's book, *Uzz, Fuzz and Buzz* and contributed to *The Merry-Go-Round* under the pseudonym of Tinker Taylor.

The designations of the survey strips are given for completeness. The main ridges descending from the centre of the island are given by a Roman capital number eg II. The second figure refers to the number of chains along the ridge from a zero post (1 chain = 22 yards). The third figure is the compass bearing of the strip in degrees. Eg II.xx.173. The situation is further complicated by subsidiary ridges.

Explanatory notes on forestry surveying are given at the back of the book.

You will find here the records of many survey trips in the mountain forests of the Santa Cruz islands and Guadalcanal. We went where few people and probably no Europeans had been before and they may give an impression of the country we saw. Those who find them boring can skip them.

Acknowledgements to the Dowdeswell Woods Song by Sam Wright, 1952, and to the original Old Trinidad (Appendix 2, page 310).

WESTERN PACIFIC HIGH COMMISSION.
HONIARA.
BRITISH SOLOMON ISLANDS PROTECTORATE.

No. 406/PF.1235

29 December, 1953.

Sir,

I am directed to inform you that you have been appointed to the Colonial Service on probation as an Assistant Conservator of Forests for allocation as a Forestry Officer in the British Solomon Islands Protectorate on the terms and conditions embodied in Colonial Office letter CDE/P/1357 of 14th August, 1953, addressed to you.

2. Your appointment will take effect from 5th November, 1953, the date of your departure from the United Kingdom. Your initial salary will be £F600 per annum, proceeding to £F660 per annum on the 21st March, 1954, which will be your incremental date. Half salary will be payable for the period of your journey to the Protectorate.

3. You will be required to contribute at the prescribed rate to the Fiji Government Widows and Orphans' Pension Scheme.

I am,
Sir,
Your obedient servant,

R.D. Fairley

for Chief Secretary.

C.J. Hadley, Esq.,
HONIARA.

Letter of Appointment.

1953

5 November

The old P&O steamer *Maloja* crept slowly out from Tilbury on its last voyage to Australia before the scrap-heap. Gazing through the murk at the south bank we could already see the glow of a bonfire and the brave stab of an occasional rocket against the opaque November evening, for ten thousand Guys were being gaily martyred in as many back yards ashore as we slipped away from England for the Islands of the bright Pacific.

Warnings had not been lacking, from those who were in a position to know, of the material disadvantages and professional inadvisability of burying myself in a remote island outpost for four or five years. But the combined influence of R. M. Ballantyne, R. L. Stevenson, and Grimble was too strong. When the time came and the job was offered I had no more difficulty in making up my mind than a swallow in the autumn. And Claire, born and bred in India, and having gone to school within sight of the Himalayas, was ready for fresh horizons, and life in another tropical country.

10 November

Letter to Aunt Erica.

So far the voyage has been uneventful. The general aspect of the decks by day is that of Bournemouth beach on a bank holiday, and it's all a bit too much like a Butlin camp to be altogether to my liking. We've discovered that the best time is before breakfast, when few are about – to go and get our exercise by skipping. Also we've had a lot of fun taking photographs, and last night we turned our cabin into a darkroom to do our developing and printing. The snap is of the sun setting over the Bay of Biscay.

19 November

Letter to Aunt Erica.

The days are passing quickly now with reading and sun bathing, an occasional swim in the small swimming bath and looking out for strange birds.

The temperature after dark last night was 86 F and Claire and I tried sleeping on the fore-deck. We found the wind a bit too much in the end, though and retreated to our cabin.

Claire is already half-way through War and Peace. *We're well supplied with our own books but there's a library too.*

We enjoyed ourselves wandering round Algiers for a few hours. At Port Said we only had an evening, and had a job to escape the clutches of would-be guides and wander off by ourselves. It was exciting, there were policemen with rifles every hundred yards, so that when you got to where there weren't any, you wondered how safe you were!

The Suez Canal was interesting. In the Red Sea we saw no life for the first day or two. Then a wagtail came aboard, and a warbler of sorts.

5 December

Letter to Aunt Erica.

Ceylon looks a good place. Inland it is mountainous and looked a bit like North Wales or the Lakes from the distance. The shore is a sandy beach with palm trees, and canoes with outriggers come paddling around. As usual it requires the greatest determination to get away from the docks without a guide and to succeed in buying only what you want to buy. As it was, a Moslem succeeded in joining on to us at last, by appearing more disinterestedly friendly than most – but he was a nice chap and took us around by bus, showed us where to eat and took us a walk to see a Buddhist temple. The temple is lovely and cool inside, only thirty-five years old, with a large seated Buddha in the middle chamber, and a passage round it in which are other images and painted scenes from the scriptures, many of which are very reminiscent of Biblical scenes. Outside this was a verandah going all round, with little chapels leading off it. From it you could see all sorts of vegetation, including a large Bo tree nearby (Buddha was supposed to have received enlightenment under one).

We were shown round by a priest in an orange gown. Half the passengers from the SS Maloja *were there, having come by taxi, and the temple must have received a lot of money. Mahommet, our Moslem guide, said however that on the night of the full moon food was given away to the poor by the priests. He said that he was understudying to be a priest too, but at his temple there was nothing to see, no fee for seeing it, and nothing given to the poor.*

Before we met Mahommet we wandered around the Pettah (native Bazaar) – can you imagine what Moseley would be like if the shopkeepers called out at you to come inside, and the larger stores had agents for fetching you in from streets away. We got 'fetched in' to the Army & Navy stores that way, because Claire wanted a straw hat. They had one. We were then made to sit down and shown jewellery. A very clever salesman tried to sell us a nice ring, explaining that he was practically giving it away for our benefit, and so that we could tell our friends, and that we could get four times as much for it in England. He was quite hurt when we said 'thank you very much, but we don't want it' after about half an hour.

11 December

Letter to Aunt Erica.

Aden is certainly a wild sort of place. It is surrounded by rather striking rugged mountains, completely waterless of course. It is on a sort of peninsula, so that looking out to sea you are looking north and can see the mountains of Arabia hazy in the distance. The boat was soon surrounded by about a dozen little brown boys or youths (we were anchored some way out), and they dived for coins. The bird life consisted of large kites in great numbers, also vultures.

We've just had two days in Adelaide – we had an extra day because of a dockers' strike. It is nearer the equator than Algiers but it really was almost cold at times, although it is summer. The city was forty minutes away in a train. It's a nice place – the city is surrounded by a belt of park land which separates it from the suburbs (largely bungalows). From the city centre you can see the hills, about four miles away.

The first day we wandered round the zoo and saw some glorious little penguins. Also there was a European fallow deer in velvet which was very beautiful, and a Canadian wapiti likewise. But we were just as interested in the Australian birds which were not in cages, and went a walk in the hills yesterday to see the country. It is so like England in many ways - barbed wire along the country lane, and lots of notices 'Private Trespassers will be Prosecuted'. On the other hand the trees are mainly Eucalyptus, there is an occasional large 'sword-cactus' (probably Agave americana), *green and orange parakeets, the 'Murray magpie' or mudlark, which is coloured like a magpie but is obviously a wagtail, and other strange birds.*

We wandered off the lane towards a coombe in the hillside and in less than ten minutes we were covered in the seeds of a kind of Geum or Avens. It looked as if I'd got bristly leggings on and Claire had a fringe all round her skirt and in all sorts of uncomfortable places. Fortunately they were easily removed with a comb. There were lots of figs growing everywhere, but of course they're not ripe yet.

We have now heard that we are definitely flying from Sydney on 19 December via New Guinea, and arriving at Honiara on 21 December.

We were followed across the Australian Bight, which was calm, by dozens of large albatross.

13 December

Letter from Claire to Erica and Mu.

Today we went an hour's train journey out of Melbourne into the country, it turned out to be quite a civilized place (Fern Tree Gully) but we quickly got into the eucalyptus forest away from everybody. We took a picnic lunch with us and had a lovely time watching birds; among those we saw were two types of parrots, several kookaburras and different sorts of treecreepers. We also came across lots of sweet-smelling white violets.

We have had a very nice letter from Mr Logie giving us names of people to contact here and in Sydney. I expect Chris told you that the house is wooden and that there have been difficulties in getting repairs done, due to lack of transport to get materials and men there and back. We are also going to have the use of a refrigerator, run on paraffin, which will make a great difference to pleasant living.

Everything seems to be very expensive here, except I believe, woollen goods.

* * *

Six weeks after leaving London we disembarked at Sydney and two nights later we were peering from the cabin of a Skymaster as the lights of that city and the Harbour Bridge spun splendidly beneath us and we banked and headed North on the second leg of our journey for the wild and slightly sinister mountains of New Guinea.

We stopped briefly at Brisbane, then slept for some hours and when the dawn broke through a distant continent of cloud we were already descending over a silver mirror towards the first pile-built villages and the airfield at Port Moresby, where we stepped out into the early morning warmth of the tropics.

The backbone of New Guinea is a mountain range a thousand miles long, with snow peaks at its Western end. We now had to cross the Owen Stanley Range, the eastern end of this barrier, and soon the shadow of our plane was flitting across the forested hollows and interminable grassy ridges of the highlands. Very occasionally we would see a track leading to a cluster of two or three huts, incredibly isolated.

This was the beginning of Melanesia, a collection of archipelagoes that lies round the rim of the Pacific basin and ends in the Fiji Islands. Compared with the sparkling atolls of brown skinned Polynesians to the north and east, the forested islands and the people that live in them are dark, though to which the name is due nobody seems to know.

We were at Lae in time for lunch and next morning boarded the Dakota for Honiara, the capital of the British Solomon Islands. On the same plane were Dick Thompson and Phil Pudsey-Dawson, two geologists also going out for the first time to the Solomons. They had been with us ever since we left England on the *SS Maloja* and I first met them in the queue to sort out the dining room seating arrangements at the beginning of the voyage. There were these two chaps just in front, one dark and the other fair. They were talking to some girl and the dark one, later to be revealed as Dick, was saying,

'. . . Iceland last summer, with Nottingham University Expedition, and now I'm going to the Solomon Islands as a geologist.'

Surely, I thought, there could not be two Englishmen who, unknown to each other, had both been to Iceland at the same time and were now both going to the Solomons?

But it was so. When in Iceland we had heard stories of this expedition camped out on the ice-cap somewhere, and here was one of them!

Dick and Phil were going out to join the Senior Geologist, John Grover, and do a survey of the Solomons. Gold had already been found on Guadalcanal, and perhaps there was more of that or other minerals. When they were not camping in the bush these three bachelors were an important feature of Honiara social life, but they were most famous for their pith helmets.

Though the old-time deadliness of the tropical sun to the white man has long ago been debunked, there is no doubt that some degree of protection is a help, and John Grover believed, probably quite rightly, that the old pith helmet was an admirable invention and ideal for this purpose. Dick and Phil were advised accordingly, and the spectacle of pith helmets in triplicate driving around in the Geological Department land-rover was one of the features of Honiara. I do not remember seeing any other specimens of this type of headgear during my time in the Pacific.

For myself, to be on the safe side, I had bought a splendid Australian cow-boy hat while in Sydney. It had a large brim and cost five pounds and probably looked far more extra-ordinary than the pith helmets. It was not a great deal of help either, as the chief use of a hat in the jungle is to keep the rain off and when it is not doing that it is better to stuff it in your rucksack. Being stuffed in my rucksack did not improve my felt one much.

Immediately after Lae we touched down at Finschhafen, then crossed the sound to the long island of New Britain and followed its jungle covered mountains until we came in low over the crater of an extinct volcano to land at Rabaul about midday. Then we crossed the tip of New Ireland and headed out to sea for Bougainville, a large island that is geographically part of the Solomon Islands, but is administered by Australia as part of the Territory of Papua and New Guinea as are New Britain and New Ireland.

And beneath the surface of the wrinkled sea that crawled below us, somewhere beyond our starboard wing-tip, lay the Planet Deep, a mysterious canyon several hundred feet greater in depth than Mount Everest is high.

After Bougainville we were flying along the chain of the Solomon Islands proper, and the shapes of coral reefs shone up through the turquoise sea, fascinating in the abundance of hidden life which I knew they supported, and the airstrips at which we landed were hemmed in on either side by plantations of coconut trees.

Now the rugged mountains at the Western end of Guadalcanal were beneath our wing-tip, the omnipresent rain forest that stretches down from South-East Asia to the Pacific struggling up to their summits. Then as we left these behind there were more and bigger mountains far away to the south and beneath us lay the coastal plain with scattered wrecks rusting along the beaches, relics of the bloody naval battles in which the Americans turned the tide of the Japanese advance in the Second World War.

At Honiara airport we were met by John Logie, the Chief Forest Officer, and the two Forest Rangers Alec Naqu (pronounced Nangoo) and Silas Ronoe, who had both been trained in Fiji.

Naqu was from the Western Solomons; he had a fine build, a military moustache, a flashing white grin and a good command of English. Silas also spoke good English and was the epitome of solid dependability and the expert on running forest nurseries, which he did at Honiara and later at Vanikoro.

The Logies' house was of the older vintage, built on piles against the hillside and looking out across the sea to Nggela, also called Florida, and the volcanic island of Savo. We stayed there with John and Elizabeth and their three children, Ann, Fiona and Miles, for six weeks until the Marine Department could provide us with a boat to take us to our final destination.

1954

1 January

The Logie's were at the Government House party last night till 2 pm so the day began a little late. A rain squall then interrupted our start, but Claire and I at last set off along the road to the dam. Sheltered again in a Nissen hut. Then we paddled very pleasantly along a stream, very clear, with fish, crabs and prawn-like creatures, until we reached the very small reservoir, in rather a pretty spot in the jungle.

3 January

Claire and I set off at about 10.30 am equipped for a day in the jungle, I with boots and gaiters, she with shorts and my small hat. Some heavy rain, sheltered in hut. Over yesterday's return route and then plunged into jungle heading SW towards a grassy hill apparently quite near – both having good sticks cut from the jungle. No paths, practically every yard had to be beaten and slashed. Down steeply, across a stream, up and along a ridge, then off to the right and into a bamboo thicket whence we emerged on the grass after what seemed like two hours. Lunch on top. Views inland limited by cloud.

4 January

Made enquiries at the customs office about getting our luggage cleared. Then spent most of the rest of the morning testing Isaac, an applicant for the job of clerk-cum-ranger, in typewriting and arithmetic. A good time was had by all. Also walked over to see District Commissioner Central about Gorosi (Dudley) who they want as juryman (or something) on Wednesday.

4 January

Letter to Aunt Erica.

The fortnightly plane arrived this afternoon and will leave tomorrow. The Logies are youngish and nice, with two little girls and a boy-toddler. The house is on a bit of a hill surrounded by trees, and one can see and hear the Pacific and see the islands of Nggela (Florida) and Savo, dark with jungle in the distance.

Much of the time so far I've been in the little wooden office down by the sea, but I've also been at the forest nursery and spent a couple of days planting trees in an area up on a hillside surrounded by jungle. There are still some Japanese bones there, where there was a skirmish in the war.

Few people swim here, but Claire and I have been swimming twice off a bit of coral reef nearby. The water is just about the right degree of coolness and the sun beats on your back. Where the coral ends it is a lovely deep blue colour, and you float off with caution and your eyes wide open in case of sharks. In Vanikoro I believe bathing is more popular.

Few people seem to get out into the bush here, just as few people in Moseley get as far as Weatheroak. Claire and I went out yesterday and aimed for a hill to reach which we had to cross about half a mile of trackless jungle. We had to slash and beat with sticks practically every yard of the way, and go entirely by compass. We found ourselves going up and down steep ridges, along stream beds and visibility was rarely more than about ten yards. We got there all right, and came back by a different route just about as difficult, but it was good fun and experience. I doubt if anyone had been there for years. I've also been out sailing in a small boat with Mr Logie and Brian Twomey the owner, a couple of times.

The Forest staff is about a dozen. The head ranger, Naqu (pronounced Nangu), is a very nice chap; he was born on an island away to the North, and had a three year forestry course at Fiji. He can also type and is a useful clerk. I have seen him make fire by rubbing two sticks together to light a cigarette.

A few days ago I had to see a boy who refused to work when the ranger, Dudley, told him to. Poku was silent and wouldn't say anything until I stood close to him and asked him if he wanted to stay working here, and then he smiled, and in the end promised to do what he was told in future and said he was sorry to Dudley. Next day, Dudley gave notice, but I don't know if there was any connection at all.

One of John Logie's house boys called Samuel wants to come with us to Vanikoro and I expect he will.

5 January

Got firearms certificate from police station and income tax office – cost 1s. 6d. Finished timber identification card key. Read some interesting files documents on Vanikoro and forest management and policy. Heavy rain in the afternoon. John busy next door with Brian while I tried using the key on timber specimens – no luck at first, but improved with practice.

6 January

Looked like rain to the West in the morning, but didn't much. Sent off a telegram to McIlrath's about sending invoice by next plane. Out to the plantation with Gabriel, Isaac and five men, cutting grass and fire lanes.

Dealt with customs and was taken down to shed by Geoff Dennis with Naqu and two of his boys – found luggage. Sent others back as too much to move today, and sorted it with Naqu.

Read *No Picnic on Mount Kenya.*

7 January

Other Isaac, John, Sali and Poku turned up shortly with trees for planting, brought in a truck by Mr Logie who went back.

Organized the planting up top, a lot of it in mounds owing to high water table, while Naqu put in some teak by the road. Poku and Sali planted the little *Cupressus lusitanica,* some forty-five of them, on a slightly rocky slope in the corner.

Trees all planted and the party ended with a glorious grass cutting session. A good day, nice people to work with, sun and rain, and a good job done, I hope.

8 January

Fifteen cases containing our personal effects and three months' supply of groceries lay at Point Cruz, where they had been unloaded. Something had to be done about getting them under cover and the PWD had very kindly agreed to send a lorry and take them to their store.

At the appointed time I made my way to the wharf and sat on a box, enjoying the play of early morning sunlight on the water. Ten minutes later a tip-up lorry with PWD painted on the door came round the corner, a crew of grinning Solomon Islanders in the back. We exchanged waves, then they drove on, and vanished among the coconut palms of Point Cruz. Half an hour later they came roaring back with a load of sand. Meanwhile another lorry had gone in the same direction.

Now I began seriously to reflect. This was, after all, an Outpost of Empire, and not England. One did not expect to be spoon-fed in the Outposts. What if the PWD officer had simply assumed that I would have enough initiative to commandeer one of the lorries that were passing all the time? I visualized the scene when I went to complain that the lorry had not come:

'Didn't send a lorry! But I've been sending lorries to Point Cruz all day! Do you think I've got time to send one with your name painted on it or something?' With a shaking hand he mops his brow. 'These chaps they're sending out nowadays, I don't know what England is coming to.' He sighs rather sadly. 'No, I really don't know!'

So the next time a lorry came by I stepped out and stopped it, addressing the driver in halting Pidgin English:

'Mifella wantim youfella takim altogether bokis blong mi

long PWD this time.'

It worked. In five minutes flat they had loaded the lot and we were on our way to the store.

It was a very surprised Jock Vincent who saw one of his sand lorries arriving piled high with packing cases, but he was very polite and kind and he made no comment until they were safely stowed away in the store and the lorry was on its way back to Point Cruz. Then he said, in his mild way,

'Of course you shouldn't really have taken that lorry you know, but on the other hand it is undoubtedly the way to get things done in the Solomons and if you keep it up you should go far.'

9 January

Got a lift out to plantation in John Grover's Morris. Met Naqu and Isaac, and completed the job of recording the position of all species planted, which they had started yesterday. Fine morning, strong sun. Planted two Kauris which had been forgotten. Then went to see Naqu's garden nearby and was introduced to various edible plants, cultivated and otherwise, including palm shoots, *Spondias dulcis* and others.

10 January

After lunch there was a very striking mushroom-shaped cloud, of presumably enormous proportions, to the north-east. It vanished in an hour or two.

11 January

Went to the Marine Department and found that I can probably send most of our heavy baggage to Vanikoro on Thursday in the *Mary*. Then had a session with Peter Flynn at the Treasury, learning what an imprest is, and how to collect revenue.

I learnt that a moth had been called after Paul Huggins,

who found it in the Himalyas in 1951. Also Naqu says there may be pygmies on Vanikoro!

15 January

Drawing out diagrams to show manufacturer's desired pattern for Vanikoro rubber stamps. Then out to nursery, sunny. Fewer *Pinus carribea* now, owing to damping off, remainder ready for planting out. Large young Gmelina waiting for removal as shade trees. Young Kauris eaten by goats.

16 January

Asked John if Naqu could come to Vanikoro. 'No' at first, but then came a telegram from DC Eastern telling John there would be no boat back for him from Vanikoro. So Naqu is to go with us and wait two to four months for the next boat back. He will be a great help to me and is keen to go, and would even prefer to go permanently. His wife and family will be sent to their home in the West to start a garden.

Discussed how to do the enumeration (see back of book). No statistics possible, which simplifies things a bit. General idea: strip enumerations at right angles to base lines along the ridges which are tied up to fixed points on the coast, eg river mouths, as being the only features accurately mapped by the Admiralty.

Most of the government offices were ex US army huts, and the Forest Office was one of the more dilapidated of these, with a decaying grass roof. We shared the building with the Lands Department, which consisted of Brian Twomey from South Africa and Geoff Dennis, a wiry Australian, who was a keen jungle walker and collector of specimens.

It was through Geoff that we got our introduction to the Solomon Islands' jungle. On those early trips we followed trails up heart-break hill-sides and down slithery slopes through the steaming forest while high overhead huge hornbills launched themselves from the tree-tops, the beat of their wings like the sudden starting spasms of an ancient locomotive. When, as often happened, we were all soaked to the skin in a downpour, it was pleasantly refreshing rather than otherwise.

These Pacific jungles are extremely safe and, on the whole, comfortable to live in. For as you go further away from the mainland of South-East Asia and as the islands become smaller, the number of species of animals and plants becomes smaller too. There are no beasts of prey and I never met anyone who had trouble with leeches. On Guadalcanal there is a poisonous snake, but on the smaller islands further East where I spent most of my time it is not found.

17 January

One Sunday morning Geoff collected us at 8.30 in his Austin pick-up. We started walking just beyond the Roman Catholic Mission and followed the path along the left bank of the Mataniko River passing two or three villages, the houses built on piles, the walls and roofs of woven leaf.

After about a mile we took to the river-bed, so often the line of least resistance through the jungle in these islands. When the shingle bank we were following came to an end we would have to swim a deep pool.

Red-barked Syzigium trees overhung the bank and shed their long stamened white flowers into the water and overhead companies of green parakeets with flashes of crimson under the wing yammered noisily away. Lower down, pied fantails watched our progress from the branches and ahead we put up flights of sandpipers and once a couple of Australian grey duck.

Claire had borrowed a pair of old gym-shoes from Geoff and now the uppers of one gave out and had to be fixed with string, then the other went the same way and they both had to be jettisoned.

Soon we came into a deep gorge, hemmed in by cliffs on both sides. We were only half a mile from our destination but the rest of the way we had to swim. As we launched out into the first hundred yard stretch of dark water we remembered that this river was said to have been infested with crocodiles before the war – we hoped the story was true that the

American forces had exterminated them for target practice at week-ends.

It was not true, however, for next Thursday I met Dick Thompson on his way back from surveying this gorge, and he had seen a croc just here!

At the end of the gorge we climbed up past a waterfall to a large cave, full of huge stalactites, from which the river emerged. We found a flat place in the sun to eat our sopping sandwiches, which we supplemented with the pith, cut by Geoff from the middle of small palm trees. This contains carbohydrate and provides 'something to chaw on.'

Close to our picnic spot, water trickling over flat rocks was being evaporated by the heat of the sun. On these rocks deposits of calcium carbonate had had the effect of making small dams. In the tiny reservoirs so formed, fallen leaves were being encrusted with the crystals and were thus being fossilized as we watched!

Refreshed, we plunged into the clear water, pale blue in the sunlight, and swam easily down with the current between steep green walls of rock and forest. The swimming part over, I had to carry a shoeless Claire on my back much of the way home!

When we got home we had an hour to get changed and be at a party (obligatory for all government officers) being held on a frigate in the bay. The hitherto clear sky was now marred by one black cloud just out to sea, and the downpour came as we were being rowed out to the ship in our party rig. It was odd how, after being cheerfully wet all day, one resented the final sousing. As we stood at last under the awning on deck surrounded by scores of complete strangers, we failed to raise any interest in the proceedings and stood solemnly chatting to each other. A senior officer came by.

'That's not the way to get on,' he said. 'You should circulate, get to know people!'

He was probably right, but we were just too darned sleepy!

Much time, inevitably, had to be spent in the office, and it was a pleasant change when I was told to go and supervise labour on an experimental plantation on a grassy hill-top surrounded by jungle just out of town.

Naqu was there, and we stood together on the very summit of the hill, where a few old bones and bits of boot, in addition to the usual war-time ironmongery, brought the last moments of the invaders vividly to the imagination.

'Excuse me sir, do you mind if I have a smoke?' asked Naqu.

'Go ahead.'

I accompanied him to the edge of the clearing, where he carefully selected two bits of wood, one flattish and the other pointed. Holding the flat bit firmly with his bare toes he rubbed the other with maximum energy up and down it so that a groove was formed which soon began to char, and then ignited. He lit his cigarette.

But most people, even in the Solomons, use a match.

19 January

Rather overcast today. Overhauled the steel measuring tape and made a list of field equipment being taken to Vanikoro. Saw a large scale map of the island as surveyed by D'Urville in about 1829.

Sir Geoffrey Clay, Agricultural Adviser to the Secretary of State, came to have a talk with Mr Logie about 4 pm. He arrived from England on last night's plane. I stayed to be introduced and then went off. Sir Geoffrey is a big, weatherbeaten looking man with a suggestion of a North country accent. In the evening I was reading *Madame Curie* by Eve Curie. A fascinating story and stimulating. It turns my own mind towards research. Perhaps I shall be able to do some interesting experiments in growing trees on Vanikoro; there must be all sorts of opportunities, if only I can hit upon something really worth while.

20 January

Reading *Problems in Tree Nutrition* between interruptions. In the afternoon I was shown how to install a lavatory etc, as a plumber cannot be got for Vanikoro.

* * *

21 January

Made out a requisition form for water pipes. Revised about colloids in Tansley botany textbook. Thought about the microscopic worlds of which our world is made up . . . Went off with Naqu along the Mataniko in the afternoon and got specimens of 'Taura' and 'Tolle' (native names told us in the village). The former the orangy barked river bank species with white flowers which we saw on Sunday, the latter Naqu's 'Kaudama' from Fiji, the shoots of which are good to eat, especially for pregnant women. Quite a few native families about, looking for snails and picnicking. Met Dick Thompson on his way back from surveying up the gorge, he says they saw a crocodile in the gorge where we were on Sunday!

22 January

Identified 'Taura' as *Syzigium Walkeri* and 'Tolle', doubtfully, as *Myristica castanaefolia*. Put some flowers of the former in a bottle with formalin.

Walked out by myself to the plantation to have a look at how things were growing, or not. Of the fifty *Cupressus lusitanica* we planted, twenty-one have survived, the rest dying apparently from drought. The Kauri, most of the *Calophyllum*, Vitex and teak are OK, some of the *Pometia pinnata* (Polynesian plum) is dead. Looked at the flower of 'pawpawndalla' (*Passifloraceae*), a most beautiful little flower. Found out about paint required and made out a requisition. Then looked at Hutchinson's Families of Flowering Plants.

24 January

By the sea in the afternoon, calm and peaceful, the mountain looking very clear. The geologists arrived for a swim. Later I borrowed a pair of flippers and their mask and went for a swim round the reef. The difference a mask makes is tremendous. It was most exciting. So many fish, and so wonderful to be able to see the coral distinctly, and any possible danger. And the flippers make swimming so effortless. Watching the scenery go by is like watching a colour film.

25 January

Looked at wood specimens acquired last week, found that *Myristica castanaefolia* fits in more or less exactly with the structure described for *M. Kajewski*. Also observed minute ants on the wood, and larger soldiers and winged forms emerging from a hole in the wood.

Overcast; set out for the reef after tea where I initiated Claire into the use of face-mask, flippers and snorkel. We both saw lots of fish: 1: three to four inches long, many coloured longitudinal stripes. 2: Two to three inches long, vertical black and orange-yellow bands, dallying among the tentacles of a white anemone and then drifting free again. 3: Carp-like, eighteen inches long, irridescent green on back of tail. 4: Four to five feet long, about twenty feet away, probably a small shark. Saw many more fish of all descriptions. Started going down to about fifteen feet, where the pressure was noticeable very quickly.

Shrike-like perching-bird; grey above, white beneath, black eye patch. Seen several times around Honiara. Also small heron-like bird seen in flight from the beach, probably a reef heron.

26 January

Continued collecting things together, gym shoes, meths etc from Trade Scheme, and packing things in the store, with the help of Naqu and Isaac. Lesson in graphical adjustment of closing errors. Also taught Naqu about fractions, and both of them about atomic structure and electrolysis. They were very eager to learn.

29 January

Lessons on how to check a chain and compass survey by

triangulation, by Brian Twomey. Provisional map of Vanikoro now completed and four prints given to me. Logie tells me I am to be a 'Deputy Commissioner with limitations' and power to perform Native marriages!

30 January

Mr Logie off early taking Sir Geoffrey Clay round Tenaru Timbers. Later on I got a lift out to the nursery in the geologists' land rover to collect a tree, and had a look round with Nelson.

1 February

Isaac has decided he doesn't want to be cut off from his father and therefore will not come to Vanikoro and incidentally has to leave the department in consequence. Trip out to the nursery to tell Nelson that he will be coming instead. Meanwhile many odd jobs to do. Called at Chinatown on the way back and got a brace and bits on requisition. Rained in the afternoon. Got eleven books from the library to take with us.

On the way to post letter, about nine pm, heard a feverish gibbering noise in a tree top. Torch beam revealed two pairs of red eyes, which apparently belonged to large bats with a wing-span of eighteen inches. They flew out when I clapped.

2 February

Nelson, who comes from the island of Malaita, told me that in his language the name of the Pleiades is Huni aro-aro. Literally this means a group of trees close together.

3 February

Preparations reached their climax on the day before our departure. At last we heard that the motor vessel *Betua* was

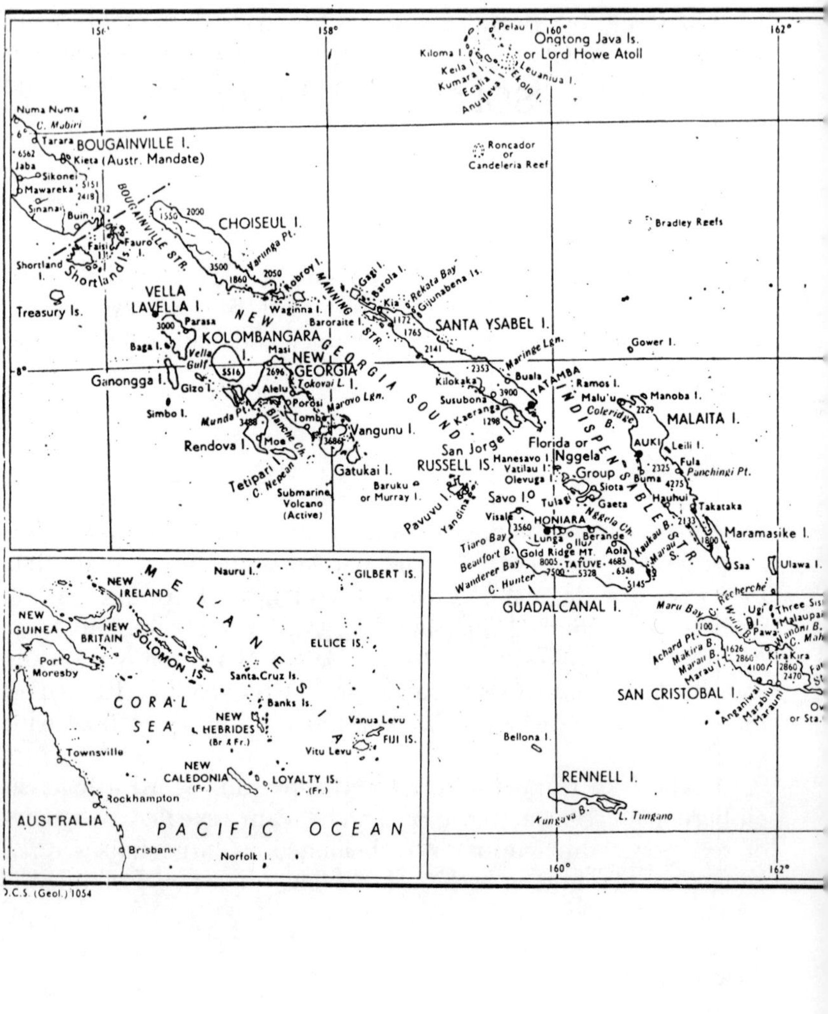

D.C.S. (Geol.) 1054

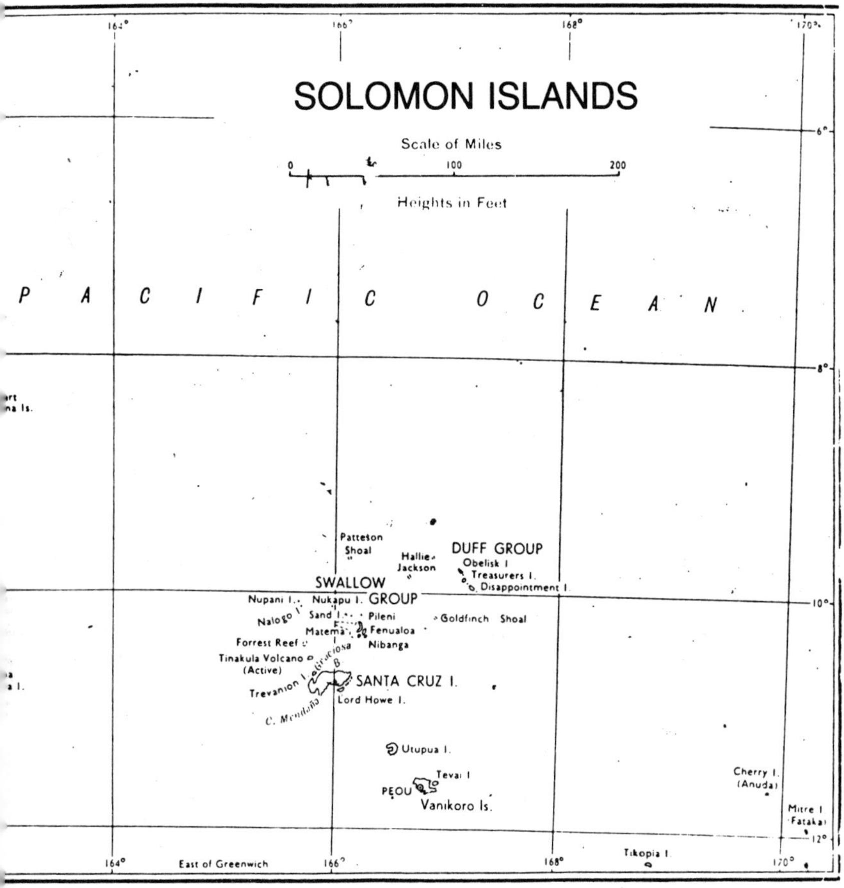
SOLOMON ISLANDS
Scale of Miles
0
100
200
Heights in Feet
P A C I F I C O C E A N
164°
166°
168°
170°
6°
8°
10°
12°
Patteson Shoal
Hallie Jackson
DUFF GROUP
Obelisk I.
Treasurers I.
Disappointment I.
SWALLOW GROUP
Nupani I.
Nukapu I.
Nalogo I.
Sand I.
Pileni
Goldfinch Shoal
Matema
Fenualoa
Forrest Reef
Nibanga
Tinakula Volcano (Active)
Graciosa B.
Trevanion I.
SANTA CRUZ I.
Lord Howe I.
C. Mendaña
Utupua I.
Tevai I.
PEOU
Vanikoro Is.
Cherry I. (Anuda)
Mitre I. (Fataka)
Tikopia I.
East of Greenwich

on its way across the sound from Tulagi harbour, on Nggela, to pick us up and everything had to be ready for sailing at five am next day.

First I had to borrow a PWD lorry to get some water piping and take it to the workshop to have it cut into shorter lengths before it could be fitted into the ship. Then there was a search for Naqu and our house-boy Selwyn, who had mysteriously disappeared, to tell them the news, which it turned out they had heard on the grape-vine anyway.

Food had to be bought for the voyage, bills paid, and the ammunition box and padlock, which was to be my safe, collected. There was an imprest cheque for £400 waiting for me at the Treasury which I duly signed for and cashed at the bank. The money was safely transferred to the box which was locked with the self-locking padlock. But on checking, the key was nowhere to be found. It had, obviously, crept into the box with the cash!

After a bad ten minutes I was just off to look for a hack-saw when Naqu miraculously found the key in the grass!

Meanwhile three lorries were busy loading and by tea-time it was over with nothing left to do but say our goodbyes and row peacefully aboard at nine pm, ready for an early start next morning.

Secretly, I had hoped to travel between islands in a shapely schooner and I was disappointed. The Government fleet were mostly of the same build: a broad, rounded, clinker-built hull with a square stern; a large flat-topped superstructure aft of the single hold, containing several cabins and a galley; tables and chairs on top of the superstructure, with a wide awning to keep out the sun; and several tons of pig-iron in the bilge to keep the ship the right way up. Diesel engines provided the power, but a solitary mast forward sometimes wore a sail in order to hinder a little the perpetual, metronome-like roll. (See illus. 2 Feb. 55.)

The general top-heavy effect was reminiscent of a Spanish galleon, like an unconscious tribute to Mendana, who discovered the islands at the end of the sixteenth century.

At dawn the mountains of Eastern Guadalcanal were to starboard, and we breakfasted with a bearded New Zealander on the way back to his mission on San Cristoval. At length we reached Marau Sound, a narrow stretch of water protected from the ocean by a long, low island, and dropped our anchor by a copra station. We had supper with Mr and Mrs Hay, who ran it and as we rowed back to the ship that night the water was gleaming with phosphorescence.

Next morning the sea was mirror calm as we left Marau Sound and far away on the starboard bow was the dim outline of San Cristoval, on which was our destination for that night, Kira-Kira.

This was the Government station for the Eastern Solomons, including the Santa Cruz Group two hundred miles away to the East, where John Bartle was the District Commissioner. We brought the mail ashore in the dinghy through the surf, there being no proper anchorage, and had supper with Mrs Bartle. Then we took back with us a large carton for John full of pineapples, pawpaws and grapefruits from the large tree by his house.

At four am we up-anchored and slid down the coast. Here and there the line of the mangroves would be interrupted by a few leaf houses and a neat coconut plantation, but behind the coast ridge after ridge of jungle swept darkly up to the uninhabited mountains of the interior.

We dropped the missionary at Wanoni, then anchored off Star Harbour at midday, where I swam through clear water to the abruptly shelving beach and made my first acquaintance with the small, grey, yellow-legged reef-heron that haunts these shores.

Now we left the true Solomons behind us and turned our bows into the heaving waste of the open Pacific and, rolling horribly, began the thirty-hour passage to the Santa Cruz Group.

I remember particularly next morning when a queasy stomach drove me on deck before the stars had paled and I wedged myself up in the bows between capstan and bulwark while the wind blew the sickness out of me, and the Scorpion burned and swung aloft. Then, as it faded and the steadfast eye of Venus hung beyond the emerald atmosphere, a point of fire shone sudden athwart the inky horizon and the sun came, seeming to my feeble eyes to quiver while resting a moment on the hard rim and sending its rays to slash with crimson each foaming crest, before climbing into a vapourous, windy, tabernacle.

7 February

With the sun came dolphins, splendid creatures of utter loveliness, racing and sporting with each other and with the ship for the sheer fun of it. A deep indigo gleam far, far below takes shape and colour as it rushes up towards you, finally leaping a fathom into the air in a rush of sound blending with the play of wave and ship. An hour they flashed and gambolled around us, until we entered into their mood and laughed aloud.

The sun was in the zenith when we sighted the cone of Tinakula, though its plume of smoke had been visible long before. This island volcano is regarded as the safety valve for the Group and there is a common belief that as long as it is smoking contentedly there is not too much danger of a serious earthquake.

Ndeni, as the main island is called, has several excellent anchorages, and it was to one of these, Graciosa Bay, that we were heading. On the relatively level land nearby, Mendana had made his disastrous attempt at colonisation, and here, on the blessedly still water between the bay and Trevanion Island, we saw the white galleon-shape of the motor vessel *Mary*, the floating headquarters of the DC. At anchor nearby lay a low grey launch, which we afterwards learnt belonged to the Vanikoro timber company. It left during the night.

8 February

Two white galleons now rested side by side in the clear water above the sand and the heads of coral. Much refreshed by a night's sleep I was rowed across to the *Mary* by two uniformed Solomon Islanders.

John Bartle, responsible for the peaceful administration of some scores of thousands of square miles of ocean and its islands sat impressively coping with affairs in pidgin English at his table under the awning. He started to put me in the picture and to give me my orders.

'There used to be a DO living in your house on Vanikoro before the war and the station was kept in good shape. Now it's all overgrown and the house is falling to bits, in fact it's a hell of a mess. Your main job is to get it all repaired and tidied up so that it looks like a Government Station again. Of course you won't be able to get it quite up to pre-war standard, because in the old days the prison was down there and there was plenty of free labour. I should think, anyway, you will need to employ six men for three months on the house and grounds and after that keep four men on maintenance.'

I thought of the typed sheet of foolscap I had from John Logie, my forestry instructions for one year; and I thought of my four hundred pounds, which would have to last for three or four months, until the next ship came.

'But I thought the idea was to use my six men on enumeration of the Kauri Pine and work on the house at week-ends.'

'You can't, man. You'll have to get the place into decent shape before you can live there and then see if you can fit in some forestry. Now I had better tell you about the set-up. There are two timber companies on Vanikoro. Ernie Haling, on the launch that was here yesterday, is the younger of the two brothers that run the Vanikoro Timber Company, which does the actual logging of the Kauri Pine. He was here recruiting labour, which is bad luck on you as he will have taken all the good ones. The other lot is the Kauri Timber Company. They have the concession and employ the Haling brothers as contractors. The manager is Mr MacEwin.'

'He's offered to put us up when we get there, and we're staying with him,' I said.

'H'm, yes. Well he is a great friend of Fred Jones, the trader, who has been out in the islands for years, and was running a store on Vanikoro long before the company came. He also has a small vessel and comes this way occasionally, trading in Green Snail and Trochus Shell (see back of book). Now the Company do quite a bit of that too, of course, and Mrs Haling runs a store. Fred Jones is an Englishman. So is Harry Chaperlin, who is the company's secretary, and keeps the office going. He's been out here most of the time since 1914. All the other Europeans on the island are Australian. Then there is a young couple about your own age, Keith and Dorothy Ward. He is the Engineer. All these people live at the settlement of Peou, just down the hill from your house.

Up in the bush there are a dozen or so Australians who drive the lorries and generally act as foremen. You'll soon get to know them.'

John then proceeded to give me the low-down on island politics, and ended by handing me a Government Telegraph Code book, urging me to keep him informed. There was a two-way radio at the meteorological station by Mr MacEwin's house.

The three main inhabited islands of the Santa Cruz Group are really the tops of three mountains, rising from a submarine range which is linked to the range of the New Hebrides beginning a hundred miles to the south.

Their names, from West to East, are Ndeni, Utupua, and Vanikoro, and it is eighty miles from the first to the last. All are rugged and covered in forest, with small populations confined to scattered villages at the coast.

Ndeni is the largest. Utupua is the smallest, and Vanikoro the highest, rising to three thousand feet above sea level. Ndeni has no barrier reef and a considerable part of the coast is rock-bound, but the other two islands are both almost completely surrounded by barriers of coral enclosing relatively sheltered lagoons with a good development of fringing reef and mangrove forest round the shore.

9 February

The barrier reef of Vanikoro was now under our port beam and we could hear the roar of breakers above the beat of our engines as Billy the bosun sought the passage into the lagoon. Two miles away fingers of mist clinging to the mountains showed where the forest was broken up into a multiplicity of ridges and outlined the rugged silhouettes of the hurricane-resisting Kauri Pines, while far away on one of the ridges a red scar showed where the timber company's road was pushing into the interior.

Safely anchored at last, we were rowed to the end of the long jetty, and walked along the trolley-way to the store at the end. The place seemed deserted. However there was no time to be lost as night was falling and our two plumbers, on loan from the PWD at Honiara, had to leave with the *Betua* next day, and must make a preliminary inspection of the lavatory in our house before getting to work in the morning. They were Polynesians, born on the island of Ticopia a hundred and twenty miles to the East of us.

So we found our way under the coconut trees to Fred Jones's store then turned inland into secondary forest for a quarter of a mile, and climbed the steps between the hibiscus bushes to our house two hundred feet above the sea. Later we returned to the settlement and met Mac as we crossed the foot-bridge over the Lawrence River to his house.

Mac shared a large bungalow built on piles close to the sea with half a dozen cats and their kittens. He was a 'Taswegian', whose ancestors originated from Shetland, and he knew as much about the sea as he did about timber. Besides being Manager he was Harbour Master and Customs Officer, and the latter duty I was now to share with him. For relaxation at week-ends he used to circumnavigate the island in his outboard-engined launch, a distance of some thirty miles or so.

Passenger vessels did not often enter the Protectorate through Vanikoro, but on one occasion when this happened Mac was invited aboard to a party and introduced as 'The Manager of the Timber Company'.

They stood there on the deck, watching the sun go down, and it was not long before a tycoon, finding Mac a sensible sort of chap, drew him over to the rail and muttered:

'Look here, you know the ropes in these islands, perhaps you can help me. I've got rather a lot of dutiable items in my baggage and naturally I don't want to pay more than I have to at Honiara.'

'Naturally.'

'So maybe you can tell me how I can, er, dodge the customs eh?'

But Mac made his excuses and slipped away. The Captain, who had overheard, came up.

'Did you know who that was you were speaking to?'

The tycoon sensed something from his tone. He looked worried.

'Surely, it was the Manager?' he said.

'Too right it was the Manager,' agreed the Captain, 'and around these parts the Manager is the Customs Officer, too!'

10 February

We woke next morning to the song of the Golden Whistler and a view of mountains rising steeply in golden sunlight beyond the palms. The path to our house was ablaze with pink hibiscus and yellow crotons and when we reached the garden after the long climb we turned and looked out beyond the white slash of the barrier reef to the immensity of the Pacific. Then we met Nati.

Nati was short for Nathaniel Siso, and he had been employed by the government before the war and had carried on as caretaker ever since.

He came and greeted us in English with an enormous grin, looking rather like a wizened boy scout in his ancient uniform.

No doubt he had saved our house from termites by his efforts in destroying their runways up the concrete piles on which the house stood, and it was not surprising that a few had gone undetected over the years, hidden away in darkness behind a couple of the many piles. These had provided the termites with a vital connection with the soil and the water it yielded, enabling them to get on with the work of eating part of our bathroom and store. But we were lucky it was not worse and after a few weeks' carpentry, replacement of the gutters and the bamboo shutters, and application of a few score gallons of paint, we had a comfortable home.

The verandah extended along the front and down one side, at the rear corner being partitioned off to make an insect-proof suite, sitting-room on the outside, bathroom and bedroom on the inside, where we spent the evenings. At the centre of the house was an enormous room which we used to eat in; the back verandah led from the bathroom to a small bedroom and the kitchen, which, with its adjacent store, formed a separate wing.

In the angle between the store and the back verandah was a raised wooden structure bearing six large water tanks, in an upper and a lower tier. From the corrugated iron roof, gleaming in a new coat of aluminium paint, the rain was fed into these tanks and thence to our taps.

The steps leading up to our front door in the middle of the

verandah is a good place to sit. The sea stretches from behind the big mango tree on the right to where the jungle mountains begin on the left. At the foot of the steps is a huge three-legged pot which we tell visitors was used for cooking missionaries in.

The morning sunlight streams through the spreading branches of the ancient Kauri Pine on to the level plot we call our lawn, gilding two massive lumps of black basalt which break its surface and being transmuted into a dozen different shades of green by as many different trees, dark mango to pale tree fern, restless in the trade-wind from the sparkling sea.

But a new sound intrudes above the rustle of the wind, a colder, starker sound. The impact of a billion rain-drops upon a million leaves. For a wall of white has blotted out the ridge across the valley and is slowly approaching, engulfing one tree after another. Soon our iron roof is joining in the mad crescendo and then the torrent is drumming into our half empty tanks. Within twenty minutes the chorus is swelled by the voice of our stream a hundred yards away and the boom of the fall where it leaps into the rocky gorge.

The old tractor track was a red gash in the jungle below our house and to the left. At this edge of the garden was a clump of what we in our ignorance, called 'sword cactus'. When we went to Tanganyika, years later, we learned it was sisal. Below it, the ground fell away in a ten foot cliff of the soft, purple, lateritic subsoil which is the decomposition product of the native basalt under humid tropical conditions. The stream, which emerged from the jungle above our house and formed the Eastern limit of our garden crossed the track just beyond this point and it was here that the gorge began. We called it 'Fern Tree Gully'.

The Solomon Islanders working for the Company had put in a pipe to carry some of the water out and give them a convenient shower-bath.

Above the track the stream was gentler and one day I built a dam across it using rocks as big as I could carry and sods of earth.

So we had our plunge-pool there under the trees and used to lie out among the ferns on the bank to enjoy the sun. It was not deep enough for a proper swim, but it was clear and beautifully cool after the hot walk up from the settlement at midday, and many days we had a dip there at dawn.

11 February

Located and unpacked saw, and got the timber carried up to the house. Had the boys washing and scrubbing the house. Went aboard the *Betua* hunting for a lost 'stock' and fountain pen. When I returned to the house about 4.30 I was told that Fakea's haversack, with a razor and £1, had been stolen. Tentative investigations by Naqu on the *Betua* having drawn a blank, I went aboard after dinner and searched all the mens' boxes with the same result, except that there was some adverse reaction, unfortunately. Before dinner looked at Wete's house and discussed desirability of a new one instead.

Letter to Father

. . . an interesting voyage, including a rendezvous with DC Eastern, Mr Bartle, at Graciosa Baoy, Santa Cruz – scene of Mendana's ill-fated attempt at colonization in 1598, and the subsequent murder of Commodore Goodenough and cannibalisation of a missionary, where no whites live now; it is however very pleasant and peaceful and there is a native hospital there. Mr Bartle gave me the low-down on the whites of Vanikoro, apparently they all hate each other, and told me to keep him informed of communist plots. I've even got a Government Telegraph Code book to do it with.

We're living in MacEwin's house at the moment and working hard on our own, which is over the river and up the hill near the boys' houses. They all need a great deal of repair. I've just had the lavatory fixed by a couple of Ticopians, and now we've got to renew the guttering, replace termite-eaten timber and generally restore the place to its pre-war status as a shining example of British what-have-you. It's great fun and I go bounding up and down the path with hammer in hand, labourers carrying planks and Claire supervising the clearing. Tomorrow we're going to build a new house for a married couple since their house hasn't been the same since a coconut tree fell on it. It will be semi-permanent, semi-native style.

This morning one of our boys had his haversack stolen from his hut. It contained £1, a razor and a bag. Since the Betua *is sailing first thing tomorrow, and the crew were coming and going in the boys' quarters when the boys were away, the crew were to my mind obvious suspects. Naqu went aboard, looked around and drew a blank, so I've just been aboard after dark with the victim, and explained it all to Billy the captain, who understood the situation and proceeded to search the crew's boxes. The engineer, fairly new on the ship, became indignant and yelled and thumped – not at me, but that he with his blameless record should be with such a blackguardly crew. Of course the crew were OK and I tried to calm him down. The captain and mate understood the situation but I'm afraid there was some ill-feeling in the crew. The haversack is still lost.*

Walter now sawing away removing bottom of rotten planks from pantry wall. Nelson removing old mosquito gauze.

12 February

The boys went off into the bush to get materials for Wete's house. So Claire and I settled down to enjoy peace in our own place for once. I put a bung in the top near water tank and then removed a leaky pipe, thus leaving the way clear for replacement of rotten timber.

Saw Wete's house, timber uprights and cross-pieces in place, leaves to be fetched.

13 February

Met Fred Jones (the English trader), who had a complaint to make about Nati, said he had come and railed at a couple from Buma who were selling Jones a trochus shell a few days ago and said that if they didn't go to Halings' store instead he would refuse to let them live on government ground. Also other accusations, harsh words and a brandished knife. Promised to talk to Nati about it.

*   *   *

15 February

Tackled Nati about Fred Jones's complaint and he admitted it, saying that Jones cheats in packing the trochus shells, not filling the tins properly, and also that his boys poach on the diving grounds of the local natives. I told him to keep his feelings to himself in future and I would let the DC know.

Walter was laid up with boils. The boys were showing a strong tendency to stay in bed, it being cold, wet and windy. Got Naqu doing the structural repairs, while Selwyn turned out to be an old hand at soldering and was put on the guttering with a blow lamp.

20 February

Most of the boys were working on the leaf house. The canvas bale, containing camp beds was carried up to the house, the plan being to move in soon, say Tuesday.

Roof cleaning, painting, soldering of guttering in progress.

21 February

We reconnoitred the stream behind the house and found a likely site for a dam and plunge-pool. Set to work with knife and shovel, heaving rocks into the water. Finally tried to move a two-ton boulder that had sunk into the deepest part of the pool, without success.

22 February

Claire's twenty-first birthday. We walked up to the new house, then to the pool where she had a dip and then lay in the sun to dry. Eight men with two tree trunks carried the stove up. Set up the camp beds. Emptied the lower series of tanks while Nelson cleaned out the open one.

Received two telegrams from Mr Logie, and in the evening Ernie Haling arrived from Santa Cruz with a letter from the headman of Utupua about an adultery case.

23 February

The fridge was carried up. Then went to where Wete and Fakea were completing the former's house and asked about the Utupua trouble. Was told that R is the 'guilty man'. Asked him and he admitted it. Telegraphed the DC in code giving the Utupua story and also the Nati-Jones trouble.

24 February

With the arrival of more personal effects, lamps and lots of tins of food, the house is beginning to look more like a home. Also the pantry is taking shape again, thanks to the labours of Naqu and Walter.

There are lots of frogs on the island, including many young ones round our house. MacEwin says there were none until four years ago, when he imported a dozen from Honiara to cope with the 'white ants'. White ants were bad then, and a 'white ant king' was employed to go round the houses every day and exterminate them (by removing their runways up the piles on which the houses are built). Since the frogs came, they have disappeared.

25 February

Left Claire packing and had some more food carried up to the house.

Said goodbye to Mr MacEwin in the afternoon, gave him a copy of the Vanikoro map.

Settled in. Opened the chest and found with great gladness my old friendly books. Spent the evening communing with them.

About ten pm we retired to bed on our new Camp-bed-cum-mosquito-nets.

26 February

I sent Logie a coded telegram about William and pay rates.

Radio and some crockery were carried up – Auntie Erica's and Auntie Mary's tumblers for lunch. Fridge not working.

Set up the radio. Borrowed a six-volt accumulator from Keith. Obtained a hum, probably the vibrator-unit vibrating, but no other noises, probably due to lack of aerial.

Naqu is accomplishing great work in the carpentry field.

27 February

Got the outflow from the spetic tank cemented in and had three chaps scrubbing a ceiling. I paid them all, then had lunch, some sweet potatoes and oranges brought up by Nati.

One Saturday I took my twelve-bore, an ancient double-barrelled hammer-gun, and set off to explore the old track. My reason knew that the jungle was neutral, Spencer Chapman had said so; but my atavistic memory didn't know, it still thought that some gibbering hairy horror might leap out of the undergrowth at me, and a gun in the hand made me feel better; though within a few days I found that a six foot staff cut from the jungle was just as effective and more useful. We are after all tool using animals, and feel better in the wild with something held in the hand. When surveying my hands were busy with compass and field note-book, while the Solomon islanders with me always had bush knives.

The afternoon sun was on my bare back and around me were the life-smells of the growing forest, the mineral smell of baking earth and sometimes the cool smell of rainwater held in the eroded gully, deep as a man, which twisted up the centre.

For an hour I climbed, until at a thousand feet above sea level the angle eased and through a gap in the jungle I could see a fair section of the reef, with the Passage and False Passage, and beyond the reef the blue Pacific rising up to meet the sky.

As I carried on there were signs of more recent company activity, bits of broken tree and raw earth only beginning to sink back into the enveloping bush.

At length another major ridge joined the one I was on and for the first time the country to the West opened out. There was Kauri forest below me now, dark blue-green against the light green of secondary vegetation nearby.

Two thousand feet above me the ridges gathered together to form the unclimbed top of the island, Mount Popogia, still covered in some kind of forest, and clear now from its usual canopy of mist.

Beyond the forest the reef at the end of Vanikoro was a white twist of foam pointing out into the burnished immensity of ocean to sun-ward, and thirty miles away lay the shallow hump of Utupua with its barrier reef, a reminder that mine was not the only island in the world.

There was a metalled road up the ridge which had joined mine, coming from the Company's base on the Sundi River down below. Following it upwards I came to a deserted corrugated iron hut, the old labour lines, and then the road ended and I climbed along the narrowing ridge to the point where operations had stopped and the primeval forest began.

The ridge, which had been broad, drew itself together and the trees were larger and of more species, joined together by lianas and with hanging gardens of moss and fern. I felt very small in the presence of this entity, and seemed to be going back millions of years. And then . . . a pterodactyl from the Jurassic age flew out of the forest nearby. Only it wasn't, of course. It was a fox-bat, or flying-fox. They have wing-spans of up to five feet.

Then down the ridge as the sun set, accompanied often by the very tame perching birds of the forest, the golden whistler and rufous fronted fantail.

In this area there was still plenty of timber, within a mile of the ridge top, that the Company had not reached, and it seemed as good an area as any in which to begin.

So in the next few weeks three or four Solomon Islanders and I surveyed a base-line up the tractor track, using a chain, a compass and an Abney level. (See reference to surveying at back of book.) The Abney level had the date 1909 stamped on it, and the compass of the dry prismatic type, had been my father's in the Great War. Both the ones issued to me by the Government had turned out to be less accurate when I tested them.

As operations got further from home, we occupied the company's old labour lines at the road-head, sleeping on the floor of the hut.

When the base-line was complete, a herring-bone network of transects was put in, the transects being ten chains apart from each other and descending from the base-line on the ridge top to the rivers on each side, a distance of up to a mile, often of very rough going as the transects had to descend steep slopes through chaotic felling damage and you were continually cat-walking along slippery tree trunks suspended over deep hollows filled with rotting vegetation. Old land-slides were common, the red subsoil thickly covered with fern and club-moss.

Sometimes, as the line plunged into a ravine the cry would come,

'Master, you makim chain fast!'

And the chain would have to do duty as a climbing rope for a moment or two.

The transects were each one chain wide, and within them all mature trees were counted, thus effecting a ten per cent enumeration from which an estimate of the total stocking per acre could be obtained. At the same time a fairly accurate map was produced, with form lines instead of contours. Whenever a secondary ridge descended from the main ridge a separate herring-bone system of base-line and transects was introduced.

The team now consisted of six men, two ahead with bush-knives, clearing a way, two with the chain and two measuring trees. I did all the booking until Forest Guard Nelson learned to use the compass and then I was able to delegate some of the transects to him. Naqu, after rebuilding part of our store for us with great skill, had been recalled to Honiara.

Nelson Kausimae Nanau was a chief's son from the large and populous island of Malaita, in the main group of the Solomons. Educated in a mission school, he spoke perfect English, and was one of the nicest chaps to work with I ever met. He must have had a pretty good share of the Christian virtues, and if he ever had a vice I never heard of it. He was gentle, intelligent, industrious and cheerful.

Claire used to camp with us in the bush, and at night we used to join the boys round their fire and listen to the songs they sang for us in Pidgin English and the various Melanesian languages; and once Nelson told us the story of his grandfather and two great uncles who one Saturday night killed and ate three English missionaries. They got indigestion through eating their shoes as they thought these appendages were part of the European's body and 'ought to be eaten too.'

Nelson's favourite song was called 'Morning Star'. Here it is, with his own translation:

MORO NGAURO IUDO MOMOMBO
When the dew has fallen
DAVA MANAFILO LIMOLOE
All the flowers awaken
DAMILIGO LIETEGI LIKA TEFE EN
All the birds are singing come to me
LIVUIE LIKA LEVENE
Say come to me
BELE MAEO MENUKO
Lips of your sweetheart
NIKE BELE MAEO MENUKO
Kiss the lips of your sweetheart
AWA ENE ISU NIU
Feeling sorry about you
NIFODO EO
I am thinking of you
FOTOBO ENE NEBU
To be dead would be better
NIRO OMO EO TAE
I see you never
BELE MAEO
Lips of yours
MATIKI MURO IVENE
Star Arise!

And this is a song for when you are far out at sea in your canoe, alone:

Time noe come long
Middle sea,
Rain and sun hardem me.
Me no savvy where
Place you go,
Oh, you ravem me true!

Please you give me
Blanket for me,
Me thankem you true
Me no forget you
Every day.
Oh, you ravem me true!

Time me catchem
Place belong you,
Boat belong you,
Salag Mala!
That's why me round for you
Oh, you ravem me true!

28 February

I set off along the track behind the house. Fantail, Whistler (male and female) and Slaty Flycatcher played two yards from me, and while I was watching, I was watched by a large cat, twenty yards up the track, it had a black face about eight inches across, with white throat. It vanished into jungle when I turned and I never saw it again. Slight earth tremor, set branches moving. Collected several flowering shrubs and trees.

1 March

Out before dusk with gun. Down to the marshes, saw several rails (purple gallinule) and fox-bats in the mangroves. Some sort of heron flew overhead.

2 March

(My twenty-fifth birthday.) Used another film, getting a record of what the house looks like.

Claire had the idea of centralising the fridge flame, and at long last the machine was actually felt to get cool inside!

Complaint from Via, MacEwin's boy, that the missionary

at Utupua is forcing his wife to live with him, and Via wants her back. Telegraphed Bartle in code about this.

3 March

I found a lizard in the copper and put it into a British Museum Kilner jar. Little fellow, tabby coloured. I went round the estate with Naqu trying to decide what our requirements are from Honiara and sent off a long telegram to Mr Logie in the afternoon. Had coconuts fetched down for us by Wete.

Collected MacEwin's tabby female kitten, nee Cessy, now called Pippa, who settled in very quickly and contentedly.

Couldn't bear to kill the lizard yet. Gave it a home in the kilner jar, with soil, rock and a bit of pawpaw.

4 March

Put Naqu and Walter onto renewing the pipes from the upper series of water tanks, and Nelson and Basil cleaning the tanks, Christian painting the roof and Selwyn the small bedroom.

In the evening went down to the marsh again. The water fowl seemed to be keeping nearer the mangroves after yesterday. I saw a serpent-like creature in the water about three yards away and shot it in the head. I wondered whether it is an eel or a sea-snake.

5 March

Last night's catch has been identified by Naqu as a swamp eel, considered by natives as a delicacy and occurring throughout the Solomons, but he didn't realize it occurred on Vanikoro. Decided to keep it and put it in a jar with meths.

9 March

Small nursery now completed by Nelson and thirty-seven *Pinus Carribea* seedlings put in.

10 March

By request down to see Mrs Haling. She told me of J's boy reported to her sick by Alan Nielen, and said that though he wanted treatment he didn't come to her because J had told him not to and he was afraid. Now being treated for pneumonia with injections. Saw him myself and confirmed the story.

18 March

Part of a turtle was brought up by Mali, for which I gave him a stick of tobacco. We had it for lunch – excellent! Five bean seeds eaten by rats. Cleared jungle further back a little and took steps to ensure a catty smell as rat deterrent, with kind co-operation of Pippa and use of the contents of her earth-box.

20 March

Up rather late. Note from MacEwin about a trip to the reef. Went out about 10.30, anchored just inside the reef and messed about in the shallows. MacE stalking fish with his spring-gun. Met the Wards and Alan Nielen in another boat. Chased a groper. Short trip outside the reef, back about 1.30 pm. Set to work on a second (lower) bean bed, and put in sixty-five French dwarf bean seeds at dusk. Five of the others eaten.

25 March

Letter to Father.

The DC Eastern and Mr Logie have now just gone on to Ticopia to see if the famine is serious after the last hurricane. Of course they may never get there – yesterday the meteorological report said 'sea smooth' and they were turned back ten miles out by heavy seas, whereas today's forecast said 'seas slight to moderate', so Heaven help them.

Ticopia is a small island 120 miles to the ESE and I hope they don't miss and have to run for the New Hebrides or New Zealand.!

An order has just come through that I am to take over the customs from MacEwin, and I'll have to go aboard every boat that comes.

We're still working hard on the house and have been living in it since 28 February. Now however there is some prospect of being able to leave the men to get on with it for some days and go on a forest reconnaissance. One of the first steps will probably be to explore the ridges in the centre of the island, including Mount Popogia the highest point, which has never yet, I believe, been climbed. I've been told that I may have difficulty in getting Solomon Islanders to go up there, because there are reputed to be 'little men' living in the mountains (that is elves or gnomes, rather than pygmies). One Saturday afternoon I did follow a track up the ridge behind the house as far as the camp where the Timber Company is working. There are some wonderful views from the ridge. It falls away steeply on either side and you look out over the jungle and one or two fairly steep looking mountains to the Pacific. When you are a thousand feet or more above sea level you can see an awful lot of ocean – a long way between the reef which is a mile out, and the horizon. If it's fine you can just see the hazy blob of Utupua in the distance.

I shot and stuffed a small flying-fox. We ate it too, and it was nice. We've also eaten turtle, which is something like veal. Behind the house is a small forest nursery and nearby we've got two bean beds. The ground is sloping so all the beds are terraced, with trunks of tree ferns supporting the lower side. There is also a stream where I've built a dam, making a pool of lovely cool water to lie in, but Claire can hardly be got right in since she saw crayfishes in it which tried nibbling her!

One of MacEwin's cats had got a family when we were there and we took one female tabby kitten. So it lives here with us and is called Pippa. It has a loud purr and also a plaintive mew. When it thinks enough attention isn't being given to it, it gets up on the roof and mews to be got down and then resists with all its might. It has already caught and eaten three rats in the house. It ate them in our bedroom-cum-living room. It also catches lizards, which I pickle for the British Museum, and moths.

27 March

Logie and Bartle back.

Logie came up, saw nursery and went with Naqu to the junction, where a line had been cut through the forest last year and eleven kauri saplings had survived.

28 March

Joined Logie and Bartle at the boys' lines for an inspection. MacEwin returned from fishing with quite a catch. Logie and Bartle up to lunch. We went through the forms I'd filled in afterwards, mostly done wrong – all got to be re-done, including cash book.

Letter to Aunt Muriel.

Claire is wondering if she could make marmalade from the oranges that grow on government ground. We get plenty of sweet potatoes and bananas from our land, and people with long established gardens supply us with pineapples and pawpaws. We've got limes just behind the house which are nice in tea or on pineapple, and two or three large mango trees which fruit in December or January.

Our beans tend to get dug up in the night by some animal. It might be a six inch Solomon Island toad, or a rat or a purple swamp hen. I've tried shooting the latter but they nearly always get away into the mangroves where it is difficult to chase them, not to mention the danger there from crocodiles.

29 March

I went to have a look at the 'squatters' village, since I am supposed to tell Ben Tua (the headman) to clean it up. I found Ramoli at Wete's with a new development of malaria and tummy trouble and took him to Mrs Haling's in case. Got the bread, and a pineapple thrown in.

* * * *

1 April

Up at five am. and left just after six with Nelson, Naqu and Clement. Took bearings at view points with 1917 prismatic compass. We reached limit of Halings' workings about 8.20 and proceeded into kauri forest. Kauri petered out after half to three-quarters mile, then mossy woodland, then, climbing still, fern scrub. Cut for four and a half hours, and discovered some good views: Utupua, Lawrence River, our house. Reached 'Banie' about one. View over Tevai, Manevai Bay, Saboe Bay. Took bearings and sketched the view.

Afterwards cut down a little into valley to the west, saw kauri on other side, but not on this side. Continued another few hundred yards towards Mount Popogia. Turned back at 3.35 pm.

2 April

Pressed plant specimens and tried to make sense of yesterday's bearings on the map.

Checked compasses and found my two prismatics disagree by up to three degrees. Borrowed McEwin's and found his to agree with the 1917 one rather than the new one.

3 April

There was a heavy earthquake shock last night.

6 April

Took Nelson and Christian up to the old strip. Opened it up, transplanted kauri seedlings and started a second strip. Left them to complete it, and a third one in the afternoon.

I found Ramoli in a bad way. Sent him to hospital, but had to get Walter to sleep with him as he thinks the hospital is haunted.

In the evening sometimes we would go to our vegetable

garden and gather a few pounds of beans from ground that we had cleared and cultivated ourselves. These, we had found from experience, were essential to our health and vigour, fruit and other fresh food not being in regular supply.

We faced the same problem in the health of our labourers, who were apt to be content with the Government ration of tinned meat, biscuit, rice, tea and sugar if they were not persuaded to grow their own gardens. To encourage them in this, Saturday morning was supposed to be devoted to gardening and later as an alternative when we got our launch, I used to tow a canoe full of boys out to the reef and they would come back in the evening with scores of fish caught by spearing.

When not in camp the labourers lived in a house on a knoll by a path that ran parallel to the path from our house to the settlement and led to the old prison where the forest staff lived.

This path was said to be haunted at night by a girl who had been kept in prison in the old days because she was a persistent cause of trouble among the boys on the station. She was of mixed blood, probably due to the French influx at the time of La Pérouse's expedition. She was known as 'The Moon-Faced Girl' and the legend was that if a man happened to meet her when coming back alone at night she would lure him into the bushes and take him as a lover and then, after a few days, the man would die.

Basil was one of my first batch of labourers and he came from a village on Trevanion Island, just across from Graciosa Bay on Ndeni. He was a gentle, harmless chap, with an amiable, slightly dreamy look in his eye and generally incapable of understanding any but the simplest instructions.

One morning a deputation led by Nelson came to my house in great distress.

'Master, the boys say something bad happened last night to Basil. He was coming back by himself and he met a spirit and fell down in a fright and was found there this morning. It was the Moon-Faced Girl.'

'Is he all right now?'

'No, he is weak and in bed, but he has taken a little food.'

'Well, who found him?' Pause for consultation.

'Sir, they say that Basil found him!'

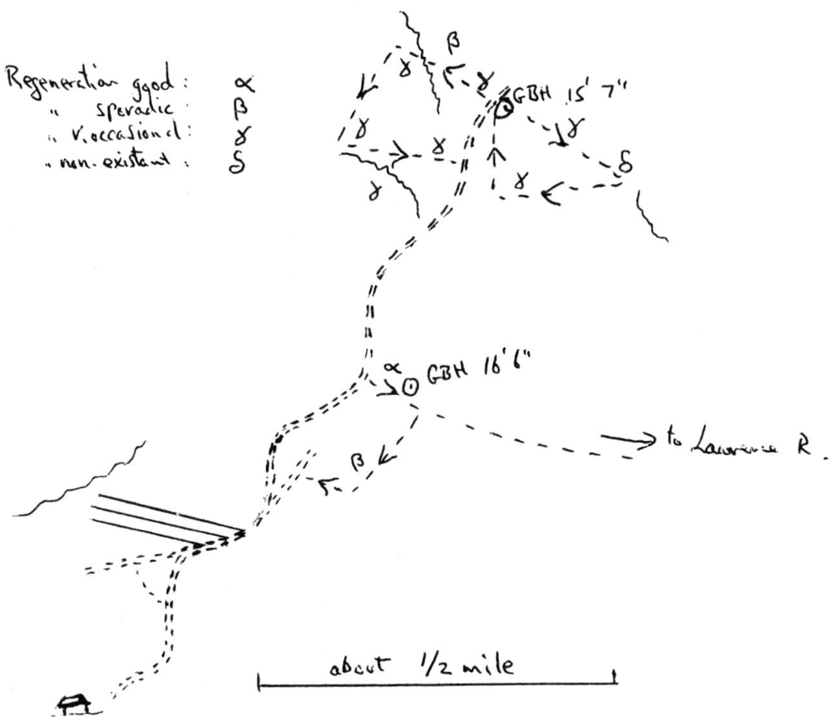

Getting to know the forest.

Happily, Basil fully recovered and went back to his village, and the Moon-Faced Girl was cheated of another victim.

I was informed that as a result of persuasion by the missionaries the price of wives in 'Village belong Basil' was now much reduced. Wives were now only ten pounds, but you could get a 'window for five pounds.' So perhaps Basil is now happily married and secure from future temptation.

7 April

Set off with Nelson at 8.30, reached the junction at 8.45 and at 9.0 halted at the view point from which Utupua is first visible. We measured a large kauri on the east side of the track, girth breast height fifteen feet seven inches. Set off SE from this tree over the ridge and down to a valley bottom, 250 paces. Only one or two kauri seedlings. Then headed west through fairly clear secondary forest. Nelson pointed out a species 'Kepi' (*Malaita*), used in canoe building. Came back to the big tree. Then headed for some big kauri on the other, north-west side of the track. Occasional kauri seedlings near relict trees. We crossed a stream and altered course SW. Few kauri seedlings although plenty of big trees, evidently swamped by ground vegetation, of which there was enough to impede progress. Saw a tree which Nelson said was 'Wowo', the same as those seen at 2000' altitude on way to Banie; also 'bush *Calophyllum*'. Headed NE along a stream where I saw a bo tree, *Fagraea obtusifolia*; a lot of Ficus and lawa (*Malaita*), the bark of which is used for fishing lines. Kauri seedlings still very occasional. Reached track again about 200 yards SW of the tree where we started.

Went down the track about ten minutes, then followed native track going south towards Lawrence river. Many Kauri seedlings along track. Large kauri about twenty yards down, girth breast height sixteen feet six inches. Headed west from this tree, still quite a few kauri every now and then. Went north a little and came out on an old extraction route. See sketch map.

9 April

The *Aros* appeared off the reef first thing. MacEwin dashed off in his speed-boat to pilot her in, but she came in without. Captain Paulsson was in a hurry, as he is due for leave at Easter. Got customs documents and mail off MacEwin. Took mail to house and read it while waiting till they should unload the general cargo. Went and helped Mrs Haling check it and also met the new nurse, Miss Tabrett, who had just arrived.

10 April

Spent much of the morning in the store trying to help rather than hinder Mrs Haling in checking goods as they are rafted slowly in from Saboe Bay. Saw Miss Tabrett, the new nurse and sympathized with the lack of bathing facilities. Naqu brought Ben Tua round so I went to the village with him and told him to have it cleaned up. Naqu helped explain. I met some more of the Europeans from the bush: two Jimmys, Trevor Pearson and a Fijian. They seem a friendly crowd.

Letter to Aunt Phyl.

How does one paint jungle, which is what these islands consist of? There are some fine colours though, especially towards sunset. The soil is lateritic (kind of clay) and purple to red, sometimes unbelievably red. There is a point on the track above the house where you can look out and see the track glowing in the sunset with a red cliff overhung by jungle on the right, a green mass of vegetation on the left, and straight ahead just miles and miles of empty Pacific stretching beyond the white line of reef about a mile away to where it meets the sky.

At last we have started a bit of forest reconnaissance. One day I set off with three boys and two dogs to get as far as we could in twelve hours, leaving at dawn. After a long walk we emerged on the shoulder (the first ever to be there for all I know) and looked down the other side on the rugged island of Tevai, and numerous jungle-clad mountains, peninsulas and inlets. I did a sketch and may try to do a picture.

At the moment I am tied to the settlement in my capacity as Customs officer owing to the presence of the Swedish ship Aros *which brought your letter, but when I start being Forest Officer again we are going to have a camp up there and try to reach the highest point, Mount Popogia, 3031 feet.*

This letter goes with the Aros. *Captain Paulsson is in a tearing hurry to get back to Brisbane, where he meets his wife and flies to Sweden for leave. He's a genial old boy, somewhat fierce at times, I imagine.*

11 April

I went and helped Mrs Haling checking stores, most of the general stores having arrived by now.

Went to fill in 'outward manifests' about 4.0. The *Aros* is probably leaving early tomorrow.

12 April

Did a few last forms at MacEwin's office and then I set off just after 9.0 with Batten and Dorothy in Mac's boat to the *Aros* in Saboe Bay. Captain Paulsson was busy loading logs with the boys. The largest logs were five tons, 440 superficial feet to the ton.

13 April

I sought out Tekusi, Dorothy's cook boy, for interrogation about a gun licence application, but was intercepted by Mr Jones enquiring about lost packages. I left him supervising unloading of the last lot of general cargo and went to boys' house where Nelson and Ramoli are making beds from materials provided. I inspected Wete's house and told Mrs W to clean it up a bit.

14 April

I returned Mac's No. 2 two inch liquid compass and borrowed his No. 1. Checked it against the Survey Department's three inch compass and confirmed the latter's suspected inaccuracy. Sent a telegram about it to Mr Logie.

Began chain and compass survey from mouth of Lawrence river with Nelson. Did ten chains by midday.

15 April

Filling in a 'G' form took half the morning. I made a trip down to Peou and then continued the chain and compass survey until 5 pm, getting one mile exactly from the mouth of the Lawrence river. Second bed arrived and we moved into the newly painted bedroom.

16 April

About three quarters of a mile up the tractor track from our house I had noticed a small footpath which led down into the jungle. On Good Friday I decided to explore it.

As I stepped from the warm sunlight my senses began to adjust themselves to a different world. When walking rapidly down an unfamiliar forest trail much of your attention at first is taken up with avoidance of obstacles and any tendency to day-dream is quickly penalized by a slap in the face or a jab in the knee. But with practice the task is taken over by eye and brain and the solitary traveller feels the eternal Presence of the jungle beating in on his consciousness. There is a moist smell of growth and decay, an infinite silence underlined by the scream of cicadas in a sun-drenched clearing, a damp and treacherous feel to a log as it supports your creeping progress over a gully, and even momentary horror when you step on a fallen tree-fern stem and vicious, biting ants spue out.

Descending through the forest I crossed several small streams and then the ground flattened out and I was in a small banana plantation and there was the cool sound of the river close by. The sunlight was pale blue in the crystal water of deep pools and flashed diamond and silver in the shallow rapids. Where it struck the shingle bank in the middle the light was dazzling after the forest dark. And through it all was the river smell, the smell of the snails on the boulders and the life borne in the waters. The distinctive smell of a tropic stream yet recognizably kin to that of an English river. So beneath the mighty tree whose very roots formed a bank ten feet above my head, I remembered a backwater of the Cherwell and a punt there with a girl in it on a day in spring.

I did not swim owing to uncertainty about crocodiles, but pushed on into the jungle the other side. There was a track of sorts and if it went sea-wards I should come out near Mac's house with luck. However it faded out in an area of jungle obviously subject to flooding, where there seemed to be random tracks going in all directions. I wondered if some of these tracks were made by crocodiles, and what I should do if I met one; and then of course the imagination starts to work and every log became a potential croc. Feeling jittery, I headed for higher ground, but ran into an impenetrable tangle of after-felling damage left by the old Company, twenty years ago. I carried on by pocket compass, South-West for the sea, and at last I saw it not too far away. By now I had acquired a stick and with it beat my way down through the undergrowth until I came to the beginning of the tidal mangrove swamp. Here it was dry and good going and my spirits rose as I followed the compass towards the sea.

Then, through the trees, I glimpsed the shipping beacon, a huge diamond-shaped piece of corrugated iron supported by a timber structure, and at last I was on a sandy beach. With relief I turned right towards the settlement, congratulating myself on the end of my little expedition.

But my auto-congratulations were premature! The beach came to an end, ahead were only mangroves. Undeterred, I pushed on into the mud until away to the right I saw the tops of some coconut trees, probably the real beach this time! When I got to it the beach was going Northwards, at right angles to the direction in which I wanted to go. However, the comforting thing about this beach was that it had fresh foot-prints going along it and all I had to do, I supposed, was follow them until they led me to a track.

I wondered idly about the foot-prints as I followed them happily along the beach. It was someone in gym shoes, probably not a Solomon Islander. Who could it be? Mac perhaps, or one of the Australians from the bush?

And then with dreadful certainty I knew who it was! It was me, and I had made them about ten minutes ago! Weariness was setting in now and I had no food with me, but I reckoned I could not be more than a mile or two from home and it was out of the question to go back the way I had come. Home ought to be West, but that way the mangroves thinned out into open water, so when I reached the end of the beach again I carried on Northwards, through the mangroves.

The tide was rising fast now, flooding into the creeks and rippling over the tree roots. The warm salt water stung on my scratches as I went knee-deep. Now a biggish creek barred the line of my advance. I toyed with the idea of plunging in, but thought better of it and headed North-West, leaving the water behind and entering thicker bush. Then I stumbled across two strands of barbed wire! Also there was a recent track which I followed. But it turned North-Eastwards, the wrong direction.

At this moment I felt very lost and tired, but not quite desperate. After all, I had a compass, and I knew which way to go and it could not be far now. Grimly I headed Westwards through the bush. More barbed wire. A track. And then, unmistakably, the roof of Mac's house through the trees!

17 April

The next day Claire and I took a picnic to the place I had found on the river. We stripped and swam and lay on the shingle in the sun. The pool was clear and deep and cool. Above the rapids was a long, clear reach, then a sharp bend where, forever beautiful, the river lost itself in the uninhabited jungle.

Many times we returned to this spot and later our baby sons used to splash in the shallows there. We never saw a sign of a crocodile.

20 April

MacEwin says he reckons I've got till Monday till the customs work is ready, so an expedition to the mountains was forthwith planned. Object: reconnaissance and enumerations, Wednesday to Saturday if fine. In the afternoon chain and compass work with Ramoli, as far as the second lot of strips cut by Nelson and Christian up the disused track.

21 April

Set off about 8.0 am with Naqu, Nelson, Christian and Ramoli, laden with bedding and food for three days. Duly reached the upper hut, where Mr Haling had kindly given us permission to stay. Sent Nelson and Ramoli on past Banie to cut a track towards Mount Popogia, and with the other two started chain and compass surveying from the road along the partially worked kauri ridge. Did twenty-six chains in all, rain slowed us down a bit in the afternoon.

Diet – biscuits for lunch, sardines and rice for supper. Shared tea with the boys.

22 April

Nelson and Ramoli went off cutting track as before. Started enumerations southward from the ten chain post down a forty degree slope to the valley and then reconnoitred the north side of workings on ridge and reckoned it would be worth enumerating there.

Later surveyed down secondary ridge No. 1, towards the Lawrence River, for twelve chains.

* * *

The chief sport on the island before the Pax Britannica had been, of course, head-hunting between the several villages round the coast. When the spirit moved an expedition would go out to the next village and return with a few heads and enough of the flesh to provide a feast for a day or two. And if on the return match one's own village lost a few, well it removed some of the dead wood and prevented over-population.

At any rate there was plenty of interest in life, deeds of valour to boast of, and if your own turn came your spirit joined the ever-increasing throng of spirits upon Mount Popogia. All that was changed now of course, and only one of the old villages was permanently inhabited. Some say that the depopulation, which is general through most of the Solomons, was caused by boredom after the banning of the National Sport.

But still Mount Popogia dreamed up there in the blue, and under the full moon the villagers would dance on the beaten earth under the palm trees, and as they chanted the old legend of the spirits who dwelt on high their song would mingle with the gentle swish of the waves along the beach and the rustle of the trade-wind in the leaves aloft. Mount Popogia was only 3,000 feet high, but still unclimbed as the ridges leading to it from the West were densely covered in mossy forest and to the East its cliffs fell sheer practically to the sea.

On a reconnaissance with Nelson, Naqu and a boy called Clement, I had reached a point 2,400 feet above sea-level where the continuation of the ridge on which we were working met the summit ridge. Half a mile beyond the limit of the company's workings the Kauri forest petered out and was replaced by stunted trees festooned with blankets of moss. We were able to find a way through this without too much cutting, but then we ran into a solid wall of giant club-moss. This club-moss, *Lycopodium cernuum,* was the same species as that which grew near our house, but what a difference! There it was soft and formed a cover over the soil about as deep as a crop of hay in an English meadow. Here its branches were thick, coarse and prickly, and the thicket piled above our heads. The bush-knives were brought to the fore and we gradually hacked our way through, until we entered mossy forest again.

Four and a half hours later the trees thinned out and there across a gulf of space, and towering above the emerald waters of Manevai Bay, was Vanikoro's sister island, the rugged peak Tevai. Away to the right was the mountainous Eastern peninsula of Vanikoro, covered in the omnipresent mantle of rain forest. But above all and encompassing all, calm, pale and terrible, streaked with amethyst, rose the tremendous circle of the sea, stretching beyond us over nearly half the curve of the planet. Nearer home was Polynesia, and somewhere over there were the shining atolls of Gilbert and Ellice, a mere thousand miles away.

23 April

It was on St. George's Day that we finally reached the summit. We set off for the hut two days previously, and Nelson and Ramoli went ahead and cut a path along the summit ridge beyond the point we had reached before.

All that day they toiled and all the next, often soaked with cold mountain rain, and cut off from the world by mist. Meanwhile the rest of the party carried on with enumeration.

The third day dawned fine, and we all left the hut and went fast along the ridge-top through the forest into the early morning sun. This was before Naqu was recalled to Honiara, and he was in the party, and the other members were Nelson, Christian from Ndeni, Ramoli from Utupua, and myself. We passed the view-point where we had stopped before and entered Nelson's path. He had hewn a great trail through the bush through which two men could have walked abreast! Progress was rapid until we reached the end of the path and emerged into an area of knee-high scrub which continued for a hundred yards or so. All around us the short bush sloped off into the mist, but ahead the ground still rose. Now we were back among the stunted trees again and the pace slowed as the knives came into play.

At 12.30 a peak was reached, and if the trees below had blankets of moss, here they had eiderdowns of it. A quarter of a mile away to the east the summit loomed through the mist across a ravine, but how long would it take us to get there? First we would have to climb down into the ravine and there would certainly be more cutting beyond. Conscious of the time, I thought it advisable to start back, and I was about to give the order to retreat when a shout from Naqu down below announced that he had found the way across and was starting to climb up the other side. We followed, and an hour later were on the top, a wooded plateau with another ridge coming in from the West, and cliffs descending to the North. All was shrouded in mist, there was nothing to see except dripping foliage. Then we headed back, through increasing rain, and reached the hut just before dusk.

There was great jubilation in the hut that night. Naqu in particular was excited at our achievement, and the tale lost nothing in the telling when he got back to the village. It was suggested to me afterwards, by an Australian, that it was a pity to have reached the top and that the peak should have remained inviolate. This is a perfectly valid argument, though it would apply equally to Mount Everest, which had been climbed less than a year before.

I never heard this point of view expressed by a Solomon Islander, however, and Ben Tua, the local Headman, in his usual enthusiastic way was keenly interested in the ascent. My chief regret was that it had not been possible to include a man of Vanikoro in the party.

* * *

Now all traces of our ascent have disappeared, and the spirits of those who died in battle range unmolested on the summit. And perhaps the grandchildren of the present inhabitants, as they dance under the Moon, will recall in their song the legend of a mad white man who came from over the sea and climbed to the top of the mountain, and came down a little madder and went away again, across the sea.

Letter to Father.

... the First Ascent of Mount Popogia, 3,031 feet. I spent the first two days doing survey work near the hut and sent Nelson and Ramoli on to cut a track towards the top. Then the third day we all went flat out, hacking our way through mossy forest, oozing wetness and dripping from pendant roots in the thick mist. At last we emerged and had a view of the ridge leading towards the top, then found ourselves in knee-high flowering scrub. This however gave way to mossy forest again and we soon came to a peak from which we could see the true summit or top of the island, also a glimpse of the distant sea through the mist. A further half hour and we were there on a wooded plateau – precipices to the north, ridges to east and south-east – but could see nothing owing to mist. I took possession on behalf of Her Majesty and left a message in a bottle to that effect, and we all beetled off home for tea.

24 April

Tidied up, packed and made the boys chop some firewood to leave in the hut in return for hospitality. Reached our house about 10.0 am.

26 April

Instructed Nelson and Naqu in reading of compass and Abney level, then left them to continue repairing Naqu's house.

In the evening, I collected lycopod with spores, I think. Chipped off a bit of rock from the lump behind the house. I think it is an olivine-basalt; how much of the rock on this island is similar and what is its structure?

28 April

The office was closed when I went down, so did compass check in the cow-pasture all day instead, with Basil as assistant. Naqu's boy came with request for more instructions, so I wrote some out; also received a present of pork, caught yesterday in the forest. Temoga brought his handiwork for us to see, four bowls and a fine walking stick with shell inlay handle, made of U'ola and Mu'awru. Bought two bowls (Claire's twenty-first birthday present!) and the stick for Daddy in his old age.

Had a shot at identifying a local timber tree, *Parinarium salomonensis*.

29 April

Sent off a telegram with yesterday's compass bearings to Honiara. Checked customs forms all morning. Inspected village and told Nati to do something about cleaning it up.

4 May

William Piaito, a Forest Guard, at last arrived, in the *Toby*. Wete also returned. Nelson and William are to live in Wete's old house. More or less finished checking customs entries by midday.

Selwyn came and said MacEwin's boy had challenged him to a fight on account of the latter's wife. I forbade him to respond, unless they have a proper boxing match, and I will try and referee! Fair earthquake shock late at night.

5 May

Ben Tua came with a story about a girl called Agnes, warning me about Willy, who is the brother of the man that is father to her child who may come and tell me that they ought to be married whereas the girl and her parents favour someone else.

Set off for the bush with Claire about 3.0 pm, the men having left before. Weather clearing up a little. Claire reached the hut OK and settled in happily.

6 May

Did enumerations on ridge IIi, to right and left at the ten chain post. Then chained along the tertiary ridge going west.

In the evening we exchanged songs with Naqu and the boys in the kitchen.

7 May

Continued with last night's line and reached limit of timber company's workings at twelve chains. Encountered some steep country and quite a few kauri. Reached the Big Sundi

Bush Party.
Back row: Wete, Naqu, Nelson.
Centre: Clement.
Front: William.

River at thirty-six chains. It was rocky, shallow and about ten yards wide. Hundred foot cliff on the other side, with a waterfall. Had lunch there, then came back, measuring the non-kauri trees like kuo, hebere.

8 May

Set out for home. There was a deputation from the village: Agnes, pa and ma, Ben Tua and ex boy friend, Lorna. All were agreed that the girl should marry Mac, who didn't appear. Lorna wanted £4 plus earring back from girl. I persuaded Lorna to give the £4 to pay for his piccaninn by Agnes and she to return the earring. All went away happy.

10 May

Naqu and Ben appeared and said they'd got a dance ready and would we come, so we went and watched. A score or so of natives festooned with aromatic leaves were leaping in a circle round a tom-tom and chanting at the tops of their voices – just like Oxford on May morning, in fact. The chant is very simple and repetitive, having a kind of childlike gladness and virility that is very beautiful. The song is either about how glad they are when the cloud lifts and they can see the top of the mountain, or about how happy the stars are, all grouped together in constellations, or about a little island hidden away in the mangroves where the rainbow sometimes seems to spring from; or it may be about the little men who live in the forest. Their footprints were last seen a year ago near the hut where we camped. I was introduced to a man whose grandfather was a friend of theirs, but I've never met anyone who has seen one. They are very very strong and have been known to move a heavy log that men couldn't move. Now they live in the Willi Willi river area where nobody goes much, but perhaps we shall see some sign when we do our survey there.

* * *

12 May

Did a 'Board of Survey', as is apparently required. Collected mysterious package from store, which when opened was found to contain one large tent plus ground sheet. Erected same after lunch for inspection, then hauled it in out of the rain.

13 May

I called on Naqu, and found him in the throes of putting in a coconut supporting pile to his house. Bit of a party in progress at same time. A lot of clearance has been effected by the villagers, but there is plenty of scope for more. Inspected Nelson's house (Wete's).

16 May

Breakfast outside in the sun.

Out to the reef with MacEwin, West end of the island. Saw a school of dolphins at close quarters and one shark. Got burned, returned into rain. Wrote letters.

17 May

Sea captains were never an inhibited breed of men, and never less so than in the Pacific.Commander N of the mission ship *Southern Cross* was no exception. She came in before noon one day and after lunch I went aboard to see the Captain about four intending passengers bound for Honiara. One of them was Naqu and he came with me, smartly dressed in his best white shirt and shorts. With the captain in his cabin I found Mac, who had been kept virtually a prisoner there since before lunch. Commander N liked to have an audience while he drank.

Mac introduced me and I, raising the subject of the intending passengers, started to introduce Naqu to the Captain. He rose from his seat, indignant at the effrontery of this ignorant young pup of a government official. He was a great red bull of a man, but such was his sense of outrage that he went slightly pale about the jowls.

'Mr Hadley,' he said, 'I have been to many places and I have done many things in my time, but I would like you to know that there is one thing I never, never do. I never, *never* meet natives!'

Poor Naqu cowered greyly back towards the stern, but the Captain pursued him relentlessly down the deck.

'And as for you, before you dare to come aboard my ship, take off that disgusting moustache, do you understand?'

He went on like this for some minutes, and eventually Naqu went ashore. Feeling cowardly, and disinclined to attack the Captain on his own ship, I waited with Mac until the eruption was over.

The rest of the afternoon I spent in his cabin, listening to his views on Life, and on missionaries.

'The trouble with these missionaries' he said, 'is that they are all so damned *holy*.'

For which he reckoned that his own earthy pragmatism was a very necessary antidote, and the perpetual proximity of the 'holiness' probably drove him to exaggerate the earthiness so that he appeared worse than he really was. And who can say but that the islanders got a truer picture of our civilization through his presence? Moreover, he had his part to play in their welfare, oh, dear me yes! While the missionaries were looking after their souls, he would be treating their bodies with simple but effective remedies. He could dish out paludrine or quinine for malaria of course, give a dose of epsom salts and treat wounds and boils. Sometimes however his services went beyond this.

'This fella comes aboard one night,' he said, 'and he came to me looking rather worried. So I asked him what was the matter.'

'"Well",' he says, '"its my wife".'

'Oh, and what's the matter with your wife?'

'"Its like this",' he says, '"I can't get her in the 'family way'".'

'So I asked him, "Do you mind if I try?" And he said no, he didn't mind, go ahead.'

'Well, I don't know if I got her in the family way,' said

Commander N, 'but I did me best!'

As the afternoon wore on I watched the empty whisky bottles multiply. From time to time he would send for one of his officers, the Mate, or the Chief Engineer.

'Ruggles,' he fumed, 'What's the water level in the fresh water tank?' – as if he ever had any use for the stuff – 'Don't know! Good God man, its your job to know. Find out!'

'Mr Stone, send for another case of whisky. There isn't another case? Why not? Drank two already this voyage? Can't have. Oh well, I suppose I must have done if you say so Mr Stone.'

*   *   *

That night all the Europeans at Peou were invited aboard for dinner. The missionaries were there this time, but still it was noticeable how the women clung together for mutual protection. And to add to the entertainment a six-foot Tiger shark was caught with a line over the side just as we were having sherry, and slain by the Captain with his .22 rifle.

*   *   *

The *Southern Cross* was due to leave next morning at dawn for the run to Utupua, and, as I was learning the job of customs officer under Mac, I had to be on board before it departed. There were also customs forms for Fred Jones which were supposed to have been completed ready to go with the mail to Honiara and I had intended to check them the previous afternoon, but, having had to humour the Captain instead, had not had an opportunity.

18 May

The alarm went off at 4.30 am and Claire lit the primus and put a kettle on for a cup of tea. The full Moon was setting in the West as I made my way down through the early-morning coolness to the office.

Then I found that I had not charged Fred Jones duty on his Trochus shell exports. So I had to go over the river to the met.

shack where the radio was to find an old telegram and see what the current rate of duty was supposed to be. But now it was nearly six o'clock and Mac was ready to start the launch and I had about three minutes in which to multiply eleven tons seven hundredweight by £25. 16s. I hoped the answer was right, that was all!

I put the forms in the mail-bag with a covering letter and then we hurried aboard the launch and dashed out across the lagoon, fully expecting to have to chase the *Southern Cross* half-way to Utupua.

'When he says six, he means it, I reckon,' said Mac. 'He'll be off on the dot and he won't wait for mail or customs or anything.'

But the ship was still there; and not only was it still there, but there was no sign of life on board! We climbed aboard, and guided by the sound of snores found our way to the Captain's cabin. In sleep his expression was amazingly cherubic. After Mac had shaken him a few times he roused himself and evidently thought that Mac was the cabin-boy, come with the tea.

Then, realizing it was time to sail, he sent a message to the Chief Engineer to start the engines. Hardly had they rumbled into life before his social instinct prevailing, he thought better of it and sent another order to have them turned off again! Whisky and cold milk were brought, and the time of departure was postponed to 6.30, and then to seven o'clock.

Meanwhile the Sun had risen and turned the lagoon to a sheet of gold, while its rays slanted beneath the awning and fell warmly on the timbers of the deck. Now he told us about how his naval career had ended when his crew mutinied under him; then we heard all about the gutlessness of the younger generation.

All this time Mac had been his chief listener, I being somewhat on the fringe; so Mr Stone, the Mate, who had been inspecting the shore through a telescope, beckoned to me, and thrusting the telescope into my hand, bade me look at the jetty and see if I did not think some drums were being unloaded from a boat.

He then whispered urgently into my ear: 'If you don't go now, we will never get away in time to reach a safe anchorage tonight.'

But Mac was the senior customs officer and was also pretty thick with Commander N, not being one of the gutless young generation; so I told Mr Stone he had better get hold of him, as I doubted if they would listen to me. He repeated the gambit with the telescope, after which Mac and I got into the launch and made for the shore, leaving the Captain asleep on his bunk.

The *Southern Cross* sailed about two hours later.

19 May

Nelson, Christian and William set off in the morning for the bush, with Selwyn to carry the tent, who returned pm. Fine day. Off to the bush myself about 3 o'clock. Got a bit of a cold and thick in the head. Hut still there, but two-thirds of the floor gone (taken by the company). All slept there.

20 May

Still fine. Found a site for the tent and pitched it by the roadside. Then set off and started enumeration line II.xx.350. Wete arrived from Peou with a note from Claire and a coconut. Found I had fever and gave up at midday, leaving the boys to go on with the line as far as twenty chains. Lay in the tent and ate paludrine. Felt much better in the evening. Talk with Nelson. Slept in tent, boys in hut.

21 May

Still slight fever when we set out, but it soon yielded to paludrine. Continued with the line and at ten o'clock reached the Upper Big Sundi River. Surveyed down the river for thirty-two chains until we reached the end of our previous enumeration line, II.o.337. Followed this back to base. Nelson now sick with fever.

pm. Started line II.xx.170. Reached about six chains, then it rained so that further work was impossible and we gave up. Mosquitos bad in the tent, gave up sleeping there and finished the night in the hut where they were not so bad.

22 May

Fine, with occasional heavy showers. Cloud cap on the mountain top, the sea bright blue. Utupua very clear, different ranges of hills standing out from one another. Lovely cloud effects, cumulus and a horizontal streaky variety.

Sent Christian down to get mosquito nets and then to come back and stay here with Nelson over the week-end.

Started surveying down the road. Reached thirty-four chains by 11 am. Then set off for home, leaving Nelson in charge. Arrived about 1 pm. Claire been busy while I was away: undergrowth cleared from mango trees, lime tree pruned, new shelf in kitchen. Transplanted beans doing OK. Reading *Don Camillo and the Prodigal Son.*

23 May

Just after breakfast a beautiful yacht appeared off the reef. Meanwhile we had a short visit from J. A. Olin and friend, the former wanting to be 'bonded out' of Vanikoro.

Went out to the anchored yacht. It was the brigantine *Yankee*, under the command of Captain Johnson, from Gloucester, New England. There were twenty-three on board, American youths and girls working the boat round the world. Shown over the yacht and met some of the crew ashore later on.

24 May

Got the chlordane emulsion base out and had William sow a bed with *P. caribbea* seed, watering with a 1/480 mixture of the insecticide. Most of the seeds were already mouldy, so I told him to sow them thick, hoping for 5% germination.

* * *

The Brigantine 'Yankee'.

26 May

Off at 7.0 am and embarked on the *Tug* with William, Ernie Haling, Ward and some other Solomon Islanders. Landed up at the Sundi River where we found Beresford. Then got a truck up to the workings. Spent the day measuring a dozen or so felled kauri with William, for form factor.

Saw the labour lines and told a gang of fellers about leaving lower stumps. Paddled out to the *Tug*, now moored off the river mouth, and reached home at sunset.

27 May

Fine. Off to the bush camp with Claire about 10 am, William following in our wake. Arrived in time for lunch. Found Nelson and Co were out in the bush, so William and I did a reconnaissance to the SW, coming back fairly early as we were tired after yesterday and the pack-hauling this morning.

28 May

Party consisted of William, Nelson, Christian and Wete. Off to do survey and enumeration in the cut over lines. Firstly went northwards from the tenth chain, then along the Big Sundi River eastwards and returned southwards along to the thirtieth chain. Poison tree by the river, 'Way-lassie' (Malaita), or 'Tar-tree' (Queensland).

30 May

In the afternoon Claire and I weeded bed in front of house ready for seed. Then went and sat on the bird-rock till sundown. Close-up of a Vanikoro broadbill, a beautiful little thing, when it is still enough to look at; also juvenile cardinal honey-eaters, fantails, a bird with white wing-bar and underparts and a juvenile kingfisher on top of a dead tree.

8 June

Nelson gave both *P. caribbea* beds a second dose of Chlordane to discourage insects. Nati is making a bed for tomatoes and repairing the stairway.

Prepared and left for the bush.

9 June

A lot of rats about in the night, climbing into my rucksack and running across me.

Continued the survey down the ridge and joined up with the others about midday. Returned to camp.

Supper: rice, native cabbage, sausages, followed by apricots out of a tin. Now I use two cooking pots and find the extra trouble well worthwhile.

10 June

Less rats. Did strip II, a short one, running into its next door neighbour to the west and with no kauri trees. Then did the other species for the latter strip, quite a list of new names. Am wondering whether these strips will throw any light on regeneration mosaics, if they occur in kauri forests. At midday Wete took sick and returned early.

Continued with Nelson and Ramoli ending up at the head of a cirque which I christened 'Twll Ddu', or Devil's Kitchen.

Returned to find Claire in residence at camp, having had a very pleasant walk up and bathe; also having brought the mail from home, which came on the *Cape Torrens*.

Pitched the tent and left the hut to the boys.

11 June

Left Claire and Wete to return to base. Did II.xxxx.123, ending up on a fifty-two degree slope into a valley containing one of the tributaries of the Lawrence River. This strip, though short, contained ten kauri, one of which had a girth breast height of nineteen feet ten inches, which is, I think, the biggest yet. Its timber height is forty-two feet, the same as another tree of girth breast height six feet nine inches, which illustrates the sort of height/girth correlation we have! After this returned to top of ridge for rest and food, then surveyed on up the ridge to fifty chains. Climbed a tree near this point and saw out over this side of the Upper Lawrence basin. Although there are some ridge-top kauri here, there seem to be few lower down, and the corresponding flank of the opposite ridge seems similar, while lower down on the same ridge the tree can be seen, giving the impression that we are here about at the altitudinal limit of the kauri as timber.

The ridge junction does not look a very long way ahead from here.

12 June

In the afternoon we wandered about the grounds with glasses and did a bit of bird watching.

A cardinal honey-eater is fond of proclaiming itself from rather a bare tree in front of the house (on top of the slope down to the kitchen garden), also an immature (or female?) of the same species. Do these birds have territory?

Pied hawk retreated in a hurry from the lawn as I appeared. The bird with white eye-stripe and underparts was in the top of the forked kauri.

Two golden whistlers were in the scrub to the left of the mango beyond the kitchen garden, much unseen scuffling and a sudden chase emerging in my direction. Probably courtship. Also today Claire watched the behaviour of the common lizard, *Emoia cyanura* (Lesson), which has a yellow stripe down the back and a long greenish tail. Two of about the same size (five inches long) were seen either fighting or courting, probably the latter as one was active and one passive throughout. The supposed male would jump on the supposed female, which would roll over in attempts to escape. A chase would then take place on a circular course and after a bout of this the two participants would take a rest, each on a separate rock, until it was time for the next round. This went on for about five minutes, after which the more passive animal succeeded in getting away, thereafter looking in all directions with every appearance of being a hunted animal. The same performance was seen about the same time (10.30 am) next day.

18 June

Nelson found a nest in a tree in which the bird with the white eye-stripe, which I think is a Polynesian triller, is sitting.

Wrote monthly report for Logie.

20 June

Letter to Father.

I'm sending a rough plan of this place. Slowly but surely it is being re-won from the jungle. Some steps have been made down the steep bank to the vegetable garden, where one of the beans is nearly as high as me, and where we also have maize, native cabbage, water melons and fifteen young banana trees. Our few orange trees have been pruned and have new shoots, some of our mangoes are bearing, and up at the nursery there are twenty-six sturdy young Pinus caribbea *in one bed and about one hundred new seedlings in another.*

A lot of survey has been done now and it is great fun plotting it and watching the map unfold itself. The country is very rough, a maze of jungle-covered ridges with occasional cliffs and waterfalls. This is the first proper map that has been made, though I am only doing the parts where there is kauri forest, and the odd lines connecting up with the coast. Previous maps have been based on Admiralty charts and aerial photographs, the latter having been lost in files somewhere in America, so that they cannot be used.

The new map (scale 1:10,000) starts off with a line up the ridge from the mouth of the river, three and a half miles inland to the first of the virgin kauri forest, and then the tale is taken up by enumeration lines going at right angles to the main line of survey, and by branch lines going along subsidiary ridges. I'm showing the slope of the country by 'form lines', which are embryo contours put in by guesswork.

My official instructions here are on one typewritten side of

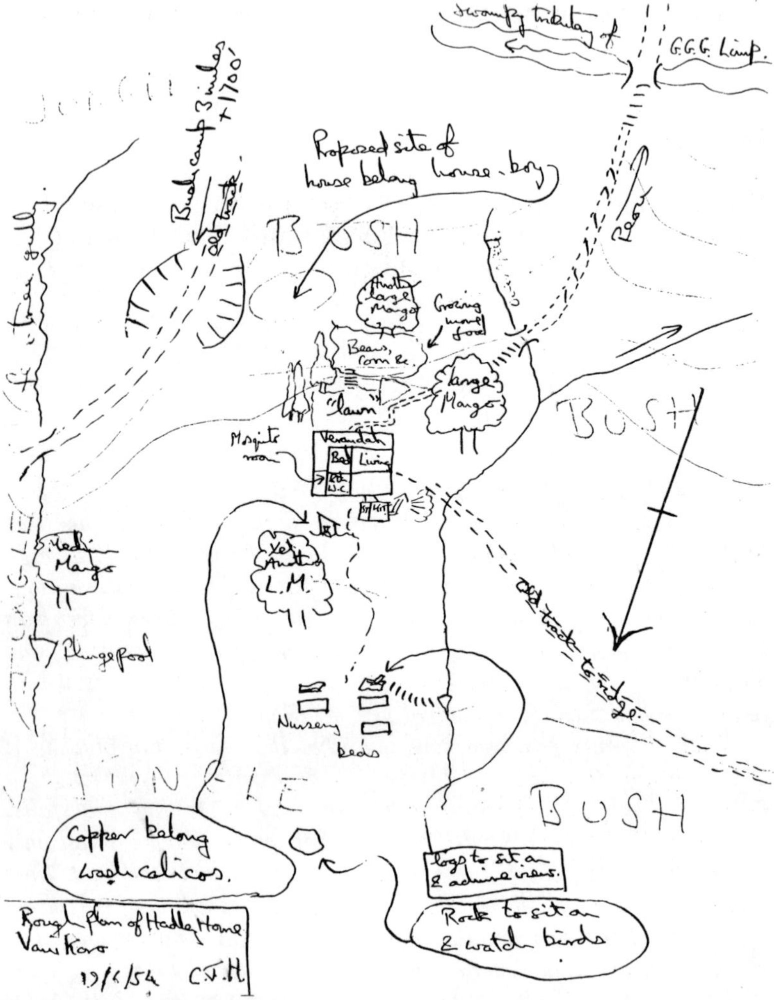

Rough plan of our house and surroundings.

foolscap, ie. general idea of what to do and how to do it, but no details, which depend on what I find when I get there. Nobody knows what ridges there are and where the kauri is. It has to be explored first.

23 June

Decided that the bird's nest in a tree nearby was deserted, so I had a forked post cut to support the tree so that I could climb it and got the one egg, 0.9 inches long, blue-green with brown markings concentrating on the round end. Blew it. Collected the flowers of the tree, also a sedge. Dinner with Mr MacEwin and the Wards. Glorious golden evening with Venus hard and clear above the sea. Distant ranks of golden-grey clouds towards the horizon, and in the foreground the clear-cut silhouettes of coconut trees. The light on the horizon changed from gold to red-orange.

When we went home it was a fairly starry night. Venus gone, and Mars high in the south-east.

Claire thinks she is going to have a baby.

25 June

Nelson brought up leaves and flowers of three different kinds of mangroves, which all have something in common with each other because they are all *Rhizophoraceae*. These were duly labelled and put in the plant press.

Saw our canoe being made.

28 June

Claire told me Keith had been knocked out while messing about in his motorboat and was in a bad way, having broken his neck some years previously. This night I dreamed that I asked Keith how he was and he seemed surprised, never having been not all right. Next day, Tuesday, I asked Dorothy, Keith's wife, how he was, and she seemed surprised and said he was OK. Meg explained afterwards that it was

Alan Nielen who had been hurt, not Keith, and Claire had made a mistake. It seems this could be a case of ESP.

4 July

We decided on a picnic to the river. Made a fishing rod out of a sapling growing in the garden, very light and about fourteen feet long. Dug some worms out of the kitchen garden and set off. Rod very trying in jungle paths! When we arrived we both plunged in forthwith. Deliciously cool, beautiful bluey colours and fish underwater, seen with mask. Caught one fish, too small and threw it back. Come lunch time, left the baited line in and a fish about ten inches long with a pug head and yellow tipped fins, otherwise brown, was caught. A fire was made and the fish roasted on green sticks, being eaten about a quarter of an hour after it was caught!

Further expeditions, down for a quarter of a mile, and up to a biggish pool we saw last time. Both stark naked all this time of course.

Set off back. Rod got bust just in time to be useful as two staffs.

5 July

Working out mean basal areas and form factors.

6 July

Finished working out form factors etc, arriving at an interim figure for the amount of timber in the Upper Sundi – Lawrence River area: 1400 cubic feet per acre. Haven't estimated the area yet.

Form factor (mean of twelve) = 0.65

Timber height (mean of twenty) = 38.8 feet

Mean basal area/acre = 56.4 sq. feet (from 102 trees in a total sampled area of 9.95 acres).

7 July

Did some plotting. Big closing error on II.o.33, decided to go up and re-do it, the weather being very promising. Took the altimeter along too. Found the hut had been taken down in the last two days. All in tent together, sleeps four quite well.

8 July

Re-surveyd II.o.33 and the river going east from its end. Back along number x. Saw a snake about four to five feet long and two inches thick, python? Flattish head, yellow underneath. Fast asleep until I woke it up.

9 July

Continued with strip xxxi 174 from ten chains. Collected two ground orchids, one orange-yellow and one white. A long strip, forty-two chains and many kauri. Arrived at the river, an upper tributary of the Lawrence, if not the Lawrence itself. Continued up the river, hoping to close on the end of xxxxi. Surmounted one waterfall after another, often a rock climb of fifty feet or so about Moderately Difficult, but hard enough for chain and compass work.

Followed a small affluent up and after about forty chains and a rise in height from 850 feet to 1370 feet reached the early part of xxxi. Back in time to start cooking before dark.

10 July

Sent the boys down after breakfast and stayed up to reconnoitre a possible site for a plantation in the worked out area by the new camp. Then descended. Spent most of the rest of the day arranging plant collection, including the two orchids collected yesterday.

12 July

Claire and I went to see how the canoe is getting on. Outrigger now being made.

15 July

Mr Haling returned from Santa Cruz with a cargo of recruits plus one stowaway, which he says I can have if required. Off to the bush, preceded by Wete.

17 July

Out with Claire in the new canoe. Rough in mid-lagoon, back to shore at the wreck. Fished and swam, great fun. Back tea-time.

22 July

Had to wait for the rain to stop for about an hour after breakfast. Then it started again just as we arrived at the scene of operations in the bush. Worked on, taking bearings with Christian holding an 'umbrella palm leaf' over me. Downpour intensified and a retreat was called, right back to Peou to await better conditions.

24 July

About noon Claire poured some boiling fat from the oven over the palm of her hand and got a nasty scald and quite a shock poor darling. Went all pale and had to lie down and have a cup of tea. We dressed it with gauze soaked in boiled sodium bicarbonate solution as per 'Hints to Travellers' and the pain went off to a large extent after about half an hour.

29 July

A lovely fine morning, the first for a long time. Sent Nelson and William off to the camp site to get one hundred kauri seedlings, after prospecting for a plantation site down here with Nelson, in the primary jungle above the Lawrence River. Afterwards thought again, in favour of secondary bush above the track.

Plotted, brought maps up to date, revised basal area figures, started report.

Considerable earthquake tremor.

30 July

Paid the boys. Nati started making a compost heap. Nelson, William, Christian and Ramoli completed the two acre plantation, one hundred kauri seedlings at thirty foot spacing, ten rows of ten each. Height of seedlings seven to twelve inches. Cost five and a half man-days.

4 August

Letter to Aunt Phyl.

I did a bit of painting when we had a fine spell and will no doubt return to it sometime. The best one was of a kingfisher sitting on a branch against the sky (from sketches made with binoculars). It was a nice simple subject with the jungle just a green blur down below.

Now it's raining hard and has been off and on for a fortnight. When it gets fine again I want to go out in our outrigger canoe and get a bit more used to the underwater world. At the moment I'm a bit hyper-cautious about invisible sharks and other things.

There are quite a few song birds here, and they are often tame. One of the most regular is the Golden Whistler, a species of which is common in Australia. It is rather a beauty, black, white and yellow. There are a few snakes about. The other day we came across a python about five feet long, fast asleep in one of the tracks we'd cut through the jungle. I poked it and it woke up and hissed at me furiously, and I fled. Also the boys found an orange tree-snake about one foot long, at had died from eating a poisonous frog. This kind of snake is poisonous but has such small fangs that it cannot inject a serious amount of poison.

I am collecting flowering plants, ferns, lizards, frogs and the odd bird, flying-fox and butterfly. With most of them, especially the plants, there isn't a hope of my being able to identify them, they may even be species not yet known; but when I think that there is all this variety just on this one small island, and that the flowering plants, or the lizards, are more closely related to forms occurring in Africa maybe, or America, or England, than to each other, I think what a long time it must have taken for it all to happen and how little we know.

The British Museum have given me two solid little boxes with drying papers and presses for plants, and a box with eight large Kilner jars and a ten gallon drum of methylated spirit for preserving specimens. I hate killing the frogs and lizards. The best way to kill a lizard is to put a bit of tobacco in its mouth and it dies very quickly. The frogs you drop into alcohol and they die a horrid death; but what a lesson to smokers and drinkers!

Claire is going to have a baby sometime around the beginning of March, so we shall all be born under the same stars, which should make for harmony.

4 August

Letter to Aunt Erica.

Many of the more educated natives can speak English and most of the rest speak pidgin English, which is the lingua franca of the Protectorate. On one island there may be twenty mutually incomprehensible native languages, so natives use pidgin English among themselves quite a lot.

5 August

Poured with rain. Cut down a Macaranga and planted an orange tree. Organized Nelson and William into punching holes in papers for filing.

6 August

Hole punching continued. Sent William and Ramoli off to bush to get one hundred kauri seedlings, Nelson and Wete to cut lines.

Started a Working Plan file – 'A plan to make a plan is better than no plan at all.'

7 August

Overcast. Inspected boys' quarters; also the canoe-house being built. Visited boys' gardens and suggested rotation of crops, native cabbage to follow potatoes.

Spent rest of morning exploring approaches to plantation strips from this end, through secondary bush.

10 August

Set off along II.L.w.150. A long way, thirty-seven chains, before we left the worked out area. Then into kauri forest and reached the Lawrence River at sixty-three chains. Lunched, and the boys collected snails and I collected a huge fern, and a flowerless aromatic epiphyte. Returned very weary and had a plunge in a pool.

15 August

Letter to Father.

We've practically finished building a very nice house for our house boy just beyond the kitchen garden. It is on mangrove piles and the framework is of mangrove except for bearers, floor joists, floor and walls which are from Honiara.

The vegetable garden is doing fine. We seem to have been having beans for over a month now, and the new lot are on their way up. We have a fine compost heap about six feet square and nearly as high as myself with a wood framework. The corn is flowering and young pineapples are already visible.

The boys have a largish communal garden down below and are allowed to do gardening on Saturday mornings. They are growing mostly sweet potatoes and some tapioca.

I at last succeeded in shooting a purple swamp hen, when I was trying to get something quite different, naturally, and it made a stew which tasted exactly like rabbit. I also stuffed the skin. Its colours are rather fine, brilliant purple round the shoulders going to blue-black further back, and with a bright red bill and red pate.

The weather here is fully as changeable as in England. You can definitely feel that it is the Southern winter now. There is never any need to wear a hat because of the sun, and this morning when we went for a walk at low tide and I had a dip in the sea, I felt perished with cold when I came out, in the steady SE trade wind. This afternoon it has been raining and thundering, so that there are ponds on the 'lawn' and the verandah is all wet. The days also seem to be very short and it is time to light the lamps after tea.

I have now got a guitar. I know there is a book of instruction that you can get at music shops in England and I think it might be a help. Can you get it and put it on my account, please?

Now for the other white men:

The trader, F. L. Jones, Englishman, has been here longest, twenty-five years or so I think, and is retiring soon. He's quite a nice little man, and has an auxiliary ketch (or yawl or something) in which he sails from group to group. He has a Polynesian wife in a neighbouring group and some children at school in Australia whom he is away visiting now. His store is by the sea, about ten minutes' walk down the hill from here.

Twenty minutes' walk from here and going left over the Lawrence River is Mr MacEwin's place. He is manager of the Kauri Timber Co. He'd be about forty, has been here a long time and is a friend of Jones. The Halings are the timber contractors, two brothers, Alan and Ernie, Mrs H, who is at present in Australia having a baby, and a boy of about six called Max. Mrs H usually runs the hospital and store, but now we have Miss Tabrett, a trained nurse from Australia, who is however going by this boat, another girl having come to replace her. Chaperlin is an Englishman about seventy-five or so, who is secretary for the Halings and lives in a house by our track on the way to Jones's store. He's lived in the Solomons since he was my age and has photograph albums going back a very long time. He keeps a fishing rod, cats and roses.

Living in the bush are Alan Nielen, a dashing young chap, fond of gin and a fast talker, also Bill, and Mr Beresford who is in charge of timber cutting operations.

Between the Halings' and Chaperlin's house are Mr and Mrs Ward, our age, he being the engineer. We've been to dinner with them once or twice and vice versa. Also with the Halings, and return matches with MacEwin. Never MacEwin and Haling together, though. We had a good party at the Halings the other night, a puzzle quiz, also ping-pong. A whole lot of chaps have arrived on the boat for the timber company, among them a fine blond specimen of Hitler Youth. He spent part of this afternoon cross-examining Chaperlin and me on the prospects of women and wine on Vanikoro, and couldn't understand why I didn't have a uniform.

Claire is kept busy organizing the house. There are always two to seven boys working on painting etc and the help of one houseboy is counterbalanced by no laundry, gas, electricity, or tradesmen's delivery. She does very well and makes it much easier for me, produces some pretty good meals, too. Sometimes the Halings' deep freeze has good meat for roasting and we now buy eggs from MacEwin.

* * *

Considering the remoteness of our situation we were very lucky in the station to which we had been sent as far as the oridinary amenities were concerned.

The Halings, who ran the Vanikoro Timber Company, also ran a store for the benefit of their employees, where you could get anything you wanted in the way of tinned food, or a shirt, a sun-hat, or a pair of boots. Mrs Haling was also a trained nurse and ran a dispensary where she treated all comers, including my labourers and the islanders. This was a big help to us as, although we treated our own boys as far as possible for the ordinary things like minor wounds and malaria, there were times when we were very glad of her help. She had one son of about six, called Max, and later she had a daughter, Kim, who was born while she was on leave in Australia. Whenever she was away for any time a nurse was recruited to look after the dispensary in her absence. The Halings also baked bread for the settlement, and in a shed by the river, next door to the generator house, they kept a deep-freeze for meat.

The carcasses came three or four times a year with the

timber ship from Australia. They had a long voyage, though, as the route was from Sydney up to Japan, then down through the Phillipines, New Britain and the Solomons to Vanikoro and so back to Australia; but if the deep-freeze on the ship had been working all right we got our meat, and then it was up to Keith Ward to keep the generator running twenty-four hours a day, so that the meat never unfroze! There were of course two generators, so one could be overhauled while the other was in use.

Keith and Dorothy lived next door to the Halings, about fifty yards away across half an acre of pineapples. Their house, like all the others in the settlement, was a timber bungalow built on piles, its red-painted corrugated-iron roof contrasting pleasantly against the background of coconut palms, hibiscus and oleander bushes and the brown and yellow crotons.

Beyond the Wards, Harry Chaperlin lived by himself in a house close to the path that led to our own house up on the hillside. He had come out to the Solomons on the same boat that had brought Grimble to the Gilbert and Ellice Islands in 1914, and in the Solomons he had been ever since. Now he was secretary to the Company and kept all their paper work under control for them, a full time job.

If you followed the path past Harry's house towards the sea you came to Fred Jones's store and his house, built just behind the beach. Here you could either turn right, behind a handful of rather scruffy huts and a neat little leaf-built church by the canoe-houses, in which case you came to a small timber built house at the edge of the jungle, which used to be the prison before the war, but was now occupied by Forest Department staff; or you could turn left and come to the Halings' store, which opened onto the jetty, and a couple of timber houses nearby that were reserved for the Australians from the bush when they came down for the week-end.

If you passed by on a Saturday night or a Sunday morning you would often be invited in for a bottle of beer. Sometimes there would only be one chap, living there for a bit while he recovered from tropical ulcers under Mrs Haling's care; or you might as easily find a dozen or more, with the Wards and one or other of the Haling brothers as well.

Ernie Haling usually took the small diesel launch, known

as *the Tug* to distinguish it from the larger *Toby* round to the company base at the Sundi River in the early morning with supplies and, if I needed to see the company's workings, I went too.

It was four miles along the lagoon, round by the mangroves and up the little estuary of the Sundi River to the workshop and the beginning of the bush road. Then you could either walk, an ever increasing distance as the road pushed on into the mountains, or you could cling onto one of the timber lorries as it returned after dumping its load of logs on the river bank.

The Australians lived in separate corrugated-iron huts by the roadside and spent their days driving and maintaining the lorries, bulldozers and log-haulers, blasting rock, building the road and extracting logs of anything up to seven tons each. Their huts were built on solid log skids and when the work required they could be towed further up the road by a bulldozer. The log-haulers, huge winches which pulled the logs up the side of the ridge to the road which was usually near the crest, were moved in the same way, leap-frogging each other as the road extended. There were usually about three in action at a time.

It was a world of red, green and blue: naked earth, forest, the sea and the sky. The trade-wind dried the sweat off your chest as soon as it was formed and at the end of the day you could feel you had achieved something solid: a new bit of road, where only jungle had been before; logs by the roadside, logs in the river, ready for towing round to Saboe Bay for the steamer. Then sunset, a shower under the bucket outside your hut and supper prepared by your cook-boy and maybe a friend to share it with. Only one thing missing, in fact.

When it rained, it was not so good. With an annual rainfall of twenty feet (yes, feet, not inches!) down at the met station, it was anybody's guess what it was in the mountains. Work might have to cease for a month or two as the road became unusable; and then the enforced idleness would allow differences to fester which would bother no one if there was a job to do. One cause of friction was a cultural difference resulting from the backgrounds from which recruits were drawn. On the one hand you had the 'fair dinkum Aussie' – a rugged Anglo-Saxon with a heart of gold sometimes from the backwoods of Victoria or Tasmania, and on the other hand you had New Australians from Central Europe. The latter were often relatively sophisticated, though they might be still in the process of learning English. They included Poles, Czechs and Germans.

One Saturday afternoon a tall, blond figure came striding towards our house on long pink legs, having walked across from the Company in the bush for a change of scene. It was Willi Kwiakovski, taut ex-member of Hitler's Youth. He was employed as an engineer round at the Sundi River and knew more about diesel than anyone on the island, having learnt it on U-boats at Hamburg in the war. Uncompromising, awkward in manner and unable to relax and absorb gallons of beer with the rest, he came in for a fair amount of ridicule and practical jokes which were not appreciated.

He used to spend quite a lot of time with Harry Chaperlin, who could understand him and see his good points, and with us, but otherwise he must have been rather lonely. He could not understand what I was there for until one day he got hold of one of my forestry text-books which had quite a few German terms in it.

'Ah!' he said, 'Now I understand what you do, why you not tell me before?'

In the end he went because he could not stand the company's method of working. He was expected to keep trucks running continuously, by patching them up from day to day, until they fell to bits. This was anathema to him. To his way of thinking each truck should come right off the road and be serviced properly at regular intervals, instead of going on until it was nothing but a battered chassis six months after delivery.

So he left Vanikoro, and made his mark instead as engineer in charge of motor vehicle maintenance in the PWD workshop at Honiara.

16 August

Some of the kauri seedlings in the plantation dead, mostly at the end of rows, in the most exposed positions.

17 August

Looked at the plantation. In one row only one seedling out of nineteen was dead, not so bad.

18 August

Went with William along his new path. It was rough going, mostly, of no great advantage. Arrived at the picnic spot and then followed a tributary eastwards, abominably slimy stones for walking on. Resorted to bare feet, but that was not much better. William took me back along an admirable, if somewhat wet, riverside track leading direct to the cow-pasture. Constitutes a major discovery, access to our favourite recreation area, formerly three times more difficult to get at.

19 August

Poured with rain. Did a lot of plotting. Boys working on the house.

20 August

Cleared up about midday, so I took William and Christian and surveyed along the River Road.

21 August

Bought new gym shoes at store. Investigated possibility of draining swamp below house and cow pasture.
pm. Went up through plantation and along last row, then up to have a look at the highest regen. strips. Finer afternoon, tended roses with Claire.

* * *

22 August

Sunday. Rained steadily all day. Claire and I did plant collection together, thirty-two species now labelled and described.

24 August

Having been shown the path going to the Ambi River, decided to follow it a little way. Got a little beyond the Oora river where the track deteriorated (or we lost it), a track that was made by manual labour in the days of the old timber company. Ended up in the mangroves. I collected a couple of species with flowers and set off back through mangroves. There were large pot-holes in swamp at one point, with coral visible underneath, a haunt of crocodiles and water snakes. This was later pointed out to me as the mouth of the Oora River.

Returned 10.30 am. Organized plant collection with Claire's help.

25 August

Christian sighted the *Citos* at 8.0 am, and she arrived about ten. Went aboard with Mr Ward. I was introduced to Mr Guest, Director of the Kauri Timber Company.

26 August

Mr Guest and Mr Becket dropped in to tell me the news about Timber Company decision relative to leaving seed trees – negative.

Showed them round a bit.

Thought much about how to get sustained yield and resolved to pay Guest and company a visit in the morning.

* * *

27 August

Off at 7.0 am in *Toby* with Haling to Saboe Bay. Saw interesting patch of dead mangrove trees just inshore. Why? Meteor?

Had to wait on *Citos* a bit, then contacted Guest, Beckett and Mac. Talked about sustained yield and modified uniform system.

4 September

Asked Nelson and William to get the men's gardens a bit more organized and try and produce some food.

A short and severe earth tremor in the middle of the night woke us up and sent us flying to the front door.

5 September

Sunday. Rained solidly all day. Pottered among the vegetable beds in the morning, leading new rivulets into the main drain, which is now a torrent.

Our stream a red and fearsome torrent. Claire ran out starko in the rain to have a look.

In the afternoon I started working at timber specimens. Tentative identifications:

Kesi: *Palaquium* sp.
Aywarawa: *Neoscortechinia forbesii*
Airate and Noora: No luck yet.

6 September

Went up the track and examined the secondary forest for Kauri seed trees, deciding on three or four places to start new regeneration lines. Nelson showed me forty pounds of rice he had from the store with cat and rat droppings in it. Arranged with Chaperlin to get it changed.

William got a large chunk of karamati timber for identification purposes.

Later I sent Nelson and company up to continue with regneration strips. Looked at karamati specimen.

8 September

Weather still holding. Sent Nelson and William up to the strips and followed myself later. Collected a couple of unknown trees, one a first storey job that William calls 'Nanum'.

10 September

Transplanted two paw-paw seedlings and dug a rose bed. Did customs forms. Nelson brought in wood specimen of Nanum.

11 September

Busy transplanting self-sown kauri seedlings about the garden. Nelson came and announced that the men were still in bed (about 9.30 am), so I roused them out and put them on gardening. Trying planting tapioca.

12 September

Eventually I was provided with a launch of my own, but until then we had to hitch-hike on the company boats or use our own canoe for pleasure.

It cost us five pounds to have a small outrigger canoe made for us. The hull was made from a hollowed-out Kuo tree (*Hernandia cordigera*), with a narrow slit along the top just big enough to take your legs, one in front of another, as you sat on top. The float, like a baby canoe, was attached to the hull by a platform and provided stability only. If you sat on the platform the float went under.

If you went straight across the lagoon to the reef it was about a mile and a half. We had been there with Mac in his launch once or twice, but thought it would be fun to go in our own canoe. So we waited till a morning when it seemed calmer than usual, although it is true that there were still a few white horses in the lagoon, then we collected some food and set off, paddling out to sea.

Soon a motor-boat hove in sight, with Lyle Beckett, on a visit from Company Headquarters in Melbourne, and Alan Nielen, a wiry, sandy-haired, blue-eyed, humorous chap who was always around when something interesting was afoot.

'Hiya Chris! Hiya Claire! Come for a ride with us?'

'Thanks, Alan, but we want to see if we can reach the reef in the canoe.'

'OK . . . Rather you than me!'

They veered off and headed for the jetty. Now we were about a third of the way across and the waves seemed to be becoming steeper. I sat behind Claire in the stern and watched the indigo ridges of water coming towards us from the port bow, flashing in the morning sun. A bigger trough than usual came along, the stern sank down, and with alarm I saw the next wave pour into the hollow log on which we were sitting. Obviously we could not make the reef and we preferred not to have to swim for it because you never can tell with sharks. Besides, our first child was now three months on the way.

So we turned her round, and paddled like fury for the shore. At least I paddled, Claire was fully occupied baling water out with a tin. But water continued to come aboard, and the lower she got the more she shipped water . . . Until at last the dreadful moment came when I realized that she was bound to ship every oncoming wave and sink.

Sure enough, two or three waves came in one after the other and down she went, with us sitting on her! We yelled for help in the direction of Alan's boat which was still just visible. Then we realized that the canoe had not sunk completely and was not going to. We sat on the partly submerged outrigger and paddled slowly towards the shore, our morale high after the initial panic.

Keith and Dorothy now appeared in their outboard-engined launch, heading in our direction. They did not realize our plight until they came close to us, then they gave us a tow to a point on the fringing reef where there were the wrecked remains of one of the Company's previous launches. There we had a pleasant party, swimming about in the shallows and collecting shells. Then they departed and we made for a beautiful hard white sandy beach by the mangroves and had lunch there in the shade.

It was the same beach on which I had followed my own footprints, five months before.

Afterwards we learned that there is an effective method of coping with a water-logged canoe, that is used by the islanders.

The thing to do is to get off the canoe so that you are swimming alongside then to grasp one of the pointed ends of the hull. You then oscillate the canoe so that the water inside builds up into a wave which eventually shoots out at one end. The water remaining is then removed by baling, after which you can climb back onto the canoe.

15 September

Rained a lot in the night, also thunder and lightning. Slept reasonably well under the circumstances. Morning overcast and a tendency to rain, but not too bad so we set off for the line that was cut yesterday (90 W at 140 degrees), and reached limit of their cuttings at thirty-two chains. Then turned back, as the rain had set in steadily. This line entered virgin kauri forest at about four chains and there is a lot of kauri regeneration, especially marked in the first part.

17 September

Claire picked kapok from our kapok tree, which has just fruited, and got quite a mass of it.

* * *

The lorries brought the logs down from the bush one or two or three at a time, according to size, and they were then unloaded onto the river bank and pushed and levered into the river. There they were joined together by a system of iron 'dogs' and cables so that a raft was formed which was then towed by one of the Company launches down the river, along the lagoon and, in the season of the South-East trade wind, past Peou and into Saboe Bay to await the ship.

On the map Saboe Bay looked like a great slipper pointing towards the other side of the island and separated only by a narrow isthmus from Manevai Bay. Rugged jungle-covered hills enclosed it on all sides except the south-west and to the north the red cliffs of the summit ridge of Vanikoro led up to Mount Popogia. During the war the bay had been a sea-plane base and had indeed seen the only military action in the Santa Cruz group, when Japanese planes came and shot up the sea-planes. It was a perfect anchorage and in the south-east season logs were usually loaded there. In the north-west season, when there was less wind, they were more often loaded from the lagoon off Peou.

The timber ships were modern Swedish liners, belonging to the Wilhelmssen Line, and there were four that used to call at Vanikoro: Aros, Citos, Delos and Milos. There were only three or four visits in a year, depending on how log production went, and these visits were naturally our main big excitement in life. In addition to the cargo the ships carried up to a dozen luxury passengers, so there would be parties and sometimes dancing on board. The ship would anchor in deep water and machinery, stores and fuel would be unloaded onto rafts made of timber and empty fuel drums. The rafts of logs would then be towed alongside and would lie there redly gleaming in the sparkling sapphire sea.

One by one the ship's cranes heaved the logs out of the sea, swung them, dripping against the blue sky and lowered them safely into the hold. Most of the logs were Kauri Pine, and when they reached Melbourne they were destined for peeling. Supported at each end by the machine, each log would be rotated like a great rolling pin while a steel blade cut a wide thin sheet of wood from the log until only the centre was left. The thin sheet so produced would then be used as veneer or for making plywood.

* * *

20 September

Every year two or three million superficial feet of timber were exported from the island. The big question, of course, was 'How much was left?'

Part of the answer lay eighty miles away across the ocean among the mountains of Ndeni, and it was not until the end of my second year in the Solomons that Mac and I went and stayed there for two months and found out the extent of the Kauri Forests on that island. Meanwhile, the opportunity was taken of making a reconnaissance to the island while Lyle Beckett, from the Kauri Timber Company's head office in Melbourne, was with us.

We went in the Vanikoro Timber Company's larger launch, *Toby*. It was a grey boat, with a mast forward, and a single large cabin in which the diesel engine was housed, along with drums of fuel, cartons of food, and our bedding. You could sit either on the flat cabin roof, or inside the cabin, or you could find a perch with the boys, forward by the mast.

Claire and Mrs Haling came down to the jetty to see us off. The party consisted of Alan Haling, Mac, Lyle, William Piaito, whose home was on Ndeni, a couple of my labourers who were bound for their home islands, and myself.

The lagoon was calm and the sky clear as we steered out past the mangroves towards the passage in the barrier reef opposite the estuary of the Sundi River. The main reefs round an island of the Vanikoro type are the fringing reef by the shore and the barrier reef forming a ring round the island and enclosing a lagoon. Other lumps of coral, however, abound in the lagoon, and we now hit one of these and stuck fast. Fortunately it was a temporary affair and we soon managed to push ourselves off.

Then we were through the passage and into the calm bright immensity of the open Pacific. We called briefly at Utupua, nosing our way in cautiously through the passage, then headed out again for the dim outline of Ndeni, fifty miles away.

As the afternoon wore on dark squalls marred the clearness of the sky, and a long, low, oily swell set the *Toby* swinging to its rhythm. Now the low wooded outline of Lord Howe Island, an appendage of Ndeni, was under our starboard beam and soon we were picking out the bays of Ndeni's Southern coast: Maunda Bay, Napir Bay. Everywhere the land was dark with its mantle of forest, the ridges rising behind to the cloudy crest of the island. Ahead of us now was Cape Mendana, the headland forming the Southern limit of a coast of sheer cliffs of ancient coral, the edge of a plateau which stretched across the western end of the island. Above a small bay at the landward end of the promontory we could now make out the leaf-built houses of William's village, Nabalue, on the top of the cliff.

We rounded the Cape and there was the little wooded island of Nea, separated from the mainland by a completely sheltered sound. We steered in, cut the engine and dropped anchor twenty yards from the sandy beach. On the other side the broken cliffs of Cape Mendana closed in upon us, the forest struggling for a foothold on every ledge and in every gully. The canoes that came over the emerald water to the launch were simple dugouts, and their occupants boys of about eight to ten years old, smiling and full of curiosity. There was a mission school here.

After dark I rowed ashore in the dinghy for a walk along the clean, sandy beach.

* * *

21 September

No European lived on Ndeni and those that visited it, missionaries, traders, or the DC, only called at the villages which were all by the sea. So I asked William if it was not possible to walk across the island from Graciosa Bay on the other side, over the coral plateau to his village near Cape Mendana.

It was easy, he said. There was a good path and the walk would only take a few hours. Since the plan was to go round to Graciosa Bay in the launch next morning I determined to do this.

Tinakula hove in sight as we left Nea behind and rounded the Western end of Ndeni. Its plume of smoke was white against the early morning blue. At the head of Graciosa Bay

William and I parted from the rest of the expedition, arranging to meet them at Nabalue next day, after they had circumnavigated the island, looking for Kauri forest from the sea.

Having packed two rucksacks ready for the trip we went ashore and met the old headman. Without success we tried recruiting labourers for the work on Vanikoro, but we did manage to collect a couple of porters for our walk.

It was raining and we had a snack under the trunk of a huge Calophyllum tree that leant out over the beach. Then we set off along the track and climbed steeply up until we reached the coral plateau at 250 feet above sea level. Now we were in what appeared to be primary forest, passing the buttressed trunks of huge trees with their crowns lost to sight far above. There was no Kauri, however.

I had often wondered about this plateau. Being limestone, surely it should be riddled with caverns?

On being asked, William admitted that there were extensive caves near his village, and twice he pointed out small pot-holes in the ground near the path, which he said were deep and dangerous. I could not have guessed that a year later Mac and I were to traverse one of the caves, and come across a mystery which was believed by the villagers to have a supernatural explanation.

We walked on through the afternoon, often splashing through swampy places. Once, away through the trees, we heard the call of wildfowl, and William told me that these were the descendants of poultry brought across from South America by the Spanish colonists. So perhaps after all there are some survivors from the expedition of the great Mendana, three and a half centuries ago. A bunch of hens!

The deep green of primary forest gave way to the light green of Macaranga growing on patches of old cultivation. Still there were a few big trees, many of them useful in some way or other, and most of them having an owner in the village we were approaching. The track enlarged, gardens appeared, and then we were among the leaf houses on a cliff overlooking the south of the Nanu River. There was some surprise at our arrival. Europeans never came this way.

From the edge of the cliff William sang out across the gorge until someone from his village appeared on the other side.

Forest Guard William Piaito and family at Nabalue.

People at Nabalue.

We descended and a canoe came across to fetch us, then, after a brief ascent, we were at Nabalue. I was given an empty hut with a raised floor of split palm stems and I peeled off my rain-soaked clothes. Later William brought me a large pudding in a bowl. It was doughy, with a pleasant nutty flavour. For drink I had the juice of a green coconut.

At sunset and at sunrise a bell rang and everybody in the village who was able to walk went to the church for prayers and hymn-singing. This they do every day of the year, and it is typical of many villages in the Solomons, where a simple, sincere form of Christianity has caught on. European missionaries may not come from one year's end to the next, for the diocese of Melanesia is scattered over several hundred thousand square miles. But of their own accord they practice their religion as a community, as we used to do in the villages of Britain, before Progress came.

The village was in a superb situation on top of a sea-cliff, looking out towards Cape Mendana, Behind was the jungle, and their gardens where the food was grown. A little below the village was a walled enclosure where they kept pigs caught in the forest, and fattened them up to eat at Christmas. To complete the comparison with an English village, instead of the Green there was a circle of beaten earth, ringed by a low wall of loose stones, where they danced, though not when I was there.

22 September

Next day I had just taken some photographs and was going for a saunter in the jungle, when the beat of the *Toby's* engine was heard and we descended to the beach to rejoin the rest of the party. Then, returning to the village, we took a guide and began to walk inland.

We crossed a river and a couple of streams and started to climb. At 450 feet above sea-level we saw the first Kauri Pine. We had reached the edge of the Kauri forest at last!

We lunched after five and a half hours' walking, then returned to the village where we were offered a green coconut each to drink. Then, after saying goodbye to the villagers, we descended to the river to have a wash from the shingle spit across its mouth. On the village side of the river several very expectant mothers were in various states of immersion. This is their chief occupation, as the water supports the burden and is pleasantly refreshing at the same time. They have to be careful of crocodiles, though.

The *Toby* was anchored a few yards off-shore, and we turned in about seven as the light was going. Three hours later I was awakened by a shout. The anchor rope had broken in the swell, and were drifting ashore in the dark! Alan was onto the engine in a flash and it started first turn: 'Putt-putt-putt-putt-kerputter-kerputter-kerputter' . . .

We steered straight out to sea in the rising wind, the *Toby* pitching viciously as we charged the steep seas. Later the motion eased a bit and I got some sleep.

A change in the motion woke me up. We were rolling fairly heavily. Alan was at the wheel and we were heading for the lee of Lord Howe Island. We were in deep water here, and there should be no danger of reefs until we got closer in. I crawled forward and stood up, hooking an arm around the mast. The crescent Moon hung out to starboard, but the sea was black, unbroken by the gleam of surf.

When the sky began to pale we turned back towards the mainland, and pretty soon we could see the dark outline of the land.

* * *

23 September

It was a fine clear morning and the sea was abating every moment, and as I stood out there, watching for reefs and breathing the cool air of dawn, I reflected that this must be one of the best of all ways to begin a day. Peril behind, and an unknown land ahead. I thought of first light on the snow-field and the sun coming up behind the Matterhorn and warming the red rocks of an Alpine col. A setting so different and yet in essence the same. This was Life.

We thought the opening ahead must be Maunda Bay, so went in and dropped our spare anchor. We breakfasted on eggs, paw-paw, bread and tea then went ashore. The beach was a fine sweep of green-black sand, with a small river each end, and inland was the usual rugged jungle country.

We soon realized however that it was not Maunda and set off again to find the larger bay, with its village, further round to the East. The village was just across from Lord Howe Island and when we stopped there canoes came out with Green Snail and Trochus shell for sale. But there was no news of Kauri here, so we went on into the bay, which was large but shallow, to explore.

Cut off from the sea by mangroves in every direction, we stopped the engine and drifted while we had lunch. Then we returned to Nabalue to collect William and a couple of porters and came back to the sound that stretches narrowly for some miles between Lord Howe Island and the mainland, for a safe and peaceful anchorage that night.

In 1945 F. S. Walker, of the Malayan Forest Service had been seconded to the Solomons to do a survey, in the course of which he had reached most of the Kauri forests of the Santa Cruz Islands. From his camp at Napir, the next bay to the Eastward from Nabalue, he had found the nearest approach on Ndeni of Kauri forest to the sea. Napir, accordingly, was our next objective.

* * *

24 September

By morning the heel of the boat had grounded on a head of coral and she had to be pushed off. Then we made for Napir and landed on the steep shingle beach, leaving Alan aboard as he had brushed against the leaves of a poison tree on our walk two days before and his face and eyes were swollen and painful. We skirted a thicket of Pandanus behind the beach and passed under the coconut trees into steamy lowland forest. Every hundred yards or so the path would swerve as it met the huge base of one of the forest dominants. Once we passed close to the little river that came out at the Western end of the beach, and parakeets flashed green in the morning sun, while startled pigeons swooshed out of the crown of a tree where they had been feeding.

'Should've brought a gun' said Mac, 'then we could have had pigeon pie for supper.'

We crossed a stream and climbed steeply up the side of a ridge. At the top, only an hour's walk from the beach, we were in Kauri forest. The crest of the ridge led us easily upwards and we walked with delight through grove after grove of the sturdy, russet and silver-grey barked trunks. In defiance of the worst a hurricane can do these trees occupy the most exposed positions where they can get the combination of high rainfall and free drainage they require. Over to the left the squarish tops of another lot of Kauri in the distance indicated the proximity of the ridge on which we had been the day before yesterday.

On the hill-top where the two ridges joined we kindled a small fire and brewed a pot of tea, then we pushed on up the main ridge, which became narrow and winding. The altimeter registered 800 feet above sea level when we came to a gap in the trees giving us a good view into the interior of the island. Below us the ground fell sharply away and as we gazed north-north-east upon ridge upon ridge of Kauri forest we had no doubt that, in view of the fact that none had been seen by the boat party on the other side of the island, we were looking upon its main development on Ndeni.

Meanwhile there was a hue and cry down the other side of our ridge where the dogs belonging to the Nabalue party had found a family of pigs. Only one piglet was caught, however, and it was let go, being too small.

As we returned to the *Toby* I collected several plants, including some of the little filmy ferns growing by the path. These were later sent to the British Museum and identified.

Leaving Napir, we returned to the sound for the night, and as we rounded the point of Lord Howe Island next morning and set a course for Utupua, it was with the certain knowledge that we had found the beach on which the survey of the Kauri forests of Ndeni must be based.

* * *

25 September

Made good speed and reached Utupua about lunch time. After lunch we went ashore and went round the village with the old headman. Later we talked to the new school teacher (ex Pawa school), and went round the village with him too.

Received presents of four paw-paws and gave presents of tobacco in exchange.

26 September

A buoy discovered by Mac was hoisted aboard. After last minute transactions, we set off back to Vanikoro. Fine, usual swell. Arrived home at midday. Claire came back from reef in Keith's boat just after.

* * *

1 October

Cat had three kittens in the night, having first woken us up about 3 am to show us her nest selected for the purpose down below the pineapples. In the morning we transferred the family to a box in the house with wood-wool.

2 October

About fourteen chaps started to make a cricket field on the old gardens site, and another chap whittling away at a cricket bat. The idea seems to have caught on.

4 October

Very rough night – earthquake to start with, followed by lightning, thunder and floods of rain. Very wet last night, too. Also this is the third day running on which we have had a considerable earth tremor.

5 October

Continued with customs.

Camp on Vanikoro had now been moved about half a mile down the ridge from the hut, which had been dismantled. We had our own tent now and the new, virgin camp site was cleaner than the old. It was nice not to have rats running over your body while you slept.

We still reaped some benefits from past occupation of the area, however. The bush had been cleared and growth around the camp was light and secondary, while everywhere there were tracks. Also the 'native cabbage', a kind of wild hibiscus, had been planted all over the place and we used it to supplement our diet of tinned meat, rice and biscuit, thereby keeping up our vitamin C.

After the first Ndeni expedition I was prevented from going on enumeration for a month by an infected toe, and during this time I had to spend a lot of time doing customs forms. It was good to be home, though. There were paths in the light woodland up the hill behind the house to explore when it was fine, and often my attention would be caught by the antics of one of the half-dozen or so species of passerine birds on the island.

7 October

Customs forms.

Thought about trying to get a job in England after this, at Outward Bound School for instance.

11 October

Self doing own customs forms, with Claire.

12 October

Still doing own customs forms, totals will not add up right. Sick of customs forms.

Prevented from going to the bush by toe, which is not yet healed.

15 October

Finished customs forms early, then spent the day inspecting local forests. Estimated 90% survival in plantation.

In the afternoon went up the hill with Nelson and looked for site for further planting. Saw site of old government house on ridge top and white man's grave.

17 October

Worked on the dam all afternoon, raised water level by about a foot, so you can now have a proper swim in it. After tea Claire came and 'opened' it with a glorious naked swim, water having cleared. Large crayfish much in evidence.

18 October

Went and had a swim in the pool before breakfast. Claire also had a swim later in the morning after she'd been down to the village and got hot. The pool is a great success in fact.

29 October

Letter to Father.

A chap called Lyle Beckett from Tasmania has been staying here and was on the Santa Cruz trip. A twenty-five foot cutter is supposed to be calling for him from Santo (New Hebrides) tomorrow, so this will go then I hope. He has been here on behalf of the Kauri Timber Company, looking around.

I have had a couple of glorious weekends damming our stream and we have now got a pool big enough to swim a couple of strokes in. The floods tend to knock the top foot off but it's still good for a wallow. When it's fine weather we have a dip before breakfast.

Forestry operations have been much hampered by rain of late, also I've had a septic toe got from a blister at Santa Cruz. Everything goes septic here. It's better now. Day before yesterday I was round at the Sundi River and up in the bush I met a Pole, who was a Spitfire pilot, working a log hauler. He was stationed in Manchester. We had iced coffee in his hut.

The warm weather is coming again now, and the sun is vertically overhead at midday. Once when I wanted to know the time I held a pebble so that its shadow was on another small pebble, and when dropped (from two or three feet) it bounced the other pebble out of the way. I wonder what sort of a winter you are in for this time. I will be quite glad to get back to seasons again.

30 October

Letter to Aunt Erica.

Pippa had three kittens on 1 October, Ginger, Blackie and Tabby, now all entering the frisky stage. When she had them, she came and got us up in the middle of the night, and then took me right down to the edge of the kitchen garden and showed me a hole she had chosen in a bush. And in the morning, there they all were. We've had them in the house most of the time since then, in a box with wood wool, but twice she took them out into the jungle again. The second time she left Ginger behind as he was too big to carry, so I had to carry him and she showed me where the family was. The last move back to the house was made with Pippa's assistance.

1 November

pm. Set off for bush.

2 November

Rain threatened, but as our way lay down towards the Lawrence River, we escaped any that fell. Surveyed left and right along the Lawrence River, contacting the other strips on each side. The river surveying was all done by Nelson, I watched and occasionally put in form lines. Returned up secondary ridge. Tired, I ate four slices of pineapple right off.

3 November

Completed the strip from above the view-point and then crossed a biggish stream before reaching Lawrence River.

Bathed and lunched in and by river. Sent Christian home to get camera and sketch block and take them to camp.

Surveyed 2000 feet up the river, then back through some very fine kauri forest.

Boys cooking shells collected in river. Tried two, nice.

4 November

Quite a bit of rain in night, very fine day however. Set off for Banie. Took a panorama at 2200 feet, looking back along the ridge, then photos in Tevai direction. Quite a bit of cloud about over Tevai. Wonderful view. Climbed a tree to look at the beginning of the ridge on the left of the Lawrence River. Then back. Got in the stream at midday. Brew of tea etc.

Then surveyed down the road as far as the small hill on the way to Sundi River station. Beautiful afternoon, brilliant sun, spatters of rain, cumuli and fresh blue sky. Utupua in the distance, sometimes obscured by a rain cloud.

5 November

Plotted. Had Nelson and company sawing and chopping timber specimens into convenient sizes.

7 November

In the evening Claire and I sorted out the dried plant specimens. We now have fifty-one species.

11 November

With Nelson, I measured trees at MacEwin's. Kauris had grown to fifty feet high and with a girth of 5' 1" in seventeen years.

13 November

Played about with identifying woods, think Airate may be *Aglaia* sp.

15 November

Public holiday. I walked round the tracks behind the house. A commotion in the top of a bush reveals a young Golden Whistler impatiently fanning its wings while its mother, no bigger than itself, brings it a mouthful of grubs.

From low down in the thicket comes a mysterious 'chuck

chuck' noise. I stalk it as quietly as possible, but conscious of making an elephantine disturbance in the undergrowth. Then I stand quite still, perceiving the second young golden whistler, feeding at ground level, which is the source of the sound, and becoming aware of all the other life about me: a black, orange-bellied lizard nine inches long poised menacingly while an unsuspecting black ant scurries towards it along a fallen branch, then suddenly swerves away from the danger; the pervasive din of the shrill cicada, dying away only to be taken up by another just behind.

Then run down to the stream and a plunge in the cool clear water of the dam while the little crayfish dashes for cover under the big rock in the middle.

Other birds seen: long-tailed kingfisher by the path, adult male golden whistler in the tops of noora trees, and a fantail.

17 November

Off in the *Tug* with John to the Sundi River. Inspected regeneration strips, John planted seedlings where necessary.

Heard Alan discussing reason for low output – too much malingering!

Looked at the felling and talked to boss-boy (Thomas) and others about low stumps.

Collected information about the set-up: four haulers, about twenty natives per hauler; three cross-cut saws per hauler each with four men, boss-boy and rope operators.

A good day should yield about three trees of say 1500 super each per hauler or a total of 18,000 super for the lot. This is equivalent to 90,000 per week, and Mr Haling's aim is 80,000 per week, which is not attained. 80,000 per week = 4,000,000 per annum, just under double the usual output, but what they hope to increase to.

Letter from Geoff Dennis, Honiara.

Many thanks for your interesting note of August last; you and Claire appear to be enjoying the isolated life in spite of the lack of more civilized amenities and the very wet climate for which, I believe, Vanikoro is noted. Too bad the sea bathing facilities are not so good,

Chris, but like all these high islands in the Pacific, good beaches are difficult to find – one has to go out to the atolls and other low islands to enjoy real reefs, lagoons and delightful white sands. Still you can enjoy lots of fun and interest with a face mask or goggles in any patch of coastal water or stretch of river. Several of us here are thinking seriously of acquiring aqua-lungs, forming a small club, and venturing into the greater depths together. Incidentally, I spent most of the last weekend in the water off the reefs at Tulagi, where a mixed party of ten of us went camping – saw three sharks, and was able to study sea-horses, blue demoiselle fish and other queer creatures at close quarters; I've returned to Honiara brown as a Polynesian.

I have been out on many walking, swimming, cycling, and canoeing trips, Chris, since you were here, including two more excursions up the Mataniko'o River to the caverns, subterranean streams, etc. and discovered an entirely new series of caves in the same area. Of course there were no women in the party on these occasions, and we went equipped with torches and candles for cave exploration. There are about a dozen of us here now who are keen on the outdoor life, and weekend trips are becoming popular.

Harking back to the subject of goggle-diving, one of the local Melanesians who is employed as a truck driver by the PWD went spear fishing weekend before last off the Japanese wreck, up the coast. Having caught a few fish, he was returning to the wreck when a large shark attacked him and grabbed him by the head. He had the presence of mind to remain quite still and rigid, instead of struggling, and the shark relaxed its grip sufficiently long for him to escape to the surface and struggle onto the ship suffering only from a few superficial teeth lacerations. As he is a member of the Malaita clan who totemistically worship the shark, and this is the second occasion on which he has escaped from a shark's jaws, he and his friends are firmly convinced that no shark will deliberately kaikai them!

You are fortunate to be away from all the 'red tape' which makes life in Honiara so intolerable at times. I'm completely frustrated in management of Lands Department affairs, like other heads of departments, since Secretariat persists in having a hand in everything that goes on and, by so doing, delays the completion of various matters for months; I have had land applications that have been outstanding for more than three years held up simply because the powers-that-be can't make quick decisions.

Congratulations to you both on the happy event anticipated in February – believe me, you'll have your time fully occupied being a papa, Chris, for several years to come. Still, I guess you will be very happy in your new status – Claire too!! John Logie tells me that she may not be coming here for the special occasion; however, perhaps you'll both change your minds, in which case I shall look forward to seeing you again.

My wife and young Tony went southward to Sydney in July. The infant is growing upwards and outwards in the temperate climate, and starts school with his elder brother at the beginning of the year.

I am hoping to make a trip to Lord Howe Atoll next month for a week's stay. The entomologist Eric Brown and I have been asked by Dr Hollins to go up there in order to confirm, by examination of the entire area, that his six months of anti-malarial campaigning there has succeeded in completely destroying anopheline mosquitoes. Fred Hollins believes that malaria has been the main factor in reducing the population there from an estimated 6,000 souls about sixty years ago to a mere 700 at the present day and considers that, as the atoll is a Polynesian outlier and remote from the high mainland islands where malaria has always been endemic, the disease was probably introduced by early European traders and missionaries; virtually 100% of the population suffer from the disease at the present time. It's a lovely spot up there – a complete world of its own, the horizons of which are the blue Pacific, and the land a string of white pearl-like sandy islands, densely clothed in feathery coconut palms, incessantly pounded by surf on the seaward side and lapped by the placid waters of the magic blues and greens of the forty mile long lagoon within its circle. The people are fair, charming, clean and friendly, fond of dancing and great fisher-folk; in fact, a real romantic South sea island.

Honiara continues to grow up, but the place is still predominantly a Government town; private enterprise isn't interested in the Solomons. In fact, the position in regard to the outside lack of interest in the development of these islands has become so serious that the High Commissioner leaves on Monday's plane for England to discuss BSIP affairs with the Colonial Office personally.

I do know that the planters have presented a petition to Government requesting abolition of income tax, as it was here before the war, and as is the present position in the adjoining Australian territory of New Guinea. The latter territory is progressing in leaps and bounds – with no income tax, low import duties and higher wages there, enterprising folk prefer the place to the Solomons.

I guess you have quite a small museum there now, Chris, judging from your description of the collecting of natural history specimens you have been doing. It's an interesting hobby, and one can never become bored if the interest in nature is retained – there's always some fascinating new thing to be discovered and wondered at if you are the observant type, and your work must give you ample opportunity to get about and see things.

27 November

Mr Logie and I had a look at the boys gardening. Saw William in hospital, having had a four inch splinter extracted from his foot on Thursday evening. He is in a very bad state, writhing and groaning the whole time, his foot very swollen. Mrs Haling says nothing can be done at this stage, except to drink a lot, as he has fever.

28 November

Sunday. Down to see William, he was quieter but had another sleepless night.

Mary arrived, running out of fuel. Aboard with Logie and Alan Nielen. Latter pretty drunk, tried to sink us on the way ashore!

29 November

Saw William, he was still in a bad way. We had a discussion as to whether to send him to Kira Kira and then Honiara or not.

3 December

Letter to Aunt Erica.

Mr Logie has been here for a fortnight, and the DC will soon be returning to collect him. Claire is also going back to Honiara, because Mrs Haling more or less insisted on her having the baby where a doctor would be available. Anyway I expect I will be going there in February, and then we will return in March.

Pippa's kittens are now in full spate and all over the place. Nelson is taking the ginger one home to Malaita, where he is now going on leave. William had an accident and got a splinter of wood four inches long and half an inch wide in his foot. It was extracted all right but he's been in a very bad way all the week, foot swelled up like a football and in great pain. He seems to be getting a bit better now however.

So now I will be without both Forest Guards as well as without Claire, and in addition I have just had four extra labourers recruited, making a total of seven, and there will be no one but me to supervise them. And I have the Customs work and the running of the Forest Department for office work, so something will get left out! I have told Mr Logie that if he expects the survey done in three years I can do it if I don't have to be hamstrung by the Customs work the whole time – otherwise it's off! So perhaps one day I will have some assistance. There is talk of Naqu coming back next year, which would be fine.

The radio has come back and this time it works, which is very nice. We get some quite decent music from Australia at times, also the BBC of course.

The tomatoes are in flower. I am so sorry that Claire will not be here to enjoy them (if they produce tomatoes), she was so looking forward to them.

The Mary *with the District Commissioner is expected tomorrow. The sea's been rough though and it may not come yet.*

4 December

Did parcel to British Museum containing swamp hen, flying fox and bat.

5 December

Sunday. Helped Claire pack a little. No sign of the *Mary*.

6 December

Motor vessel *Mary* sighted soon after breakfast. Down to

meet John Hearth and deal with mail.

Boys carried cases down and Claire left finally before sunset, feeling well and looking happy. Also going: Logie, Hearth, Nelson, William and Christian. Christian is to be Claire's personal servant.

7 December

pm. Off to camp sending three boys first.

10 December

Fine morning. Off along the ridge as far as C51. Sat up in a tree and reviewed the situation. As a result of my cogitations set a course of 120 degrees through the jungle – skirting the upward limit of kauri forest at 1500 to 1550 feet – Kauri few, big and very mossy. One specimen with girth twenty feet eight inches. Reached point above stream – no kauri visible on other side except lower down. Measured fifteen below girth limit trees on the open ridge top, with the idea of obtaining growth records. Then continued surveying road to Sundi River from 3,000 to 5,000 feet downwards. Thence to camp again – picked up rucksack and down home. Fine evening. Selwyn in occupation. Cats hungry – they drank two saucers of milk right off.

Supper: Sausage (tinned), English potato, onions, beans, Pawpaw. Some good music on the radio afterwards, 'Scenes from Childhood', Schubert.

11 December

Tidied things up. Selwyn fetched some meat for lunch.

12 December

Sunday. Rather wet. Read novel most of the time. Getting own meals, Selwyn having a day off.

Letter from Claire to Aunt Erica.

I expect you will be surprised to see that I am in Honiara. I can hardly believe it myself. It was all decided rather suddenly when Mr Logie came down to Vanikoro about three weeks ago. He brought a lot of mail from you all including your August letter and note enclosed in Chris's letter for me. I wish we had had more leisure to enjoy them. Still I expect Chris is re-reading them now. I am staying with the Logies until after Christmas and then probably moving into a small house on my own, the idea being that Chris should join me in February. I do hope this doesn't fall through as I should hate to be on my own for long.

Now to tell you a little about our journey down here which was quite interesting except for the first twenty-four hours when I was seasick. We (that is Mr Logie, the District Commissioner for the Eastern Solomons and I) left Vanikoro on Monday in pouring rain and headed out into the open sea. Instead of making for Santa Cruz, which is usually the first halting place, we made straight for the island of San Cristobal which we reached on Wednesday morning. We had lovely weather this day and cruised gently along the island, calling in at a couple of Roman Catholic Mission stations on the way, reaching Kira Kira, the DC's headquarters in the evening. We had to stay here until Friday afternoon as the ship had to take on a load of copra, but I enjoyed it very much indeed. Kira Kira is a lovely place, the only European house being the DC's, the rest consisting of post office, police station and native jail, native hospital under a native doctor etc. The whole station is in a lovely bay with the surf breaking continually on the white sand. The next morning we paid a visit to a nearby village where they have been preparing a feast since July. One hut has been built to store the food which so far consists of huge puddings made up of a mixture of coconuts, nali nuts (rather like brazil nuts and delicious roasted) and taro. Thirty four pigs have also been collected. All the neighbouring villages will come, but instead of staying and feasting on the spot they take the food away with them. I believe it is meant to be in honour of the old chief who died last year, but it is also a means of the new chief gaining popularity by his lavishness.

How I wish that we were able to get about more at Vanikoro. We left Kira Kira on Friday afternoon and arrived here on Saturday morning after another day of perfect travelling weather. At the moment is is very hot and sultry here, but perhaps I notice it more as at our house on the hill we nearly always get a breeze. I expect you will be getting some more photos soon as Chris packed up a whole lot of negatives to send to Tiggie.

I'm delighted everyone is looking forward to the prospect of another Hadley in the family. So far I haven't prepared a thing. I've been waiting for material, etc., but I've brought my sewing machine and everything with me so must now make a start.

Baby clothes here are down to a minimum as it is too hot to wear much. To start with, anyway, I'm just making simple cotton nightgowns and a couple of warm jackets just in case it gets a bit cold. I don't know if I ought to get a shawl though. I have a small crib blanket.

16 December

Rained a lot in the night.

Set off about 7 am. To strip II xxxi 350, down same, then across the forest between strips and out on number xx, found a suitable site for a profile diagram, 200 feet by twenty-five feet and spent the rest of the day doing it, with Johnson, Menau and Melobou. Rained on the way back.

19 December

Letter from Claire to Tiggie.

I feel awful not having written for so long, the only attempt at an excuse I can make is that we had no boat for a long time, and then Mr Logie came and at the same time the house-boy went off to collect his wife from another island.

I find the gay life of Honiara rather tiring after Vanikoro, especially now with all the Christmas festivities, still I am keeping very well. Your idea of 'it' being 'them' HORRIFIED me, as I am sure that one will be much more than I can cope with . . . The only garments it possesses so far are some vests, even the nappies are still in the post. It would be too bad if it arrived unexpectedly. As you say, we are having an awful job with names. Do pass on any ideas . . .

Christmas Party
Front row, left to right:' Max H., Mrs Haling, Unknown, Alan Nielen with bottle, Ernie Haling.
Second row: Keith and Dorothy Ward, Willie K, Bill Powell, Margaret Vincent.
Third row: CJH, Ned
Back row: ???   Alan Haling.

25 December

Christmas Day. Went to Church at 8.15, the service was taken by one of the met. boys. Down to Halings' for Christmas dinner at 12.0, eighteen there: Chaperlin, Europeans from the bush, Wards and Margaret Vincent. Came away about 3.0. Then Willi came up with a plan to go to Buma by canoe tonight. We got all ready and went down there, but there were too many unknown quantities for my liking and I called it off, with the support of Nati.

Down after dark to watch dancing to tom-toms and singing. Returned with Bob and another chap, and we talked till 2.0 am. Then listened to the Queen, but could only hear odd phrases.

26 December

Set off a little way up the track behind the house. Returned and cleared fungus out of binoculars with spirit. Heard a recording of the Queen.

31 December

Went on with the plotting all day, sending the boys to lengthen some of the existing strips to 1,000 feet. Nati painting as usual. Had a lemonade with him for elevenses and listened to some local news. Temoga's wife has just died of a coughing sickness, which is sad as she was a very pleasant and cultured sort of native, also one of the last women of the old chiefly line at Buma.

Nati's wife comes from Tanema, and he attributes her light colour to French blood from La Pérouse's day.

Just going to bed when Willi Kwiakowski came up to celebrate the New Year. Sat up till 12.0. Rather sleepless night afterwards.

1955

1 January

After visiting the men on the gardens, went and talked to the Wards, Dorothy, Margaret and Keith – partly because of a hint dropped by Willi last night that I am unsociable – that I am 'too much Oxford and do not talk enough'. I think this is partly Willi's imagination, with his Germanic ideas of the need for impressing other people, but I know I do not talk enough for some people and am annoyed if they should mistake the reason. I just prefer to be silent and always have.

So I dropped in at Ned's for a New Year glass of beer with Mac, Chaperlin, Alan Nielen and Willi, and after an afternoon walk around the plantation had supper at the Wards and spent a very pleasant evening there playing Scrabble, Housey-Housey and other parlour games.

2 January

Sunday. Rainy still. Read *War and Peace* most of the time, good company in this isolation; also had the cats for company. Collected tree fern, ground fern and a grass. Willi turned up in afternoon on his way to the bush. Showed me his photographs, of his home farm in the Moselle area, of his many girl friends, wife (dead), and little girl of eight.

Rain continued. Rough on the reef, and white horses. Wind NW, sheltered here. Some chance of a hurricane.

3 January

Wet all day, and gusty, sea often not visible. The storm

reached its maximum in the afternoon and more or less died out by evening.

4 January

Sent Johnson, Melobou and Bema to camp up river and to start building a hut. The other boys went too, helping to carry stuff, and came back later.

I did some money calculations in response to a telegram requesting information about last year's expenditure.

5 January

Sent Ramoli, John and Metoa to take my stuff up to camp. Followed myself in the afternoon. They have already, after one day, cleared a camp site on the river bank (spot selected by me), erected the tent with a betel-nut palm-wood floor six inches off the ground and built a charming little leaf hut, of very solid structure, with three little beds, each about two and a half feet high with palm-wood tops. Identified the camp site as being further upstream than I thought before. Now I have a whole tent to myself and am much fresher on arriving, having not carried a pack. This sort of organization pays! Took me a year to find out, though.

6 January

Fine. Along river to strip 70 W. Explored neighbourhood of stream crossing strip. Surveyed a line of the Northern boundary of kauri between 70 and 50 W. 25% of the kauri there termite infested.

7 January

Off to profile diagram on 90 W. All worked hard all day, measured girth, height, lower limit of crown etc. for 148 trees. Then set off home and got back well before sunset. Selwyn produced supper. Full moon.

8 January

Earthquake at sunset – worst yet. Leapt out of window, pantry in quite a mess, tins all over the place. Selwyn stayed in the kitchen and held the cupboards up.

11 January

Set off upwards from river at end of 16 W to explore virgin country. Reached ridge and continued through kauri forest SE. Found a sleeping snake three feet long, new species. Killed it and sent it home by Bema to be put in spirit.

12 January

Started as yesterday, but surveying with chain and compass. Reached a point 4440 feet from the start at 1300 feet above sea level, a little beyond yesterday's lunching spot. Here the ridge meets another, T-fashion. Banie (?) visible ahead. Saboe Bay down to the right. So the watershed is reached. Down just before sunset.

Supper: beans from the garden and a tin of spaghetti in tomato sauce. Pineapple. Tea. For lunch I had two slices of bread and butter and finished a tin of bully beef begun yesterday.

13 January

Again fine. Straight up to last night's leaving off place. Reconnoitred ridge to the right (North-West), soon reached sub-montane forest at 1300 feet above sea level about 1000 feet from junction. Kauri ceases. Climbed tree and looked down on Saboe Bay to the left, the ridge we came up to the right, and behind our ridge ascending, joining another and going in the direction of Banie. Dense fern undergrowth here. Surveyed ridge going down West from junction. Kauri all the way. Came out by steam onto Lawrence River only 200 feet from our starting point yesterday, nice and near to camp. Total distance of circuit, 8110 feet. A good two days' work under good conditions.

Read *Social Life in the Insect World*, by Fabre.

Breakfast: Bread, last of the butter, slice of pineapple, tea and lemon.

Lunch: Two slices of bread.

Supper: bully beef and rice. Tea with lemon and sugar.

13 January

Letter from Claire to Aunt Erica.

Chris is still down at Vanikoro but will probably be up by the end of the month. A report came in last week that they had quite a severe earthquake down there; no houses were damaged, but heavy furniture fell over. I'm wondering if we have any china and glass left! Before Chris comes up here I have heard that he will have to visit Ticopia, one of the remotest Solomon Islands (the natives are Polynesian instead of Melanesian), to see if they have suffered any ill effects from the earthquake. I know he will be very glad of the chance to go down there as they are a different type of people, being tall and golden skinned.

I have just finished making the sweetest baby's dress, the only trouble is that it is definitely most suitable for a girl. I would have liked it to be all right for either sex, but I just happened to have the material – a rose printed on white cotton!

I have also had a dressmaking session for the Logie girls' dolls. There are three children altogether – two girls and a boy just two and a half – so there's always plenty going on in the house.

18 January

Last night telegram came – boat coming for me 26 or 28. Slept badly.

Fine. pm. Set off for bush having first had to go up to the strips and get hold of Menau and Melobou, the latter to work at camp and the former to carry my pack.

19 January

Tired. Up to the ridge. Surveyed what Ramoli and Bema had prepared, sub-ridge 1. Finished it early in afternoon. Read Evelyn Underhill.

20 January

Much refreshed after good night. Dreamt of earthquake in which portion of island sank several hundred feet. Set off for sub-ridge 3 and surveyed along it until it petered out at 1300 feet. Followed another ridge back in a north-easterly direction to main ridge at 3,000 feet. Thence back to camp, quite early.

Rice and bully beef. Chat with Ramoli, Bema and Melobou.

21 January

Woken up by duet of Golden Whistlers. Had a plunge in the river pool. Rice for breakfast. Went up 10 W, throgh some good kauri forest. Across to strip O, back by steam. Rained as we returned. Back home.

28 January

Motor vessel *Myrtle* appeared to the south-east soon after breakfast and Naqu appeared a bit later. Got everything ready, then decided to leave for Ticopia tomorrow at 3.0 pm. Mac coming too, probably. Big mail, letters from Claire, Auntie, Grisha, Mullards.

In the afternoon, I instructed Naqu on the job he has to take over.

29 January

Further explanations with Naqu. Set off for the boat about

Ticopian welcome.

Pagan chiefs at Ticopia.

Chance meeting Ticopia.

Mariners at Ticopia.

2.30 pm, finally leaving about 4.0 pm. The boat began pitching soon after leaving the lagoon, and we had a fine view of the rugged Eastern peninsula of Vanikoro. Then I began to be sick, and continued retching at intervals all through the night.

30 January

Sunday. Arrived at Ticopia about 8 am. A beautiful place, sheer white cliffs and rugged interior. Began photographing Polynesians as they came around. Mac busy trading and his old friends Philemon and Moses turned up. I was feeling weak after last night, but I had a slice of paw-paw and went ashore and did a 'royal progress' through the island, first to the Christian chief, Arike Tafua, sat together on a bench surrounded by about 200 natives – some fine people and charming picanins. Then to the pagan villages and a similar palaver with the three pagan chiefs: Batowma (number 3), Barafica (number 1), and Bofaranene (number 4). Then on to the lake which the island encloses, a crater lake I suppose. I walked round it escorted by picanins. Some striking coastal scenery and several species of wader, quite tame. Then we went back to Philemon's house, where we ate breadfruit, taro and a pudding something like porridge and peanut butter, followed by a coconut to drink.

After dark, watched a little dancing, then slept in Philemon's house, I being eaten by hordes of mosquitoes.

31 January

Breakfast in Philemon's hut. A daughter of the family had 'got married' at last night's dance and crawled round the hut to say a tearful goodbye to her people. Went along the beach, bathed, rested. Then back to the boat for a shave. Meanwhile Mac was in Moses' house, busy trading for mats, dance bats, spears and arrows. Then I had a walk along the beach with binoculars and a playful group of kids, including an albino (poor little chap, no pigment in the blazing sun).

Said goodbye (not simple), and left at 2.15.

The earthquake had not caused any damage at all.

1 February

Vanikoro in sight at daybreak. Did a couple of sketches of the Eastern end.

Breakfast at home, then saw Naqu about final arrangements. Said goodbye to Mrs Ward and Margaret Vincent and was given a box full of pineapples. Left at 12.30 pm. Reached Utupua 5.30 pm, went ashore and greeted headman. The object of this visit was to take Ramoli home. We left almost immediately and caught a three foot king fish in the lagoon which we had for supper.

Heading for Santa Cruz.

2 February

Up in night looking at stars. Off Trevanion Island in the morning and achored in Graciosa Bay. Went ashore with the dresser and saw the hospital, which was nice and clean.

3 February

Santa Anna visible about 2 pm, and then we obliquely approached the dark mountains of San Cristoval on a course just north of west. We arrived at Kira Kira at 9.15 pm as predicted, it being a lovely evening with a three-quarter moon. John Hearth met us on the beach and invited us to sleep ashore, which we did.

4 February

At John's suggestion I borrowed a tenon-saw from Robinson (of Ticopia) and started pruning an orange tree near the house. At lunch we had arguments initiated by Willi, who having decided that he had 'had' Vanikoro was coming back to Honiara with me on the *Myrtle*. I went on pruning the tree until it was finished and then had a pleasant dip in the sea. John told me later that this afternoon a boy was badly injured by a shark.

Myrtle in Graciosa Bay, Ndeni.

Below: Mouth of Lawrence River Vanikoro.

6 February

Sunday. Set off on *Myrtle* at 10 am, taking with us William, who had been at Kira Kira hospital and still had a plaster round his foot. We passed Campbell's place and stopped briefly at Wyman's. Then over to the island of Ugi and the Pawa School, where William had been at school. We left at 5 pm.

Continuation of letter to Father dated 10 February.
. . . stayed three nights at Kira Kira, a delightful place where I spent my time pruning orange trees. It has somehow caught the atmosphere of a pre-motor car English village, large stately trees, leaf roofs instead of thatch, hedges, a football field, cocks crowing, woods in the distance, and somehow the native people have an independent English look about them. After that we called at the Pawa school on the island of Ugi, which is the number one mission school of the Archipelago and produces a large proportion of the native leaders and occasional candidates for universities in New Zealand. We were shown round by Father Rawcliffe from Gloucestershire, Miss Salt from Berkshire, and another English woman. It was nice to meet such people, they are the best kind of missionaries. It is a lovely place, with sleek brown cattle grazing under the coconut trees and acres of hillside clear of bush and covered in smooth clover. Grass lawns are rarely much good here. The pupils work on the gardens in the afternoons and the school is nearly self-supporting for food.

7 February

We arrived at Honiara at about 10 am. I saw Logie, took William to Kukum and then the luggage to our house in a PWD truck. Reunion with Claire, she looking very lovely and sweet. All very happy.

8 February

Honiara weather, ie. fine and sunny. Wearing dark glasses but no hat. At office some of the time. Out to the PWD with Logie to get a table and chair, and established myself in the old geological department. Saw Dick Thompson, who now has a beard and a motor-bike.

After work went a stroll with Claire to Point Cruz, and later made lists of names for our infant.

10 February

Dressed up in palm beach suit and went with Logie and Geoff Dennis to Rove to be present at the opening of the Advisory Council by HE. A bit of pagentry – inspection of guard of honour, fanfares. Then listened to his speech, which was interesting.

Letter to Father.

. . . we stayed a night in a native hut with the family (about twenty people). They are Polynesians there, light brown skinned with features similar to ours. The children are a delightful lot and always laughing. I hope to be able to send you some negatives if they come out, they've been sent to Australia. I think I saw more naked rock in Ticopia than I've seen in the past year. The island is a volcanic crater, a ring of mountains with a freshwater lake at sea level in the middle – excellent for swimming. There are 1,700 inhabitants, one Christian village and three Pagan. We went from village to village, preceded and followed by throngs of children dancing and chanting at the tops of their voices, and shaking hands with odd bods every one hundred yards or so. Then we sit on a bench under a big tree with the chief, and 200 to 300 natives of all ages and sexes sit round in a circle, and we talk to the chief through an interpreter in Pidgin, then we exchange gifts. I dished out £1 worth of tobacco and was given a mat in return, and after a bit of talk we were each given a green coconut to drink. At the end of the day we had each drunk six!

11 February

Letter to Aunt Erica.

Nelson, who went back to Malaita on leave because his father had died, has now resigned as he wants to look after his people. A pity, as he was an excellent chap.

12 February

Letter from Claire to Tiggy.

I do hope you will believe me when I say I have only just received the nightdress and baby's dress you sent. Thank you very much for both. I think both will have to be kept for best.

There has been a terrible delay in parcels lately, and now I believe the nappies I ordered have been sent down to Vanikoro! Usually all parcels have to have the duty paid in Honiara. Luckily Mrs Logie has said she can let me have some old ones if mine don't arrive in time. In many ways Honiara reminds one of rationing in England, at the moment, as the stores are short of all sorts of things. No potatoes, eggs, cleaning powders, and just before Christmas sugar and flour were rationed – all due to dock strikes in England and Australia, chiefly Australia.

Chris will have told you about our tentative plans for leave in 1956. It's strange to think that in a few more months we shall have to start pestering people for passages. At the moment I quite like the thought of coming back here for a further two years. I hope I still feel the same way when the time comes.

The house Chris and I are now living in is rather like an old English cottage – it has a leaf roof and instead of roses climbing over it there is a large Bougainvillea. It is wonderful to have Chris up here. Today we had lunch with the Logies, and then Chris and I went for a swim – yes, both of us, although I'll admit mine wasn't frantically energetic, but it was very pleasant.

Monday 14. Wash day – but thank goodness I don't have to do it. Let me tell you a little more about the house. The chief wonder is that it is standing as about half the wood piles are eaten by white ants and are free to wave in the breeze. There is no open verandah and the front door opens into a wide L-shaped dining and sitting room (sitting room has two cane chairs!). Off the dining room end are two bedrooms, one double, one single, and a bathroom. In the other direction is the store room and kitchen. One is inclined to feel sea-sick when in the kitchen as the floor is at such a peculiar angle – white ants again.

In front there is a small garden enclosed by shrubs and trees, which make it private in what would otherwise be a very public place. There are also some paw-paw trees and a lime tree in the garden, so we are hoping some of the fruit will ripen while we are here.

Chris says that the painting at Vanikoro has been finished at last. I hope it isn't covered in mud wasps' nests by the time we get back.

13 February

Sunday. Photographed back and front of house; also Claire. Went a walk together through Coronation Gardens, up Wireless Ridge and then down the road to the Roman Catholic Mission. Turned right along the track and left it at the bridge. Sat by stream in the shade and watched birds:

1. Small bird, flocks in top of tree. Blue back.
2. White cockatoo.
3. White bird with grey mantle.
4. Slender black bird, size of jackdaw.
5. Slender bird with forked tail and long sickle shaped wings. Light grey eye-stripe and jaw-stripe. Probably whiskered tree swift.
6. Dumpy black and white bird with orange bill.
7. Parrot, green, orange band at shoulder level. Olive green on nape.
8. Honey-eater, grey above, yellow below; supposed male had glossy blue throat.

16 February

Out in the truck driven by John Logie, with Silas and three labourers and fifty Gmelina stumps. We were held up by the bridge at Rove Creek, which was being repaired, so we left the truck and got some prisoners to carry the stumps. Watched planting. Saw the plantation – all the *P. caribbea* we planted last year seem to be dead, but *Calophyllum, Vitex cofassus* and *Pometia pinnata* survived. Collected a few flowering plants on the way back.

17 February

On my return from the office I went for a stroll along the shore. Golden plovers and snipe as usual. Also a dove-grey wader larger than the snipe and heavier build than the plover, with yellow legs, fishing at the edge of the sea, with the snipe. Kingfisher, by sea, small, brilliant blue on the rump, wing darker. Rich red underneath. Blue head, very flat. Long dark bill. Thin white collar. Shy, compared to the white headed variety, flew off when I was fifty yards away. Probably River Kingfisher.

18 February

Continued calculating to begin with, did it all wrong as it happened! Out on bicycle to Rove, chaps carrying stumps for planting.

Read John Logie's plan for a 5,000 acre *Cedrela odorata* plantation for a plywood factory.

In the afternoon we went out to Rove again. John followed as the last trees were being put in. Says all this has been planted in the wrong place!

To library with Claire, returned thirteen books, some of which we had for over a year!

22 February

Bicycled to Rove to plant three *Planchonella obovata* seedlings from Malaita.

Some light rain. Obtained the forest areas from the new map with a planimeter.

26 February

About eight o'clock – Claire's labour pains beginning at last, next generation on its way.

27 February

Letter to Aunt Erica.

The baby came last night about 10.45. She didn't feel it coming until about supper time, and when she was pretty certain I rang up the hospital (from a phone box a little way from the house) and then the taxi to get us there. The taxi didn't turn up however and half an hour later it was almost over. I dashed out to let the hospital know our change of plan, if you can call it that, and then met the taxi which had now come (apparently it had come before, when I was in the house, but gone away again!) – and when I got back I was greeted by the sound of yells (not very loud). Claire sitting on the floor in the corner of the bathroom holding this pink object and looking very happy.

Then Dr Payne arrived from the club where Sister Woods had phoned him and shortly after the sister herself with bundles of stuff and a jug of hot water. It is a boy.

Then they took her off to hospital. She's got a room to herself where she can hear the waves on the beach, which is only a few yards away, and she can sit on a long chair on the verandah by the sea. I'm glad it wasn't born in hospital, though.

27 February

Sunday. Fine morning. Picked some flowers from the garden and walked out to the hospital to see Claire. Spent the morning there, back for lunch.

In the afternoon short swim at Rove, then out to hospital on John Logie's bike with a rucksack of books and things. Read to Claire on the verandah out of *Venture to the Interior*

Baby sucking rather half-heartedly, inclined to fall asleep.

28 February

Letter to Father.

I suppose you will have got my wire, sent this morning, ages ago – but I can hardly believe it. Anyway it's a boy and weighs 8lb. 5 oz. He spends most of his time yelling, except when being fed, when he immediately goes fast asleep. He has good long toes for climbing trees and bow legs for riding a horse. The facial arrangements are a mixture. Nose like Auntie Erica's (so Claire says), with Claire's wide nostrils. Fat cheeks, flat ears, blue eyes, sandy hair and no teeth. His name isn't certain yet, but it may be Michael John.

I have now surveyed an area of 850 acres of mountainous jungle country, worked out most of the results and written a report for HE. There are about nine million superficial feet of kauri timber there, enough to keep the Company occupied for four and a half years at their present rate. You will be interested to know that the instrument used for all this was your prismatic compass (from World War I). The Forest Department hadn't got one, the Survey Department one was crocked and Mac's liquid one was difficult to use in steep country. Also the Abney level I use has the date 1909 stamped on it.

There are several miles of ridges and rivers not included in the 850 acres, and there is a lot more kauri forest to be done.

2 March

Letter to Father.

Since you mention the debit side, I would put high on the list the lethargy of this humid climate and the absence of seasons. I am always wanting to drop off to sleep here and often sleep solidly for an hour after lunch. It's worse than Oxford!

7 March

Out to Kukum to see the floods subsiding from the nursery and to take a new charcoal drum out.

Collected Claire from the hospital.

Willi, and later Janice Jackson, Dick, and Phil came to see the baby.

9 March

Toe sore (foot-rot). Off on bike to Kukum with plane, brace and bit. Organized carpentry – Paul and Co. planing timber, Silas and Co. sawing posts and me drilling holes in them. Did about six dozen during the day, and cooked sixty in creosote pm.

Enjoyed the fresh air and exercise.

Later – walk to beach with Claire, baby in pram. Fairly rough, pleasant swim in the breakers.

11 March

Foot sore and left groin swollen in sympathy, feeling weak.

12 March

To hospital about foot, penicillin injection. Started registering birth.

Out to Kukum, inspected ditch with Logie and Sharp. Back to Honiara. Foot hurting.

In the afternoon rested and read. Foot much better for resting.

14 March

Rainy day again. John drove Claire and me to the hospital for our respective inspections, I my ear and feet. I am to have daily treatment at hospital for coral ear.

To Trade Scheme about shotgun for Namas, only 4-10 available, sent a wire enquiring if this is OK.

p.m. Lift out to hospital, ear treated. Then busy fixing catch for lock on office door. Finished 'Hornblower and the Atropos'.

16 March

Interviewed Alan Mala prior to his being taken on as Forest Guard.

Got provisional driving licence and made 'L' plates.

18 March

Altered name on birth certificate to Michael John.

Right foot sore, behaving like left foot last week. Out to

hospital pm. Later, out to airfield in truck with Brian – driving lesson. Got on OK. Drove back. Brian in for a beer.

22 March

Feet hurting, I think from the Whitfield ointment I'm using for foot-rot.

23 March

Bought 4-10 gun at Trade Scheme for Namas, also elastic spring-gun for underwater hunting for myself.

Out to Kukum. Saw Brown, entomologist, was shown some of his insects and introduced to *Amblypeltis cocophagus*.

24 March

All day on ditch with seven Solomon Islanders. Feet giving Hell.

One Solomon Islander with European hair, had an English grandfather, interesting. His colour was dark.

26 March

Letter to Aunt Muriel.

(58 Mud Alley, Honiara). Today I've been bathing at a place called Rove where there's a bit of coral reef. I was using my new spring-gun which I have bought for shooting fish. It works by elastic on the principle of a catapult. I didn't hit anything of course but had a lovely time looking down into an under-water ravine and watching for targets, while lots of tiny bright coloured fish swam round me. I lay on the rock half in the water and rose and fell with the waves. Using a mask you can see everything under water as clear as daylight. Sometimes the water would go all cloudy with millions of little particles – I wonder if it is plankton.

28 March

Working on the ditch. Discovered an inconsistency in three peg-levels. Logie came out about 2.30.

Claire and I had teeth inspected at hospital – no action needed.

Mail from family, also a letter of appreciation from MacDonald at the British Museum.

Letter to Father.

(58 Mud Alley, Honiara). Yes, I still write to Dave Pedder. He is at Kitwe in Northern Rhodesia and in charge of the forests of the copper belt. He seems to appreciate the countryside but misses the rain and mist of his homeland.

At the moment I am recovering from a vicious attack of foot-rot which developed when I arrived in Honiara, I think because of wearing hot leather shoes to the office. I am also dosing a 'coral ear', another fungus which I have been enjoying for nearly a year. The other day I called on Mr Brown the entomologist who has a laboratory near Honiara, and is doing very interesting work on Amblypeltis cocophagus, *the bug that eats coconuts so that they drop off too soon. I'm going to look for it on Vanikoro and send him specimens if it is present. I met his wife and family who all go with him when he visits other islands and help collect insects. He has a beautiful collection – scores of each kind, and several species of ant since these affect the coconut bug.*

I have sent a box of plant specimens (seventy different species) to the British Museum, also I am in touch with the bird man and sent him a stuffed water hen, and a flying fox and a bat to be passed on to the mammal department. I have a cupboard full of Kilner jars with frogs, lizards and snakes for Mr Parker the reptile man. Also I've been sending fungi to the Forest Products Research Institute in Melbourne, who send me notes and identifications in return.

Naturalists are interested in an isolated island like Vanikoro, for one thing organisms have had a chance to evolve on their own into different sub-species, like the St Kilda wren.

* * *

31 March

Fine. Off in geological land rover with Dick, Phil and Mike Hamilton. Dropped them at the departure point for Gold Ridge Lodge. Photographed the party. Then to sawmill, took picture. Picked up chap from plantation further down the coast, who wanted a lift to Honiara. To Grass Hills, rail terminus for Tenaru Timbers, walked two miles up railway to rail-head. Met foreman and saw what there was to see. Good forest, 90% Mangifera, with *Pometia pinnata* and koila. Sixty foot boles, all size classes. Took pictures, also of a canoe being made. Rode back together on train. Saw five foot crocodile. Sleeper trouble on the way down, put right on the spot. So back home about 2.15.

Reading *The Stars are Dark*, Peter Cheyney.

2 April

Visited Brown, the entomologist, who gave me eleven specimen tubes.

In the afternoon, to Rove, alone. Goggle-fished, saw a five foot shark.

4 April

Heard that we are to leave on the *Noula* for Kira Kira at noon tomorrow. Both busy getting ready and collecting things together.

In the afternoon Claire and baby went to hospital for final examination.

5 April

Lorry came at 10.0 am to collect stuff, meanwhile got £400 odd and locked it in a box.

We set off about 12.0, getting everything in the small boat, including a wardrobe.

6 April

Claire slept in cabin, I on top of cabin. There was a lot of pitching between Guadalcanal and San Cristoval, but weather fine.

Arrived at Pawa simultaneously with the *Myrtle.* John Hearth and Mr Skipper there.

On to Kira Kira, had lunch there and settled in. Others arrived later.

7 April

Later in the morning Claire and I had a very pleasant swim in a rock pool by the sea. Saw a common yellow-grey fish six to twelve inches long with horizontal stripes on the body (not the head), also a blue fish two to three feet long.

Later a French Sister arrived from along the coast, escorting a sick Sister to Honiara. She has been in these islands for thirty-one years. Skipper and the Sisters left on the *Noula* after supper.

Saw a tree with huge buttresses and pinnate leaves by the shore. A huge spider about four inches across was using the buttresses to support its web. It had a yellow abdomen and black legs with yellow joints.

Letter to Aunt Erica.

Michael has been extraordinarily good since leaving Honiara, hardly been yelling at all until midday today. At the moment he is on the verandah floor under an umbrella with a mosquito net draped over it as there are a few flies here.

John Bartle went home on leave some months ago and has since returned to Honiara and got a job there. John Hearth replaced him and we are staying with him at the moment. Mr Skipper, another Government officer, is also here now, and is going back to Honiara on the Noula *tonight.*

I think we will be leaving here on Saturday for Vanikoro, going on the Myrtle *with John Hearth who is going to do a tour of the district.*

The Logies are leaving the Solomon Islands on 26 April. They are going on leave to England before returning to Kenya. They will fly to Auckland and then have a week in New Zealand before going across the Pacific to Panama and back that way for a change.

We have had news of a chap in the Uganda Forest Service who has applied to be Mr Logie's successor, K. W. Trenaman, with a wife and three children. I should think if he comes it will be about October or so.

Last night Claire and I had a swim in a pool in the river, and midday today we had a sea bathe, only a few yards from this house. We found a pleasant pool with a sandy bottom about two feet deep for wallowing in. The waves just reached it and round the side the rock had been rounded into hollows for sitting in.

Willi's latest feat is to get fined five pounds for smuggling a pair of binoculars. The binoculars, worth about £35, were confiscated too. He says he will 'get even with them' in the end though.

We now have a new Forest Guard, a young chap called Alan Mala. Like William Piaito, he was educated at Pawa. So now, with Naqu, I shall have three assistants to organize the labour. I'm hoping to recruit six more boys at Santa Cruz, bringing the labour force up to twelve.

8 April

Nature notes: rain-tree, *Samanea saman*, large and spreading, with pinnate leaves and pink flowers; a small monocotyledonous herb, grass-like leaves and flowers with three purple petals; a herb with bright red flowers and fuzzy leaves.

Birds: small kingfisher very common here, tame, perches in trees. Slaty blue back, front sometimes buff, sometimes white; a finch-sized bird, dark blue or black with red eye-spot; a black and white wagtail, 'Murray magpie', with white eye-spot; glimpse of a cardinal honey-eater; wader by the shore, heard in the night but not seen.

Kingfishers at Kira Kira:

1. Fairly large and dark. Blue back, wing and head, some green in wing. White collar, buff underparts. Mobbed by cardinal honey-eaters.

2. Smaller, seen with 1. White underparts. Back and wing a blue-grey colour. Also seen by itself.

3. White underparts. Wing and head bottle-green, back

brownish-green. Blue streak on wing in flight.

Both 1 and 3 have a black line through the head continuous with the bill and thin white nostril lines above the eye. Markings on the breast of 3 are paler. I think they are all one species, 1: male; 3: female; 2: juvenile. White collared kingfisher, *Halcyon chloris*.

9 April

Left Kira Kira 2.0 pm. Called at a station at nightfall, then headed east into the ocean.

10 April

Easter Sunday.
Letter to Aunt Erica (sent 19 April).

. . . in the morning we caught a sword-fish about seven feet long. There was great excitement, the ship was stopped and it was gradually hauled in, white underneath and with almost luminous purple bands across the back. The boys stabbed it through the heart with harpoons and then it was heaved aboard with a mighty effort and left a portion of the deck to itself to jump about in. So everybody had a good meal, but unfortunately the ship's fridge wasn't working properly and some of it had to be thrown away next day.

Letter continued on 11 April.

Tinakula visible in the distance towards evening. Felt our way in to Lowa anchorage after dark.

A bird appeared astern just before the fish was caught. It had a forked tail and was black, with a white belly. Probably White-throated Storm-Petrel.

11 April

Ashore after breakfast with John. Only one recruit from Graciosa Bay. Left John and with Michael as guide, crossed to Taumotu (Trevanion) Island by canoe.

Continuation of Letter to Aunt Erica.

I walked a long way trying to find labour. I came to a village on the far side of Trevanion Island where you could see Tinakula on the horizon (quiescent). It was Christian's village and I met his father and mother who were very pleasant. His younger brother, about thirteen, was just coming back from fishing. He looked a fine boy, alert and intelligent. He and a couple of his pals were keen to come to Vanikoro as labour, but when we returned to the ship it was finally decided that they were too young, and the native dresser said that Christian minor had asthma. Anyway, I got six more labour, so now I have a dozen altogether and two forest guards. Naqu has been ordered back to Honiara.

12 April

Breakfast in Utupua lagoon, dropped a man there, left sharpish. Choppy, pitched a lot. Tummies okay by now, though.

Saw several flocks, each of one hundred or more, of Brown Boobies – heading in a westerly or north-westerly direction.

Arrived Vanikoro in sunshine just before midday. Lunch aboard. Tea with Halings, then home at last. House lovely. Bear-pool full, both had a dip, leaving Michael in the mosquito-room.

Later to boys' house, then saw Mr Filewood, the new manager and Mr Moody. Introduced them to John Hearth. Organized rations for the new men. Saw Naqu and Nati. Good to be back.

We now have: one Ranger, two forest guards, eleven labourers, and one houseboy with his wife.

13 April

Issued new labour with knives, blankets and mosquito nets. Set them on making new beds for the nursery. Saw to Mala's rations and got a large cooking pot for the men.

* * *

14 April

Wandered round home plantation. Most of the kauri put in recently seem to have died, but most of those put in originally have survived.

A female Golden Whistler, feeding at fern level low down by the stream flew off. Lower down a male and female were feeding together in the tops of the noora trees. A fantail and thickheads were there too.

15 April

A large sack of kauri cones has been brought back from the Sundi River. Some boys are now extracting the seed and others are fetching palm leaves and making them into pots for kauri seedlings. Received a telegram to say that Naqu is to go back by the first ship, this is bad news.

The boys returned from the bush camp, having made a new hut with eight beds.

16 April

Down to see the boys gardening. A pig eats their potatoes and they are planning a pig-hunt.

Naqu bequeathed me his two-man western type dug-out canoe, better than the outrigger, I think.

18 April

Sent two forest guards and ten men off to bush camp. Went up myself to look at some strips. Some more planting necessary there, also some more cutting. Found an old track running West, much sign of pigs there.

Pinus caribbea plantation doing badly, only a few left alive. Saw a young pig along the track. Watched male and female broadbills in the plantation. The Vanikoro broadbill is known only from this island. It is five and a half inches long and the head, back and throat of the male are blackish-blue with a chestnut belly and a broad grey bill. The female is paler.

20 April

Meeting on our verandah at 8 am, of all who had matters to discuss with the District Commissioner. About twenty Solomon Islanders, Jones and Haling. The chief business was the shell fishing dispute. The DC got the facts and then made an interim injunction based on pre-war practice. He will hold a proper court in November.

23 April

Decided to go up to the bush camp today for a week, with Claire and the baby. This project was postponed till Sunday and on Sunday, being wet, was abandoned. However, got things ready and sent Mala and Bema up with them in the afternoon for 5s. each.

Norfolk Island Lily (*Phormium*), with lovely flower in dam by nursery. Left baby at Dorothy's and went canoeing. Reached sandy beach and swam. Coming back, the canoe sank when in the river mouth and we had to swim it ashore.

25 April

Set off for bush about ten, first sending Pippa and little Blackie off in a wooden box, the idea being that they are to rid the camp of the rats with which it is so infested.

Left William with instructions about what to do while I am away, and arranged to buy an adze from Mr Jones for 5s. to make a canoe with. Reached camp about twelve I reckon.

Let cat out of the box. Very timid, gave her some milk. Then she went off to explore, preceded by Blackie.

26 April

Fine morning. Plunge in the pool. Fried an egg for breakfast.

One man stayed behind sick. Set off to the ridge to the south of the river and did strip at 2,000 feet, 235 degrees. Then strips on sub-ridge one at one hundred feet, north and south. All in forest containing a good proportion of kauri, though not of good form.

Lunch halt by stream south of sub-ridge one, during which seven boys caught by hand eleven fish, in about half an hour.

Continued, rain came. Very precipitous terrain. Cut strip northwards towards camp, reached end of Naqu's old strip at 1,000 feet 235 degrees. Then homewards down a rocky stream and gully, arriving just before dusk.

Supper – fish (cat had the head), and mixed vegetables from a tin. Rain stopped afterwards, fine evening. Crescent moon going down above the trees.

27 April

Went 4,000 feet along ridge, then cut a strip down to the 'Valley of Lost Horizon', on a bearing of 130 degrees and found some noble kauri trees. One mighty jungle King was 150 feet high, girth fifteen feet six inches and timber height fifty-five feet.

Pause for lunch, during which four fish and two eels were caught. Spotted a gleaming yellow mineral in the rock and collected specimens.

After supper, the boys told me that there was a flying fox in a tree over the river. I shot it, but it had to be knocked down from the tree with sticks. It was an adult male. I skinned it for the British Museum and gave the meat to the boys. Its mate was nearby and came flying back very boldly.

30 April

After breakfast Johnson came to announce that they had caught a pig (by a noose round its leg). So I went down with the gun and shot the poor brute, four cartridges of number one shot before it expired, having been shot through the eye. It was a large animal and had been troublesome, eating our boys' potatoes.

1 May

Sunday. Had to get up in night, cat with milk surplus owing to having left kitten up bush. Claire milked her while I held.

5 May

Letter to Aunt Erica.

When I went to the bush I had Pippa taken too, in a wooden box, with her new kitten Blackie. The idea was that she should catch rats, there are far too many in camp, and she did catch plenty. On Friday I took Pippa home but left Blackie as she'd got a den in the jungle and didn't want to come; but I don't think the separation was a good idea and Pippa has gone back this week with William and company.

Michael is doing fine and now weighs ten pounds twelve ounces.

12 May

A FINE day. Finished yesterday's ridge, down to the upper fork in the Lawrence River. Then up into the unknown between the arms of the fork, found the LAST RIDGE (we hope) and surveyed it to 2,500 where there is a junction.

Returned, slipping on a rock in the river and thus smashing the Departmental Aneroid Barometer, a feat one feels would be more appropriately performed tomorrow.

13 May

Friday. Set off up the last ridge and reached 4,000 feet, then returned to camp and on home before sundown.

3 June

Re-did the plan of home plantation, then out to record a couple more lines.

Was coming back along line sixteen when I saw in line

fifteen a Slaty Flycatcher on its nest, about six feet above ground level. Still building, no eggs. Both parents there. Only call note a 'chrrp'. Seemed a bit anxious at my presence.

Collected a ground orchid with small orange flowers.

Michael's weight: twelve pounds twelve ounces.

6 June

Sent William and six boys to camp to get on with survey, and Mala with two boys off in Nati's canoe to get bamboos. Had a look at the Slaty Flycatcher's nest. Continued recording trees in the plantation.

Explored straight up ridge behind house, Found two big rocks, one with a new species of large (four inch) brown lizard on it. Up to the first rock with Claire and the baby later.

7 June

Went into the forest above the boys' house and collected about eight different kinds of fungus to send to Melbourne. Described and packed them ready to send.

10 June

Sent Mala and five boys to cut lines on other side of river. Followed with a chain and compass, surveying a new ridge and putting a new area of secondary kauri forest on the map. Plenty of regeneration of all sizes there. Collected.

To the bird's nest. Sitting. One egg, pellucid cream tinged with pink, red-brown markings at one end, about three quarters of an inch long.

11 June

Went bird watching above the nursery and later on to see the nest, bird still sitting. Saw the change over.

Pippa came back! (Of her own accord, having disappeared from the bush camp three weeks ago.) Enmity between her and Blackie.

14 June

Sent Mala and boys off to bush. Down to Peou, saw Chaperlin, Nati and Dana.

In the afternoon I set off for bush, pack having been taken by Walter.

15 June

Started surveying the unexplored ridge going westwards from IA at 3,000 feet. Full complement of boys:
Mala, Bema and Luke ahead, cutting a track.
Mennau pulling chain. Walter clearing line of vision. Menepa attending to near end of chain. Camis holding my field book.

Followed a branch ridge, reached stream to north. Back across country to camp, over two ridges. Expedition ended in rain.

16 June

Continued with main branch of yesterday's ridge. Got to 4,000 feet, just reached area worked by old company. Mala went ahead cutting track, followed stream down a long way and had to come a long way back along river. My party went across unknown country, boys afraid of being lost, onto ridge IAi, down a strip at forty-seven degrees, from the top had a very good view of this part of the upper Lawrence River valley, with the forest-clad mountains above. Magnificent and lovely, river far below, wisps of vapour drifting past the trees. Clear-cut outline of kauris against mist-filled coombe above.

* * *

Archdeacon Reynolds Christens Max Haling and Michael held by Claire.

22 June

Up to the Sundi River with Mr Haling and Max in the tug. Mala and Bema came too, bringing the small canoe, just in case. Saw a large sting-ray in the mouth of the Sundi River.

29 June

Day started off rainy. Later set off home, leaving Mala to carry on, because the *Baura* is reported in. Claire returned from Peou with the mail shortly after I got back.

Then I went to see Archdeacon Reynolds, who came on

the boat, and arranged the christening of Michael. The ceremony took place in the church at 5.15 pm, and two Solomon Island babies were baptized at the same time.

Letter to Father.

. . . two native babies were christened at the same time, David and Nesta. They were sucking away at their mothers while Michael was being christened and returned to the same occupation after their turn to shut them up. Michael was looking round in wide-eyed wonder all the time and only yelled when he got his dose of water (from a large shell supported on a font made of a tree-fern stump). His godparents are David Pedder, Henry Taylor and Vicki. David is still in Kitwe, Northern Rhodesia and a bit fed up with too much town life, trying hard to get sent to an outpost somewhere near the Congo and Portuguese West Africa. He had a good camping holiday at Easter, by a 120 foot waterfall with scenic gorge and hill country.

1 July

The slaty flycatcher's egg has hatched, one chick.

Letter to Aunt Erica.

Michael is very conscious of people now and looking about him and smiling. Anything put in his hand is clutched and, if approved of – eg. an Hibiscus flower – is thrust into his mouth. We took him on a picnic up the river to our usual spot last Sunday – he travelled in a calico slung from my shoulder. He enjoyed every minute of it and was very interested – twisting his head right round to watch me making a fire. He got a bit of sunburn, too.

Selwyn has a lot of fun playing with him and often goes to wheel his pram up and down the verandah in the intervals of getting lunch, especially when Michael has been yelling a bit. In fact natives in general are very fond of white children. Max Haling is about five years old and the only other white child on the island. He goes around with a faithful native retainer of his own age who is I think paid for it to keep him out of trouble. He pushes Max's motor car and goes swimming with him. Max also goes up to the bush for the day with his father in the boat. He will go to school in Australia at the end of the year.

The Citos *is due in tomorrow with Mr Filewood's wife and eighteen year old daughter. We are all going to a party of celebration at his house tomorrow.*

. . . recently I noticed a Slaty Flycatcher at its nest. It is a small grey bird with an erect tail like a wren's. The book says that this bird only occurs on Vanikoro and its habits are unknown, so I'm lucky to have been able to follow its life.

When Naqu was here he lost the outrigger canoe which I had made last year. This was annoying but he started another canoe made of a karamatti log, not an outrigger but boat-shaped. Dana has now completed it and painted it white. It is a slender craft with beautiful lines and should be capable of carrying four or five people.

I am sorry you are not here to see Michael. Just now I'd been sitting here writing and hearing a sound of paper being rustled. When I went to see, it was Michael lying on the camp bed on the verandah and he'd got hold of a bill of lading I'd put down there and the little soft chewed up bits were lying all round and a long strip was lying round his neck. Fortunately it was not important.

2 July

Letter from Claire to Aunt Erica.

We have just heard that the Citos, *which was due today, will not be here until 5 July so we have a few more days in which to answer mail brought by the* Baura. *Did Chris tell you that it might possibly be bringing him a small launch or similar craft to help him with his work? The big dug-out canoe that Naqu started when he was here was finished last week, and very fine it is too. It has been made so that it can take a sail if necessary. Our picnic by the river with Michael last weekend was a great success. He took an intelligent interest in all that went on, lying on a bed of palm leaves with his head inside Chris's hat to keep off the sun.*

How you would both love Michael. He looks adorable with his bright blue eyes, fair hair, dark eyelashes and little pink cheeks. He is very strong and is now trying to sit up; he can't get very far unaided yet but enjoys being propped up for a short time. I now give him his bath in the kitchen sink. He used to use an enamel bowl. He has great fun splashing with his legs. His only blemish is a red birthmark on the back of his head. How sweet of you to make something for him. It hasn't arrived yet but I expect it will be on the Citos.

5 July

Lovely fine day. Lagoon flat calm. *Citos* came in about 9.0 am. Went aboard with Claire later on. Collected my £600 from the Captain, also the Forest Department planimeter.

Checked cargo coming ashore, in the store with Mrs Haling. Temoga brought four combs of bo wood which I bought for 6s. each.

Continuation of Claire's Letter to Aunt Erica.

. . . it brought no mail from Honiara which is very surprising, nor any of the stores for us that I had ordered from Australia – most annoying as a lot of it was baby food. I hope Mrs Haling can let me have some. She has a little girl Kim, aged nine months, and Max aged five.

6 July

Letter from Mr Donald suggesting that we have a proper launch with inboard engine. Agreed!

Down again to clear up question of medical supplies. Wrote Dr Payne a letter, to be sent with Mrs Haling's bill.

Party on board *Citos*, went on Mr Jones' *Endeavour III*. Buffet supper, danced. Back about one o'clock. Selwyn and Hanna sleeping in our kitchen so that Michael wouldn't be alone in the house.

7 July

Checked cargo in morning.

Jones came and wanted me to find a box of torch batteries of his in Halings' store. Mrs Haling wouldn't open the store for me or let me have the key – she said it was a private store. I said it was a government store. Certain amount of ill-feeling.

Referred to law-book afterwards.

8 July

Saw Haling – he denies that it is a 'bond store'. Feeling uncertain about the facts, I gave in and peace was made. Jones' missing case turned up after all!

11 July

Windy. Bush parties postponed owing to uncertain weather; also most of the men have colds. Men potting kauri, using leaf pots, in nursery hut.

Below: The view from the verandah of our house, Vanikoro. The tree in the foregrounds is Spondias dulcis *(Polynesian Plum) Young Kauris and tree fern beyond.*

12 July

Foot-rot worse, weather worse too, so gave up idea of going to bush. Men working at nursery.

13 July

Finer. Prepared to set off for bush. To see Luke, who is sick with a pain in his chest and a nasty cough. Sent him to Mrs Haling.

Steady rain set in soon after my arrival at camp.

14 July

Finished the strips on Ridge I C. Returned to camp feeling very tired and went to bed, with fever. Started vomiting at dusk, very weak. Restless night.

15 July

Still sick. Packed up, left camp to the boys and tottered home down the river. Soon after arrival, went to bed. Took orange juice and sulpha tablets. Better later, up for supper.

18 July

Still wet. No one going up bush this week.

Dana very sick with pneumonia, had him carried to hospital on a stretcher. Mrs Haling gave him 300,000 units of penicillin. Luke to stay with him. Mayo with malaria. William with cold in bed.

Put rest of boys on a) repairing leaf-roof of canoe-house, b) putting iron roof on kitchen made by Naqu.

Michael's weight: 13 pounds eight ounces.

* * *

20 July

Hannah sick, fainted, taken to hospital. Selwyn crying and very worried. She had penicillin, then back home. I do not think that she is all that bad. Dana much better.

23 July

Down to send off a belated telegram about aliens on Vanikoro.

24 July

Sunday. Off into the forest above the nursery. Watched fantails, whistlers and a flycatcher, then continued up the hill to the path and so down to the house, making a pleasant round.

After lunch went down to the shore with Claire and the baby, watched a reef heron feeding on the incoming tide. Then Claire to see Mrs Haling and I to see Dana in hospital, who thinks he wants to go home. Tried to dissuade him.

2 August

Bema caught a large snake in the river bed. I think same kind of tree-snake as before only bigger and blackish. It was caught by means of a noose in a bush rope at the end of a pole which could be slipped over the snake's head and pulled tight. It then coiled itself round the pole and Bema carried it back to Claire like this. She put a bit of tobacco in its mouth to kill it, but it got free and a chase ensued across the verandah.

Also saw in the bush today a small ash-grey snake, probably having just shed its skin.

7 August

Sunday. Fine. Examined walking stick and bowls, identified

them as *Intsia bijuga* and *Campnosperma brevipetiolata* (?) respectively. Sketched and painted the Slaty Flycatcher's nest (now disused, collected and dried). Found a tin for it and packed it.

8 August

Sent Mala and company up Lawrence River to finish survey. William experimenting with getting teak seed to germinate – boiling some and stratifying it.

10 August

Left at 7.45 am in the launch *Delaware*, with Mr Filewood, his boys Henry and Tabwaa, and William, Metoa, Menepa and John.

Weather fine.

Reached mouth of Willi Willi River, ran aground on the reef and stalled the engine, which would not start again as the batteries were not properly charged. Poled her up the river for about a quarter of a mile, to the limit of navigability. Then at 11.0 am abandoned the launch and set off up the river, which was similar to the Lawrence, but if anything a bit steeper. Going mainly east, then a bit south-east. Bends higher up, but general course south-east. Kauri on ridges to left and right. Quite a few *Dacridium* by the river. Halt for lunch. Boys caught an eel later on. Halted at 3.0 pm at 1,000 feet above sea level by aneroid. Then I explored to the north-west of the river while the rest of the boys were making camp. Slipped and made a deepish cut on my right shin. We had distant views of abundant Kauri forest on ridges to the north-west and there was a fair amount of medium size kauri on the ridge we were on.

Camp consists of two leaf shelters, one for us and one for the boys. Some rain in the night, a bit came through, but slept well.

* * *

11 August

Set off up the ridge on the left bank of the river through medium kauri forest. General direction south-west. Ridge veered to south, going up all the time. Struck out across the trend of the country, going south-west. Guided by the sound of blasting from the Company's road-head, Herbert and another Australian there. Found a leaf insect and collected it. Looked at regeneration lines and the new hut with William. Then borrowed the red motor-boat and went to the Willi Willi, leaving all my boys but William, and the kit, at Sundi River. Passed Jones in the *Endeavour III* on his way back. Arrived at the Willi Willi and the tide was out, so borrowed a canoe from a boy who happened to be there and sent Henry and William to fetch *Delaware*, which took some time. Then we man-hauled *Delaware* across the reef on its side in six inches of water and started home with it in tow. I was at the tiller of the red motor-boat. The stars were coming out as we rounded Lale Point. Tabwaa and Henry were reef-spotting and giving me steering directions, but we scraped coral once. There was not much wind and it was fairly calm, but I was a bit cold without a shirt. At last we saw the lights of Peou and entered the river, reaching home about 7.30.

12 August

To Sundi River with Filewood in *Delaware*, myself in the red motor-boat. We collected my three boys and all returned in *Delaware*, slowly because the boat was filling up partially owing to a broken exhaust and the engine was flooded.

22 August

Told Chaperlin about HE's [His Excellency the High Commissioner for the Western Pacific] visit. Saw Filewood, discussed arrangements. Better to have dinner at his place on 30th, easier for people.

Several chaps sick, rest weeding path. Did forms.

Wet morning, fine afternoon.

23 August

Fine. Organized the weeding of the path with William in charge. Calculating koila and karamati volumes for remaining areas of Lawrence River.

Finished *I'll say she does*, by Cheyney.

24 August

Fine again. Got things together and set off about 9.0, stopping for tea at the Filewoods then on up river with Lionel. Left river at ninety chain strip, up ridge through good kauri forest, east, then south east, through fair forest and so to camp. Both had a good swim in the lower pool.

25 August

Up the ridge starting at ten chain West, Lionel counted seventy-three kauri trees before emerging on worked out ground. Hut site very overgrown. Up ridge then down subridge II2, where Lionel counted eighty odd trees. Got a dozen *Dacridium* seedlings from one path. Lunch on right hand branch of Upper Lawrence River. Overcast. Up one ridge and down another (Ici and Ic), and so back to camp. Tea, followed by a swim.

Michael weighs fifteen pounds.

26 August

Lovely morning, no cloud all day. Plunge in the river before breakfast. Forest looking its best in morning sunlight. Lionel counted over one hundred trees, good ones. Reached viewpoint and saw into Saboe Bay.

Telegram – leave in March!

Eight sackees of Haling's turned up with request for attention.

27 August

Alan Haling says sackees are no-excuse time-breakers. Sackees content to abide by this appellation, staying in Tati's house.

Wrote invitations to cocktail party on *Kovala* for Acting HE. Post-prandial tea under shade of Flamboyant tree.

28 August

Sunday. Still very fine. All set off to the river, Michael being carried in a calico as before and yelling rather a lot after arrival. Both had a couple of swims, water seeming quite cold. Michael was introduced to the river as far as his bottom, but the cold was not appreciated.

Did a painting of the picnic spot with tree-roots on the opposite bank as background.

A white heron with yellow legs and arched neck circled over.

Poku came, with wife and three children, wanting to build a house in the village. This is OK.

30 August

Had to speak to District Commissioner, Eastern on wireless about impending arrival of *Kovala*. Arranged tea party for HE as *Kovala* expected at 3.0 pm, but it didn't arrive until 5.0 pm. Met it in *Delaware* with Lionel. DC came up to talk business briefly, covered main points.

Cocktails for all on *Kovala*, followed by dinner for government party at the Filewoods'.

31 August

H.E. to Sundi River with Haling, left 7.30. Late start for us in *Delaware* owing to engine trouble. We missed the tide and had to push her over the bar at the Sundi River.

Lift with Bob in the road-metal truck, caught up with HE's

party as it was about to come back. Back for lunch, *Delaware* conking out as we reached Peou.

Letter from Alston, BM, with a list of fern names (of my collection), including *Selaginella* species nova.

1 September

Sent men up to fetch tent back and it rained all day, poor chaps. Dealt with official mail.

2 September

Still wet. Paid men.

Sent off telegram about Santa Cruz expedition which is proposed.

7 September

Letter to Father.

An unexpected mail came yesterday and brought us these photographs. The cause of the mail was that when the High Commissioner called at Ticopia he found one hundred-odd people very sick or dying and Dr Payne was sent down straight away. It is an ironical fact that the cause of the epidemic was almost certainly flu, brought by the mission ship.

20 September

Delaware not functioning, so set off in the *Black Witch*, rowing, with two boys and Lionel, and three boys following in the canoe. Fine morning. No transport at Sundi River till after lunch. Rain set in pm.

Reached Phil and Herbert's hut at road head and walked to new road beyond Lemon River.

Games after supper – two new ones: 'button' game, very good indeed; also 'Twist' card game.

Slept in Herbert's hut.

21 September

Sent six boys home, then off with Lionel, William and the other six boys along a ridge in kauri forest running north from the road head. Then down north-easterly to the Willi Willi River and found the tent in a good place on a slight knoll by the river. Lunch at 10.30 am, then back west to the ridge and down through fair kauri forest, patchy, but many very good trees. All the time I was pacing and taking compass bearings for a rough map.

Down the ridge, northerly, by river, then west across to branch ridge. Here we were rejoined by William who had followed down another branch going west from higher up.

Saw a brown tree snake about two feet long; also the nest of a slaty flycatcher, six feet above ground and the bird nearby. The branch had been accidentally cut off by Johnson, so I bound it on again, hoping that the bird will not desert.

Then we returned to camp, having got a good idea of the lie of the land.

22 September

Fine morning. Left Johnson in camp, and Henry was sent back to get Mr Filewood's towel.

Set off NE, crossed the river and up the ridge. Followed river south-easterly in kauri forest, then across north-easterly to the main divide. Down it going north, height about 1200 feet above sea level. Forest very good, large trees of good form. After following this ridge for half a mile we had a superb view of Nanua, and later on we had a view inland of Mount Popogia. I drew a panorama. Then we returned across country to the river just below camp, had lunch, and went down to the pool for a good swim.

23 September

Went eastwards from camp until we reached the main divide, followed it up to 1500 feet above sea level, then back across country. After lunch returned to the road-head, and thence home. It was fine all day.

24 September

Sorted plants collected yesterday and started making a map of the Willi Willi.

26 September

Letter from Claire to Erica and Mu.

First of all I must tell you that Michael's little blue rompers have arrived. They came last mail, but I didn't get them till after the ship had left. I have recently made him a bib with an embroidered fish on it. He is just starting to crawl – if you can call it that; he puts his arms forwards and then drags his legs up. You can imagine what a state his tummy, hands and knees get into, especially when the red dust that gets walked in everywhere is mixed with his teething dribble!

Last week Mr Haling decided to go to Buma to see if they had any trochus shell ready for him, so as Mrs H and their two children were going they asked Michael and me, Dorothy Ward and Mr Chaperlin to go with them. I thoroughly enjoyed the trip as I have not been further than the Sundi River. We went past Nanua, of which we have heard so much, and it certainly does look delightful. It was much larger than I had expected it to be, and it also had a lot of trees – apparently it takes about half an hour to walk right round – it also has golden sand beaches. I do hope we have an opportunity to go soon. We were to have gone last weekend with the Filewoods but the weather wasn't suitable. I didn't go ashore at Buma – none of us did – as we discovered everyone had gone off diving for shell out at the reef, but I did at the other two places we called at on the way back. At Buma there were six or seven leaf houses, all looking very clean and neat above a sandy beach.

Lata, one of the places where we went ashore, runs a flourishing market garden – all growing out of sand and coral! It makes our efforts here seem very paltry. There they grow tomatoes, sweet corn, spring onions, beans, Chinese cabbage and several varieties of sweet potatoes. The great pity of it is that the tomatoes are attacked by some insect so that many of them go rotten before they are ripe. As you will gather from the above, the profusion of everything was amazing.

Michael behaved very well during the trip, playing, sleeping or eating. He is just cutting two more teeth, the upper ones on either side of the front two (he hasn't these yet but I think he soon will as they are looking very pronounced through the gum).

Letter to Aunt Erica.

Last mail I heard that Mr MacEwin (who we thought had disappeared for good) is going to do a 'comprehensive' survey of the kauri forests in Santa Cruz and the Chief Secretary had agreed that I should accompany him. I was to tell them when I could start, so I told them, by wireless, the beginning of October, and also said that I thought it would take at least six months, though I can't imagine Mac spending more than a month on it. What is strange is that Mr Filewood, the new manager, hadn't heard anything about it. Anyway we hope to know soon what is going to happen. If it is to be for more than a couple of months I shall probably take Claire and Michael, and we would stay at Nabalue, William's village.

Another thing we must think of soon is getting things put away in the crates for when we go – though we may leave them here locked up in the store.

Pippa is due to produce her third family any day now.

A few weeks ago Mr Jones left on a trading trip and took Selwyn and Hannah with him at our request, since Hannah is to go to her home island to have a baby. Selwyn and Mr Jones and the rest are expected back soon now. Meanwhile a couple of our labourers have been doing houseboy for us.

Recently Dr Payne came dashing through on his way to Ticopia. H.E. had arrived in the aftermath of an epidemic of common cold (brought by Archdeacon Reynold's ship) and had sent for him. He found there had been 120 deaths, mostly the very old and the very young. He also took a large consignment of rice for Ticopia from the store and promised that a ship would come to replace it by early October, so we are expecting a ship soon. They have run out of ration biscuits for the boys, so they have extra rice, and now that is nearly exhausted I believe. However there's always coconuts!

Last week I had a very good camp with Mr Filewood in a new and pleasant site on the Willi Willi River. The weather was gloriously fine and we saw a lot of new country and quite a bit of timber. One day we looked down on the island of Nanua across the lagoon with its dazzling beach, shady trees and the pale blue water over the coral reef round it. We might have seen the Toby, *but didn't, as that was the*

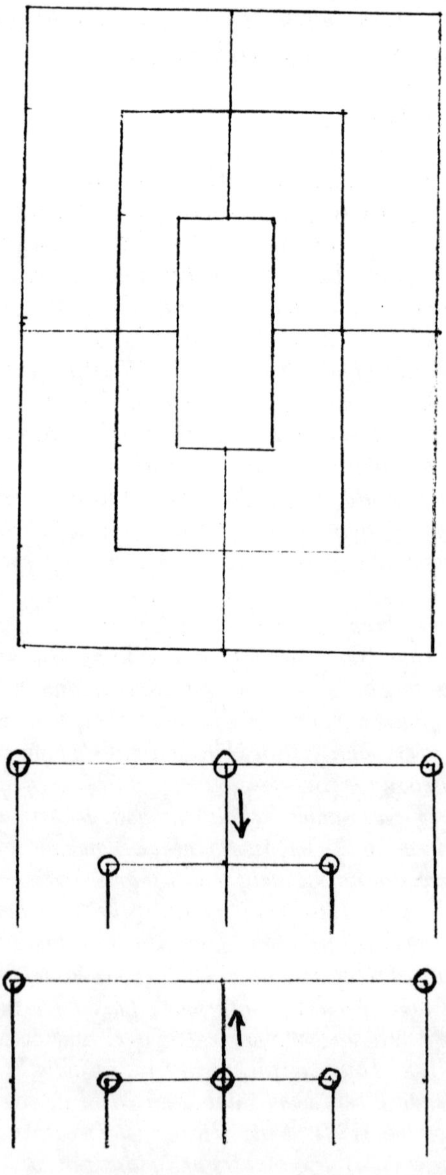

Buttons Game.

day Claire and Michael had their trip to Buma, but I didn't know about it till later.

When Mr Filewood and I set off that week the Delaware *wouldn't start (as usual) so we had to row round to the Sundi River (four miles, but boys did most of the work!), and missed the lorry going up the road. So we didn't get to the road-head till 2.0 pm, and by then it was raining hard. So we stayed the night with two Australians in their huts and went on in the morning. I stayed with Herbert Schneider, a German ('New Australian') from the Black Forest. He is a very nice quiet chap and I enjoyed looking at his photograph album. Some lovely picture postcards of the country round Berchtesgaden and the Zugspitze. He was in the war, I think in Normandy after 'D' day, as a boy – 'They put me in the front line and the second day I was captured and very glad too!' After supper the four of us played 'Buttons', which Herbert brought from Germany. It s a bit like draughts, but more interesting. The 'board' (on the back of a writing pad) is like this – only bigger of course. Two play, each with nine buttons of different colours. You take it in turns to put one button at a time on each intersection or corner, and if you get three of your own in a line you can 'take' one of his. Then when all nine are down, you can move them about, one space at a time – until you have only three left, when you can 'jump' to any space you like! The art is to get so that you can open and close a line every other move, if not every move, and every time you close it you take one – but beware when he has only three left! It can be as difficult as chess. This is a good position, if he lets you get into it. N.B. A counter which is one of three in a line cannot be taken, unless there is no other counter to take. It ends when he has only three left and you manage to take one, because with only two he cannot take and you have him, (or do you?)*

(4 October) Pippa's family has arrived – two tabby and one ginger. After we had turned her out from behind the books in the bookshelf, she carried them away into the jungle somewhere. We think that little Blackie, Pippa's daughter, will also soon produce kittens.

29 September

Up at 4.45 am – roused Mala and left quay in the tug at 5.0 am. Put up a 'curlew' on Peou beach – decurved bill, white rump, large, call could be a curlew's. Several more there I think, with sandpipers.

Round to Lavaka and there disembarked, tide fairly low. Greeted by Tati. Straight off along track to beginning of ridge, pacing and taking bearings. Reached kauri forest after a mile. Passed through just under two miles of good ridge-top forest. Eventually joined back-bone ridge at about 1600 feet above sea level and followed this until we reached our track of last week. Thence down to our camp, tea and a swim in the river.

30 September

Alan and Lionel headed straight for the road. I went to have a look at the slaty flycatcher's nest first, deserted unfortunately. Also saw a bird which could have been an immature cardinal honey-eater – scarlet rump, grey body and pale colour, but I do not think it is a jungle species; also shape of head and bill a bit different. Saw one the same last week on the ridge at 1500 feet above sea level.

To road-head, cup of tea at Leo's. Then paced up the road a bit, then across country for about a mile on post-exploitation area. Counted kauri seedlings.

Back by jeep and tug.

14 October

Boys cutting lines. Went a walk among the ridges, it being fine, seeing regeneration areas. Thought about possible stocking densities and silviculture.

15 October

Started packing for Santa Cruz.

On Ingau's demand met three canoes returning from poaching his reef and sorted out the situation.

Shooting at lizards in pasture – no luck.

17 October

William and company getting nursery into order and sowing 600 kauri seed. Mala cutting lines in a fresh regeneration area.

Later William cutting lines at the second bend in the track behind the house.

Caught a gekko under the house, put it in spirit.

19 October

Dorothy called in afternoon – arrival of *Citos* now postponed till Friday midday at the earliest.

Collected some seed from flamboyant tree and gave Dorothy three dozen to take home to Australia. Sowed eighteen in nursery.

20 October

Boys making partition out of leaves in the dining room.

21 October

Read up Leyton's soil notes, then out looking for mull and mor soil. Found mor soil on an old kauri ridge with regeneration – one inch of raw humus thickly rooted, blackish, and reddish soil. Mull in non-kauri forest – crumb structure, coffee colour, earthworms. Collected some micro-fauna and examined it.

Letter to Father.

The Citos *is coming at last tomorrow and bringing MacEwin with whom I am to go and survey Santa Cruz. Mr Jones has agreed to take us, for a price, in his ketch* Endeavour III, *so with luck we should get off early next week. I hope we will get back by Christmas, though if we really stay for two months the chance is slender.*

I've had a job these last few weeks to keep my men employed –

we've run out of virgin forest to survey within a day's march, and it wasn't worth chartering a boat for a long trip with this business in the offing. As usual nobody knew anything about what was happening, since I was told at the beginning of September that Mac was ready to leave Australia immediately for Honiara!

Mr Filewood has been warned that he is to take over the store from Haling as per letter on Citos, *and one wonders what the reaction is going to be. Lionel says he's going to convert the bridge over the river to his house into a drawbridge! But the old situation of all goods coming ashore into the store and Jones accusing Haling of pinching his stuff, and me trying to see fair play and getting cursed by both sides was not much good. There was a real row last time the* Citos *came. I gather Haling is going soon anyway.*

22 October

Citos came in at dusk and went round to Saboe Bay. Mail came after supper.

23 October

Sunday. *Citos* came and went away again – too much wind and too rough for unloading.

Golden plovers on lawn. These birds were about all evening.

Selwyn in trouble due to horse-play with Europeans from the bush, Phil in particular. I had to go and confront a dozen or so Australians in the house by the store and see 'fair play' – they gave Selwyn's clothes back to him after he apologized for disrespectful behaviour (which was probably invited by *their* behaviour). My own conduct was disapproved of – 'When a white man sticks up for a black man against another white man, there's something wrong somewhere' – agreed by all.

Letter to Aunt Erica.

The Citos *came in last night at sundown and went straight round to Saboe Bay for the night. Early this morning it anchored off Peou and hooted a bit, but there is such a gale blowing and the sea is so rough, even in the lagoon, that there is no question of unloading. I'm rather pleased actually, since it's Sunday, and unloading means work for the Customs officer! At breakfast time it up-anchored and went back to Saboe Bay in despair. MacEwin is aboard, and in a few days we shall be off to Santa Cruz in Mr Jones's boat. I hope we will be back for Christmas, but I do not think you will get another letter from me before then, so I will now wish you a very happy Christmas, just in case. I think Naqu is on this boat too – to take over while I'm away. I forgot to tell you that the mat Michael was on in the photograph was the one given me by the Chief at Ticopia. He is the one with the fan in the group under the tree – the paramount Chief. Unfortunately he died in the last epidemic.*

While waiting for the Citos *to arrive I kept the boys in Peou and they have been doing silviculture in the secondary forest, that was felled in the 1920s or thereabouts, nearby. On the ridge tops sometimes there is quite a dense growth of shoulder high kauri saplings and if you cut down the 'weed species' that are keeping them shaded, then they will grow much faster. A tree like that is capable of growing three feet in height every year.*

The last boat brought us a whole lot of library books from Honiara so we've been having an orgy of reading.

I wonder if you or Dr Stone can think of a cure for the middle finger of Claire's right hand. Months ago the cuticle disappeared, then the flesh round the base of the nail began to dry up. The nail is now all rough, dry, scaly and dented, and the flesh inflamed and sore. Occasionally a little pus comes out. We thought it might be an infected nail bed, and Dr Payne on his flying visit prescribed a penicillin injection – but it didn't do any good. We've tried vaseline, icthymol, and Zipp ointment for periods of three days or so without effect. It is a minor complaint, but worrying when it refuses to clear up.

Both my foot-rot and coral ear have at last cleared up, touch wood! The foot-rot yielded at once to Mycozol, a preparation containing salicylic acid, an effective fungicide. The coral ear yielded to constant drying out with cotton wool on a matchstick.

Addition from Claire, 25 October.

Just heard we have been 'wait-listed' for the Oronsay, *sailing from Sydney 7 April.*

There is no real news I'm afraid – Chris will be off to Santa Cruz shortly but Michael and I will stay here as it is only for two months. Also M is due for two more anti-diphtheria and whooping-cough injections and I don't want him to miss them. He is getting some more teeth and will soon have three at the top; he is also experimenting in kneeling and standing up – holding onto something of course.

Pippa took her three kittens off into the garden the day after they were born, and we have not seen them until today when she brought them under the house for more shelter. They are lovely fluffy little things but rather wild, they spit a lot when picked up.

24 October

Citos came and unloaded, the ship's officers checking the cargo while still on board. Some of it had been left at Honiara. I saw Mac at a gathering at Jones's place and learnt that we are leaving next week and will be back for Christmas.

1 November

Fine, down at 8.0 am with Claire. Sat in canoe house awhile, then I went aboard *Endeavour III* and we left Vanikoro, putting on a foresail outside the reef.

We had refreshments when we reached Utupua, then Mac and I went ashore and I walked to a sandspit where about a dozen waders were feeding. At least nine of them were golden plovers; two smaller birds with white belly and wing bar, brown collar and red legs were I think redshanks; also a solitary grey wader perched on a stump, a bit larger than a golden plover, small white patch on belly, black line through eye, longish slightly decurved bill, yellow legs. Two herons flew off – one pure white, yellow legs.

3 November

Up anchor and then stopped at Nagu – opposite Lord Howe Island. Sea became fairly rough. Stopped the engine to let the generator cool off and had much trouble starting again so we put the sail up. Mac and Fred then cleaned the plugs and at last the engine started. On to Nabalue, where we saw the chief and left Walter, Camnis and Mayo, then round to Napir. Looked at hut behind the beach, then landed the bulk of the stores and carried it to the hut. Then left the boys to sleep ashore, went back to the ship and round to Maunda Bay for the night. Took a spell at the wheel. Anchored just inside the eastern side, by a small leaf house on a steep bank about twenty feet high. Went ashore, ate pawpaws. *Pometia pinnata* trees there.

4 November

Mac gave Jones a lesson on engine maintenance and I listened in; after which the engine started first turn. Round to Napir – as rough as yesterday. Went ashore with remainder of cargo, checked and listed all stores.

Jones came ashore for lunch, then he and Mac left for the Reef Islands. Pitched my old tent in Walker's old site – at the crest of the shingle beach – only a few feet above the surge and thunder of the great seas beating on the shingle. A bit exposed to the south-east but safe, I think, from all but tidal waves and hurricanes. Also had the fly-sheet of one of Mac's tents pitched as a dining tent. Went along to the river for an all over wash, and ate when darkness had come (chicken noodle soup, potato, onion, Trim luncheon meat).

5 November

Stiff south-easter, squally. Set William and the boys onto making furniture and in the course of the morning they made a sturdy little table and two benches with backs in the dining tent.

7 November

Gave out rations, dressed cuts. Finally left about 10.30 with Benjamin, John, Metoa, Luke and Clement. Kept pacing and compass data. Up kauri ridge to old view point, then down half a mile north east, along a stream to a confluence and camped by the bigger river (fly-sheet only). Later on reconnoitred half a mile down this river, which flows NNE.

8 November

Up ridge to NW, plenty of kauri. Joined a bigger ridge at estimated 1200 to 1300 feet above sea level and kauri petered out. Continued northerly about a mile from camp, where a boy climbed a tree and had views of Maunda and Graciosa bays. Collected plants and went back to camp, then returned to base via two new ridges. Estimated eight miles of walking these two days.

9 November

Fine still. Swim in the sea followed by freshwater bath in the river before breakfast, which consisted of coconut, banana and tinned peaches.

William and company continuing survey, other boys clearing round base camp. Plotted all Monday and Tuesday's data, producing a useful map, with many question marks.

Sea bathe and freshwater bath again in the evening.

Reading *Tudor England*.

10 November

Quick plunge in the sea before breakfast. Then sent William and the boys up to camp with a cargo of rations and the two remaining tents.

Went along the beach for a proper swim, freshwater bath and shave later in the morning when the sun was quite strong. Found my belt which I had lost yesterday.

Benjamin and Melobou in camp all day – the former with a boil on his leg, the latter with tummy-ache, for which I gave him Epsom salts.

In the afternoon I saw grey wader with red legs and white belly patch on rock by shore.

12 November

Watched bird like a small heron by the shore: grey, yellow-grey legs, orangey feet, noticeable in flight. White streak along side of chest, white speckles on primaries, purple head. Probably little mangrove heron.

13 November

Sunday. Along the rocks, low tide, at SW end of beach. Back to fetch goggles, having found a lovely deep rock pool. Explored all around and saw lots of fish, including one about nine inches long, brick red with bright purple eyes. Rain pm.

Letter to Aunt Erica 12 November.

I have now been here just over a week and the survey is well under way. Mac came too but went off immediately again with Mr Jones to the Reef Islands and possibly the Duff Islands where I have no doubt they are having a good time.

My tent is pitched on the crest of a shingle beach a few yards from the sea. There is no sheltering reef here so when there's a south-easter we have the full force of the waves on the beach, but most of the time it's been fairly calm with the surf a subdued and rhythmic roar. The beach isn't much more than a quarter of a mile long and is set in a deepish cove facing Lord Howe Island, two or three miles away. Each end of the beach a river flows out behind the shingle. The one at the NE is the best and my usual gambit is to have a good wallow in the breakers and then a soap down in the river across the beach. No sharks or crocodiles to speak of, but Sunday night William caught a turtle six feet nine inches long and eight feet in girth – quite a small one, apparently! With its front flippers roped up and a circle of Solomon Islanders round it by lamp-light, it proceeded to dig a hole two feet deep with its back flippers and then laid 104 eggs, which are a welcome change of diet! We put two good ones and all the undersize ones back.

The woods around are filled with the cooing of doves and sundry other birds. I shot a couple of pigeons for supper last Sunday. They are very good eating.

We are very comfortable at Base Camp with tables and chairs made out of packing cases. Three miles inland I have established another camp in the middle of the forest, by a river, and had supplies carried up. So I'll be working from there next week. There is some distant kauri across the valley that I shall try to reach, and maybe have a small camp there. Meanwhile the routine chain and compass work is being carried on by William.

I am hoping Claire and Michael will contrive to turn up. It would be lovely for them, and there are no mosquitoes. It's just as well they didn't come out on Jones's boat however, as it was rather rough then and also a bit cramped. It would have been miserable trying to look after Michael and being seasick at the same time. Also there was one nasty moment when the engine was stopped to let the generator cool off – and then wouldn't start again, and on a lee shore – though fortunately a fairly distant one. It was only that the plugs needed cleaning however, and after half an hour of sickening wallowing we were off again.

We were three nights on board before we got here and every night we found a calm anchorage and usually had a good swim in clear water over a bright sandy bottom.

The best place was in Maunda Bay where there was somebody's unoccupied leaf house on the shore on a steep bank above the sea with two or three grand Pometia pinnata *trees and pawpaws with the fruit rotting on them. So we helped ourselves to some very welcome refreshment.*

I've been eating and drinking a lot of green coconuts here. It is a good food, full of vitamins and saves opening tins (we have plenty of tins and *coconuts).*

I don't suppose I shall be able to post this till near Christmas, when I hope to be back on Vanikoro.

14 November

Sent letter off to Claire by Chief Maleuto, urging her to come if possible.

Left at 1.30 pm and arrived at camp II about 5.0 pm.

We had some heavy rain in the night and had to shift our positions owing to flooding.

* * *

15 November

Weather cleared up a bit. Left Benjamin and Bali to make betel-nut palm beds in our tent. Set off NNE, crossed three ridges with kauri on and then reached a fair-sized river about one mile from camp. Here we ate and had a leaf shelter made.

16 November

Wet night, but slept dry owing to beds. Waited for the rain to stop and left camp about 10.0 am taking the fly sheet and a quantity of rations. To the River of yesterday, waited out another shower in our shelter, then the boys made camp (camp III) a bit upstream on a flat bit of bank. Fly sheet for us, with betel-nut leaves to lie on. Boys made themselves a leaf shelter.

17 November

Off up the ridge, going north exploring further virgin country. Had a fine look-out over a basin with many kauri ridges. Down to the Bwonjia River, a fair sized one, where the boys caught a fish about eighteen inches long and about five pounds. Up next ridge, going north-east in plenty of kauri. Reached a hill top at 1040 feet above sea level. No decent look-out, but glimpses through the trees east and north east, looks as if no further ridges capable of bearing kauri.

Back in record time through pouring rain. Found messenger party from William at camp – news of boys having arrived to build house.

18 November

Left camp at 9.20 and walked down river, keeping pacing and compass data. Fine, swim in pool. Boys followed with loads. Arrived at path 12.30. Boys stayed to cook a meal. Went on with Bali, got lost, reached base camp 1.30. Rough sea. Rested all afternoon.

19 November

Plotted data all day. Mac organized the boys putting down shingle etc.

Heavy rain in afternoon. Mac out with gun, but no luck owing to rain. River in spate, bay mud-coloured. Many pieces of timber washed down. Thunder.

20 November

Sunday. Calmer, quite fine. Along to the rock pools on the point, Mac bringing two Solomon Islanders and the gun. Both did a bit of goggling. Swam an underwater tunnel. Back for large meal – camp pie, sweet potatoes, followed by rice pudding with raisins.

21 November

Slow, steady drizzle most of the day. Mac and I made a 1:24 scale model of the house the boys are to build out of cartridge paper.

pm. Adjusted and corrected pacing and compass map. Still raining.

22 November

Rainy morning, but cleared up a bit by midday. Traced a copy of the map for bush use. Mac sorting our stores and checking rations. One and three quarter bags of rice apparently pilfered.

Left base camp at 2.0 and reached camp II at 4.30, going up the river.

23 November

Terrific storm after breakfast. Thunder and rain. River rose three feet in ten minutes. Bush party therefore cancelled.

Weather cleared up about 10.0. Made a rice pudding, while the men went out to catch snails and eels.

24 November

Fine. Went up ridge going north-west, through kauri to the central back-bone, where we had a good look-out over Graciosa Bay. Continued northwards to another peak and a good view of kauri forest a mile to the north-west. Lunch there, then eastwards across country, ending by going down a ridge to the river through very good kauri forest. Arrived about 5.0. Boys built two leaf shelters. Blue skies, fine weather, very pleasant spot for a bivouac. Swam in the river.

25 November

Down river a little, then up ridge north-eastwards, then across a saddle going south-east, past a kauri of estimated thirty foot girth. Arrived at point reached Thursday last week. Thence down ridge southward. For part of the way we followed an old track which is said to have been made by a race of men who are now extinct, but formerly inhabited the interior of the island.

Home swiftly along the river, a different one to last week.

26 November

Fine. William came down from the bush. Mac and I spent much of the time collecting transparent pebbles from the shore, of which Mac now has a fine collection. Also did a bit of plotting. Framework and floor of house now completed.

27 November

Sunday. Slight but distinct earthquake shock in the early hours of the morning.

Collected and sorted a few pebbles, read *Two Gentlemen of Verona*. finished painting my sketch. Rained off and on.

28 November

Started wet. District Commissioner's arrival anticipated, and ship sighted before midday. It turned into Napir after our signalling with sheets. Claire and Michael not aboard as I had hoped, letter however. Sent telegram hoping she will be able to come. Passages on *Oronsay* confirmed, plane from Honiara 3 April. New Forest Officer on his way.

Letter from Claire dated 24 November.

Mr Jones arrived back here the day before yesterday and told me he had landed you at Napir in some rough wather. I do hope it has been good since then as I know how much it can help or hinder the work, and I do want you back for Christmas. Do you think there is any chance of this happening? Things are coming to a head here – Mrs Haling has said that she and the children will probably go out on the Aros.

Mr Tedder and family arrived here on 12 November, children both boys, aged one and three quarters and three and a half, wife very nice. In fact she suggested that I go down to Ticopia with them – this was said at Sunday lunch and we left at four o'clock, so you can guess what a rush it was to collect everything that M and I would need. Michael was a trouble at times especially at nights as he wouldn't settle down, due I think to the old trouble – his teeth, his fourth upper one is just coming through. In spite of this the trip was wonderful.

At Ticopia we went and said hallo to all the chiefs, crawling respectfully into their houses, being careful to shake the sand off our feet first. At the first place we were given coconuts to drink. We didn't see very much of the lake as Jim was kept very busy, and Margaret and I couldn't go by ourselves because the children couldn't walk that far. We swam in the sea as often as possible but found this was only practicable at high tide, as otherwise it was too shallow.

We also went down to Anuda or Cherry Island, which is a perfect gem of a place, practically the whole island is a garden. We had to go ashore by canoe as the reef is very close in so the Mary *can't anchor inside it, and there is no passage for a dinghy. It was quite exciting waiting for the right moment.*

We only spent the day there, as quite a wind sprang up, making it unsafe for the ship – also giving us a rough trip back to Ticopia. On the night before we left to come back here,

Jim showed some coloured slides to them – some taken in England and Australia and some of Ticopia taken on his last visit with Mr Minnit. They were very excited by them and on the shore, while waiting for the dinghy back to the ship, they made up a song about it. Thirty families are to be moved to a place in the Russell Islands, and when we left some of the men and one of the chiefs came with us to inspect the place.

Jim went off to the Duffs after arriving back here, leaving Margaret and the children with me. It has been great fun and the house will seem very empty after they go today.

The day before yesterday the new High Commissioner and his wife came down – very nice, party on board as before. They are calling in on their way back from the New Hebrides on 4 December, to see the timber workings.

29 November

Set off mid-morning, going up Eastern River. Lunch by it, collected an orchid, then crossed the divide to the east and down a track the other side. Camped in new area by white rocks. No kauri. Got the local Creation Myth out of Benjamin. Saw a four inch gekko with a tail with nine white bands.

30 November

Bali back to base with swollen knee, accompanied by Clement. Off north-west to crest of ridge. View north-west and north – no kauri. Thence south-west to hill top reached previous trip. Measured large kauri – twenty-eight feet three inch girth base height. Cut finger, bound it with leaf and a handkerchief. Benjamin and Dick down to camp III with loads, John and I on north-westwards through kauri. Lunch by stream. Found a good ridge, followed it up to a fork, north-west and east branches, kauriferous. Returned to camp III by south-west ridge and stream. John caught seven fish and one eel. Ate two fish for supper; also rice and condensed milk. Sketched camp and river.

1 December

Up river, carrying own pack. Reached 'T' junction, took right fork. Left stream by ridge going north, which eventually became the main dividing ridge. 140 odd kauri counted, good form. Very good forest, to both right and left. Lunched off sardines and a tin of pears. View of Lord Howe Island, and (?) a ship.

After another mile, we could see the peak on the central backbone of the island just ahead, so we left the packs behind, pushed on and reached it at 1700 feet above sea level. Magnificent views all round – Graciosa Bay, Tinakula, NE end of Santa Cruz, Maunda Bay, Utupua and Napir. Returned. Then down ridge to east to small river and a camp site.

2 December

Up ridge behind camp, going south-west through some kauri. Regained main ridge and collected pen-knife which I had left at yesterday's luncheon spot (used for opening tins).

Explored ridge going south-east – linking up with peak reached on Wednesday and thus completing traverse of the north-east rim of the main kauri basin. Explored ridge going east from hill-top, good kauri. Rain – retreat to camp III. River in flood. Read *Voyage of the Beagle* and rested.

3 December

Fine, down river to a previous crossing point, then off into 'Mesopotamia' country and traversed kauri ridges heading towards the coast. Down into camp II river and thence home, just beating the floods caused by renewed rain.

Mac still in a bad way with sore ankle, also oedema – putty-flesh on leg.

4 December

A shout from the boys soon after dawn heralded the

Base Camp, Ndeni.

approach of *Endeavour III* and Mr Jones on a short visit. No family on board, alas – but he hadn't come direct from Vanikoro and is due there tomorrow after a night at Utupua. Sent a letter to Claire – but I am hoping that she and Michael will arrive in the *Kovala* tomorrow morning. The new HE is supposed to be doing a tour of the timber workings today. He has been to the New Hebrides.

5 December

No sign of the *Kovala* all day.

Did the pay sheets and paid everybody.

9 December

Letter from Claire to Erica and Mu.

I do hope this reaches you in time for Christmas. There is just a chance it may as a trader is calling here tomorrow and he might be going up to

Honiara. Incidentally I am hoping that he will take Michael and me to Santa Cruz to join Chris. It is now arranged that Mr Jones should pick them up on 31 December, so I feel it would be nice to be together if it can be managed. Chris says they have made a nice little house with verandah and separate dining room – I feel I must see it all. I shall take the camera I think. It is simply pouring with rain. The hills are completely blotted out. If it's like this tomorrow I shall be in two minds about going to Santa Cruz even if he will take me. This is supposed to be one of the finer months here, with hot days, blue skies and calm *seas.*

11 December

Fine, calm evening, sat on beach while darkness fell. Boys returned from Nagu and Nabalue, bring us a lot of cabbage, a bunch of bananas, three pawpaws and a basket of pana.

Earlier in the day I drank and ate a green coconut. At supper we ate cabbage. This to correct possible vitamin C deficiency.

12 December

Woke in the early morning with slight fever. Both groins swollen, and glands on sides of neck. Thick head, weak. Took four nivaquin, then paludrin through the day.

'Quake about 10 am, felt by Mac and the boys but not by me. Said to have been preceded by a roll of thunder or muffled explosion.

Letter from Claire dated 9 December.

I hope I will be able to give you this myself, but it's just in case something stops me from coming. Mr Campbell is expected tomorrow, and I will see if he can bring me, I hope the weather improves, it has been very wet for the last few days . . . I feel I must be with you, especially for Christmas. This is a time when a family should be together. On Monday I was talking to Mr Jones and saying just that and his reply was that we will have plenty in the future together. I feel that now *is important . . . 14 December. Don't be too disappointed that I have not come, although I feel I am letting you down. Campbell arrived yesterday, but I have heard that he is going to the Reefs and only might call at Graciosa Bay on his way home. With M this makes too drawn out and undecided a journey.*

13 December

Slept uneasily, then woke in the early morning with dysentry and glandular pain. Dawn broke fine and it kept fine all day. Sulphaguanadin stopped dysentry. Fasted most of day.

14 December

Slept very soundly till early morning, then woke thirsty. Very weak indeed, lay flat out most of morning. Still lovely and fine. Able to contemplate the thought of food. Had some pana and cabbage midday. Fish for supper.

15 December

Feeling stronger, though with a thick head. Pigeon and paw-paw for breakfast. Walked a little way along the shore and sat and watched crabs. Returned before lunch (pigeon).

Supper – pigeon.

16 December

Very weak again. Flat out on bed all day. Couldn't eat anything to speak of.

17 December

One turtle egg in the morning, otherwise nothing. Very weak still. Sent for Assistant Medical Practitioner, David Dawia, from Graciosa Bay.

18 December

Sunday. Ate some tomato puree, then a concoction of pana, and later some fish caught by Benjamin specially, which was very good.

William turned up with lemons and oranges. Some lemonade was brought to me, which was very welcome.

19 December

Assistant Medical Practitioner arrived, accompanied by Chief and retinue. He diagnosed my trouble as a virus he has known Europeans to get and lasting usually a fortnight, so mine should be on the way out! I hope. He prescribed a further fortnight's complete rest. A month doing nothing at Napir – it would have been so much better had I gone home with Jones, I could at least have been home for Christmas.

Melobou fell sick today.

20 December

Stronger, able to walk about a bit.

Luke fell sick today.

22 December

Bath and shave before breakfast – beginning to feel well again at last! Fine. Spent morning painting at north-east end of beach. Quite pleased with the result – a painting of sea, river and jungle, with a 'Lesser Bittern' (? Little Mangrove Heron).

23 December

Remainder of boys except Benjamin left after breakfast for Christmas holiday. Cooked scones for breakfast in pan – good.

Did plant collection for an hour or so, then took a walk along path into jungle and tried without success to recognize some lowland forest dominants. Looking for *Dysoxylum sp.* specially.

Ben's friend came from Nagu with bananas, two pineapples and a paw-paw for us. Then they both left.

Collected flowers of a littoral second storey forest tree very similar to Frangipani in its scent, leaves and sap, but with twenty feet of trunk.

25 December

Christmas Day. A very wet day. Boys all away, doing all chores ourselves. Finished painting sketch made in bush.

For lunch we had Cafe Royal first of all, made with Jones's rum, then pana, followed by bananas and cream.

Started painting another sketch made in the bush.

Supper – Chivers' potato and tinned carrots.

26 December

An old native turned up from nowhere and tended the fire in return for food.

Letter from Claire dated 24 December.

. . . *Must rush as Jones said he might be off today. I don't know when he will be seeing you but happy Christmas and New Year.*

The Aros *is also leaving today. There was a party on board last night and in the end I decided to go, I wore my short white dress. It wasn't dancing like last time – the passengers mainly elderly and tended to be rather stiff at first, but Phil Haebeck came to the rescue and got everyone singing songs. He really can be very funny. I was besieged with offers of escort home and thought Mr Chaperlin's the least hazardous as everybody else had had quite a bit to drink.*

Over Christmas I am staying at the Halings' so I won't be on my own, though I shall be thinking of you and wishing we were together.

* * *

Letter from Claire dated 28 December.

. . . Christmas lunch at the Halings' went off in what I expect was the same manner as last year. Nobody left the table until about four o'clock and even then some stayed until nearly six, when it was time to go to the Filewoods' party. This followed almost the same pattern as the one on board the Aros, *with the addition of dancing – we must try and improve as it is so much more fun then. I suppose we will have to give a party before we go, what an ordeal.*

Did I tell you before that eight blankets and mosquito nets have arrived for the new boys you bring back.

Last night Mala and some of the boys came up to sing songs – I gave them some money to get tobacco.

Letter to Father dated 12 December.

We have had a lovely little leaf hut built here for us with a raised floor and a verandah.

Also we have done most of the exploring we intend to do. We have had five bivouacs altogether up in the bush. There is still some measuring work to be done but it has been very wet and we have been having a much needed rest last week.

It is a shingle beach here with a river flowing out at each end. Unfortunately there is a crocodile which is sometimes seen on the beach at night, or cruising past across the bay, so we haven't been doing much sea bathing recently. There are some lovely rock pools and chasms round the bay though that are good for a safe swim.

Letter from Claire to her Father-in-Law dated 21 December.

Mr Filewood's cows have arrived at long last, brought by the trader who I thought might have been able to take me to Santa Cruz. There are three young cows and a bull, so with luck we may be able to have fresh milk next year. They were brought ashore in a dinghy, so you can imagine how small they are still, but they look all right.

27 December

Boys arrived mid-morning. Odd-bod left at William's request. Bush party postponed owing to weather, otherwise I was ready to go, but not strong enough yet to cope with bivouacs under lousy conditions.

Turtle-egg omelette (eight eggs) and cafe royal for lunch.

28 December

Relatively fine. Set off with the boys on the long march up river to camp III. Had to carry my own pack. Lunch halt on the way, fine weather held. Ate scone cooked by Mac with condensed milk – very good.

Tent brought and pitched in new site. My old bivvy full of termites and ants.

29 December

Left Benjamin in camp, to make me a betel-nut bed, get firewood and catch fish. Down river, then up old ridge to point 740 feet above sea level and thence started a line across very steep country. Only did 1800 feet owing to topography and me still being weak. Returned along previously explored stream to camp.

Ben had caught ten fish and two eels. Boys caught another fifteen eels on the way back.

I reached camp before the boys and had a snack of pineapple and cake and then a rest on the new bed, followed later by two of the fish with rice. Fed the fish bones to the crayfish. Boys well feasted, snails also. Had some myself. Opened a tin of pears and gave the boys half.

30 December

Tummy unsettled in night. Feeling a bit wobbly, but went upstream with the boys to the scene of work. There I cut my head on a snag, being accident-prone due to weakness, handed over to William and returned, thankfully, to camp, just beating the rain.

On the way upstream, a bird's nest was pointed out – on a branch ten feet above the stream. Open, about three inches across. Two white eggs, rather elongate shape, about three quarters of an inch long. Said to belong to Cardinal Honey-eater. Glimpsed bird later, but not to recognize it.

31 December

Feeling stronger, fine day. End of yeterday's line too far, so set off for the other end and worked on back-bearing from there. Ran out of kauri in about 1,000 feet, made the total strip a mile long on the surface, but not on the map. I back along strip, picking up a curiously shaped piece of Lingi (*Pterocarpus Indicus*). Boys returned via ridge and we re-united at the big tree by the starting post. Measured heights and girths of an additional twenty-one trees (mostly of very good form, one of timber height sixty-two feet), in an area 600 by 100 feet. Then returned, tired to camp. Ate a good brew of rice and condensed milk, followed by tea. Then scraped and polished my bit of Lingi.

Boys caught some fish and I had some for supper. Continued polishing wood with wooden knife-handle by kauri-gum flare at boys' house. So ends the last day of this Santa Cruz survey, a good day, and the last of 1955.

Opened a tin of pears, had two, and gave the rest to the boys to celebrate.

* * *

1956

1 January

Quite cold night, bracing morning. Warmed myself by the boys' fire before plunging in the river. Breakfast on a rock – rice and condensed milk, orange, tea. Collected two tree ferns and an *Angiopteris* on the way down river. Arrived for lunch at camp. Mac not too well, neck swellings like I had.

Collected a blue flowered rosette plant from the coral at the south-west point of Napir.

Got a few local names of trees from Benjamin and John.

2 January

Shout announced the arrival of Jones's boat while we were still in bed. Snack breakfast and hurried striking of camp, embarkation and away to Nabalue. Ashore to explore the cave, half an hour walk with a few boys including William. Magnificent entrance to underground river, very high roof. Followed river's even course upstream for half a mile, where we emerged into the ravine again. Three species of bats seen, one small one collected by picking off the wall. A still smaller eyeless one seen by Mac, also a larger one. Swifts on nests a quarter of a mile from daylight. Collected one adult, one juvenile and nests. All kept alive.

Footprints seen on the shelves at the sides – some big, some medium, some small, probably a woman's. Some a few days old, some recent. Boys say nobody has been here since 1948 and attribute the footprints to spirits. Saw prints on ledges where our boys had not been. Return to ship. Then to Nagu and anchorage. Ashore for pigeons, but no luck although

Mac got a small red-polled parakeet.

Slept on deck under the stars. Watched stars until moonrise about 11 pm. Then slept.

3 January

Left anchorage by moonlight at 4 am. Stayed abed on deck until the sun had risen and was fairly high.

Breakfast – beans and coffee – in Utupua lagoon.

Claire met us on the jetty. Very happy reunion!

4 January

A lovely fine morning. With Claire for a dip in the bear pool. Then a leisured breakfast.

Gave out a requisition for the new boys' rations; also issued the three of them with knives. They had blankets and mosquito nets last night.

Michael crying a lot because of the two strange men in the house.

Later on down to the beach for Michael's swim; also swam myself.

Selwyn sick – lit fire myself.

Talked till 10.30 before going to bed.

5 January

Another fine day. Brought accounts up to date in the morning. Iced coffee with Claire for elevenses. Tinkered with pressure lamp. Checked knives, blankets and mosquito nets after lunch. Then fetched Selwyn up from Mala's house and gave him a telling off for bad behaviour and a month's notice.

Put remaining swift and bat in spirit.

9 January

Down to do Jones's customs forms. Did some in his house, some in Filewood's office.

11 January

Luke making pots and potting kauri in mixed ash and burnt-over soil.

Working at corrected scale for paced map.

Fine starry night, star-gazed. Venus bright after sunset now. False Cross, Nubecula Major and Minor and Canopus in the south. Jupiter rising in the west. Found the constellation of Fornax. Terrific shooting star – pink-purple and then green, thirty to forty degree arc, north-west from zenith.

12 January

Still plotting data. Mac measured most of the areas in the afternoon. Results obtained:
Total area of kauri forest on Santa Cruz – 2.8 square miles.
Total volume of kauri – 32 million super.
Volume, mean tree – 3,500
Mean timber height – 46 feet
Mean basal area – 49 square feet
Timber trees per acre – 5

13 January

Did my own travel allowance – £38. 2s. 0d. for the Santa Cruz trip.

15 January

Packed trunk ready for dispatch via Trade Scheme to England.

Nellie, Ben and company came about Nellie's marriage, Ben wanting ring.

16 January

Deputation from Brown and Tati about shell poachers.

Included queries on this subject in letter to District Commissioner. Sent trunk down to be put on board, *Mary* having arrived. *Mary* departed with Jones and Walker, Mac remained.

17 January

Earthquake shock 7.15 am.

Mac left before breakfast and departed in *Endeavour III*.

Working out comparison of Santa Cruz and Lawrence River data.

19 January

Up to the sample plot after the boys, taking Claire and Michael. They sat in the shade for a little, then watched the work and had some palm to eat. Later they went home, Menepa carrying Michael. Had paths cleared and a shelter made. Measured ten kauri trees before lunch and eleven after. Looks as if there is a good curve relationship between top height and girth in this forest.

22 January

Sunday. Went down to village in the morning, trying to interest inhabitants in lizard catching, but without success. Then had an exciting but fruitless lizard hunt of my own by the lower bridge.

23 January

Set boys to catch lizards.

Called at Halings' and was given two pineapples. Inspected Haling's trochus shell and found four under size in about fifteen minutes' search. Asked Haling about shell poaching and he says he had Tati's permission to work his reef.

Day's haul of lizards: six *Emoia nigra*; two 'blue underneath'; one 'green underneath'. The 'ace catchers' are Peter Menepa and Dick.

24 January

Up at 6.15 am to catch boat to Sundi River, but it didn't leave until 8.45 am in the end. Spent the time sketching the wharf and *Endeavour III*.

Left boys and packs at the workshop, and set off with Mala, doing pacing and compass as far as the first plantation. There we were overtaken by Bob Michalek in a road metal truck bringing up the boys and he took us on as far as the track to camp. Mala and I then inspected the strips on the north side of the ridge, which were pretty good. I estimated fifty seedlings per acre on the present system. The strips are continuous on the north side down to a mile from base. Returned to camp along a strip on the south side with thirty seedlings. Shoot growth of liberated seedlings since October is about an inch.

26 January

Fine. Surveyed by pacing down road, Nelson carrying my pack. He later had a lift down on Bob's truck. Looked at four of the old lines, which are up to 0.15 miles long by pacing. Kauri growing well, with an average of fifty seedlings per acre in strips.

27 January

Weather doubtful at first, but decided it was probably fine enough for a family trip to Sundi River. We all left house about 9.20 am. Saw dolphins on the way up. The tide was still coming in and we had some trouble crossing the bar, but we only had a short time to wait for the jeep when we arrived. Up to Ray Colton's house where we ate our lunch. Walked to road-head, which was very muddy, then on to hauler and watched it working. Forest looking rather fine, dark green trees contrasting with the red road. We made a short excursion off the road at considerable hazard. Then to the house of Phil Haebeck, who has a document he wants the DC to sign. Potted and changed Michael in the shade by the house. Travelled down in a full jeep, passing Bob's truck, which is now out of action, in addition to both caterpillars. Had good views of the Lemon plains and Utupua. Waited by river then back by launch, leaving Claire's glasses' case on the river bank and shedding Michael's hat into the sea, I stepping on a mirror belonging to an old boy in the latter crisis.

28 January

Letter to Aunt Erica.

The turtle was cut up and cooked and taken away to the village for home consumption. Such occasional finds form a substantial part of their diet. We had a few eggs.

Christmas at Santa Cruz was rather lonely and very wet. All the boys departed to the village to feast and we had to fend for ourselves but since cooking meant leaving the mess tent, not much was done owing to the rain. However Mr Jones had kindly left us a present of a bottle of rum with which we enriched our coffee and this brightened the scene and gave enough energy to cook a bit of pana (kind of potato).

Before and after Christmas Mac was out of action for five weeks with tropical ulcers, and I for three weeks with a kind of virus disease (so the AMP – native doctor – said), which left me very weak and caused glandular swellings in the neck and groin. However I was strong enough after Christmas to make a trip to the bush and do some enumeration that more or less completed our survey such as it was. It achieved its object, and we know the extent of the forest, roughly, which was what we set out to find.

On my return from the bush, where we had a very jolly New Year camp with glorious weather in a pleasant place by the river, the Endeavour III *arrived punctually at dawn on Monday, but Jones was not aboard owing to sickness. After loading we couldn't make Utupua that night so went along to Nabalue by boat and then persuaded the boys to take us to the limestone caverns. They have never before been visited by white men and are probably very extensive. They are formed by rivers, and we followed an underground river from a very high entrance upstream along an even bed for half a mile (by pacing) till we emerged into the sunlight in a gorge the other end. The cave was last visited by a party of Solomon Islanders in 1946. Half way through I climbed onto a broad shelf at the side where the boys had preceeded me and they showed me human footprints in the mud (we had hurricane lamps). Some were fresh, some a day or two old, and some appeared to be dancing. There was the print of a large man and also one of a woman and an intermediate one. The boys are emphatic that they are made by spirits, and have a legend about it. I also found prints on a ledge where the boys had not been.*

On the wall were thousands of bats, Mac reckons of three kinds; also a species of swift, sitting on their nests. We picked two of the latter and one bat off the wall, and kept them alive to Vanikoro. I stuffed one swift, but unfortunately Pippa ate it in the night. The other, and the bat, are safely bottled in spirit. Who knows, they might be new species. They will travel home with my reptile collection, seven kinds of lizards and two kinds of snakes, to the British Museum. We are uncertain when we shall leave Vanikoro, but it may be only a fortnight. All our five cats will have to be left to fend for themselves on rats, mice, lizards and eels in the jungle as there is a cat surplus on the island. Blackie has just had a family in the bush, but we think they must have died, as Blackie is in the habit of feeding her own brothers and sisters, and has been since before the family came.

29 January

Letter to Father.

The local headman, Benjamin Tua, has asked me to obtain for him the following book:
A Shilling Arithmetic, *by Charles Pendlebury MA and W. S. Beard FRGS, London 1930. With Answers, 2s. 3d. If it is possible to get it and send it out to him I would be very glad –*
Benjamin Tua, Buma Village, Vanikoro.

Only the other night Claire and I got the star map out and made a voyage of discovery among the undiscovered constellations and nebulae overhead. While I was looking at Jupiter with binoculars there was the most tremendous shooting star you ever saw. Claire saw it best. It came from the zenith and was brilliant with a bright pink trail at first, and by the time I saw it, as it fell northwards, it was green. It was Saturday night, and we heard a great shout from the boys down on the beach, and apparently they went on nattering all night about it.

Looking forward to leave very much and hoping to spend as short a time as possible in Honiara. The Senior Agricultural Officer is on leave, so now there is nobody who knows about me at Honiara.

The new CFO is on leave in England and I am to see him and give him the gen on my return. He is Trenaman from the Uganda Forest Service.

2 February

Very wet all day. None of the boys showed up. Plotted map of Sundi River area from paced data. pm. traced it, made a record form and wrote instructions for the boys in my absence – 'Sundi River Area 1956 – Reafforestation Scheme'.

7 February

Prepared contract of employment forms. Saw Tati, also Nelson Teilo came in the afternoon about shell poaching.

8 February

Saw Nati at Filewood's house, also Nelson Teilo. Asked these two about shell poaching.

Packing reptile bottles.

10 February

Re-drafted and finally typed Santa Cruz report.

14 February

Helped William revise 'how to fill in forms'.

15 February

Left William preparing specimen forms. Out to see boys working in home plantation, then took them to the higher area and set them to work there. Then looked at the natural regeneration on the other side of the road, and the potted kauri which is growing OK.

16 February

Packed specimen boxes and started to pack remaining books. Claire packing kitchen things.

Long coded telegram from Secom about future of the Forest Department here while I am absent. Answered it with Claire's help, took till 10.30 pm.

17 February

Sent off telegram to Secom.

William nailed up one or two boxes. Claire finished packing big chest.

I re-wrote 'Instructions for 1956' and got William to study it.

19 February

Sunday. Busy time preparing to depart. Finally left about noon, and then we had to come back for Mac's brief-case! We reached Utupua at sunset.

20 February

We all slept on deck in camp beds, very comfortable.

Breakfast going along the lagoon, thence out to sea. Left Santa Cruz some miles to starboard. Tinakula in eruption. Boobies seen round the ship.

Tried sleeping on deck but was soaked in a squall and later on retired to the bunk.

22 February

Arrived at Kira Kira in the early morning. Telegram dated 17 February from Secom telling me not to leave Vanikoro! Contacted Secom (Bartle) by wireless at Kira Kira and was told to come on to Honiara.

Left again for Honiara at 11.0. Contacted Jim Tedder near Maru Bay for a short talk, then at dark left for the crossing to Guadalcanal, taking Andramine tablets. All day it had been smooth, since we were in the lee of San Cristoval.

23 February

Fairly rough in the night, but calm when we reached the lee of Guadalcanal. We reached Honiara at 11.0 am and were met by Mr Hill, Chief Agricultural Officer, who took Mac and us to the hotel, where we had lunch.

Mr Hill called for me in the afternoon and after a brief chat in the Agricultural Office we went to the Secretariat. There I had a talk with Sandy Peebles and John Bartle, who decided that William could *not* be left with £400 and discussed means of closing down the station. Radio contact with *Ambose* hoped for tomorrow.

24 February

Round first of all to Agricultural Department then saw Geoff Dennis. Interview with Chief Secretary (McLeod-Smith). Radio contact failed, and it looks as if operations will continue on Vanikoro!

26 February

Sunday. (Written by Claire.) Michael's birthday. Thought about going to church and Chris checked the times – nothing on in the morning. Went to Rové and all had a swim and ate grapefruit on the seat. Came back in time for Michael to have a sleep before going out to lunch. Collected by the Browns about 12.35 in the Landrover. Talked about mountains and natural history – good rock in the Seychelles. Chris went to see his plant collection before we left about 2.45 pm.

Letter to Tiggie from Claire.

. . . we got as far as Kira Kira and found a telegram waiting for us (Vanikoro's radio being out of action) saying not to leave yet as they didn't want us in Honiara until 18 March! Chris got on to the Chief Secretary by radio and asked what were we to do, come on or stay with the Tedders as they had offered to put us up. Anyway we've come up and are staying in the hotel as there is no house available at present, but we are hoping to move into a brand new one right on the sea shore in about a week's time. I hope we don't have to stay here longer than that as it is not very comfortable. In fact for the three nights we have been here Chris has not slept on a hotel bed once – his caves in at odd angles – but has slept either on the floor or on our camp bed which he put up last night. There is no wardrobe and only a small chest of drawers, and we have the camp beds, sewing machine, tin box with sheets, towels and material in it, box with forestry data in it, nappy pan, rucksack, as well as three suitcases with our own and Michael's things.

We celebrated Michael's birthday today with a visit to Rové about three quarters of a mile along the road from here. Have we told you about it? A small stream comes out to the sea and a coral terrace has been made at one side with a leaf shelter and cane chairs. There is a little bay and beach for swimming and the stream mouth forms a good pool for children. We spent part of the morning there and then Michael had a sleep before we went out to lunch with the entomologist attached to the Agricultural Department and his family. Very nice people. Sorry I haven't met them sooner as they go out on leave on Tuesday. Chris had met them before when he had been out at the forest nursery which is near their house.

Michael has had quite a few presents. We gave him a blue and red

The old engine, Vanikoro, relic of a former era. See p. 273. 8 Feb. 58.

rubber ball and a doll rattle, Mr MacEwin a lizard that you blow up, and Ted and Laura sent him a little yellow bear that we have kept until now as it arrived just a week before we left Vanikoro. Cigarette tins and cotton reels are still among his favourite toys.

For my birthday Chris gave me a little ivory figure of a Chinese philosopher who is supposed to have lived 3,000 years ago, and a pair of blue embroidered slippers. My trouble is now to find something for him. Sandals, perhaps, as his footwear is in a very bad state.

27 February

(next two days written by Claire). Chris at Trade Scheme most of the morning, getting a box for the turtle shell and measurement of the other cases.

28 February

Got a statement of cash affairs at Vanikoro typed and to the Treasury, handed over the Government Telegraph Code

Book. *Delos* not loading until Thursday; started writing report on Vanikoro.

29 February

Discussion with Peebles, Financial Secretary and Val Anderson on the forest this side of Gold Ridge. I may go up there next week. Spent morning writing a short report on what is known about it.

Labelled cases for shipment on *Delos*.

After supper Claire and I went to the new cinema and saw two films, both westerns.

2 March

Wrote letter to William to go on *Delos*. Out to PWD to get six twelve inch files for William, wrapped them up and had them posted. Got two boxes from Trade Scheme for seed.

5 March

Letter to Aunt Erica.

It was rather amusing, when we got to Kira Kira I had an urgent telegram from the Chief Secretary saying that I must not leave Vanikoro . . . As far as we were concerned however, it was a case of taking advantage of the ship provided for us by the DC, as you can never rely on getting another one on Vanikoro.

I had left William and company, on Vanikoro with £400, to get on with it, and they were making a fuss about it; but in the end, when they found they couldn't do anything about it, they were perfectly resigned and happy!

Honiara is busier than ever and has blossomed out with a cinema and a motor bus, so we are quite a big city. The motor bus is a sort of pocket one that would just about fit into my bedroom at 121. The fare is one shilling, wherever you are going – which makes it much simpler for the driver and more profitable for the owner. They don't have tickets.

This morning Claire and Michael were in Trade Scheme and got picked up by Mrs Payne the doctor's wife and taken a drive out to their house by the hospital, where she had a nice morning. They are going out again on Wednesday.

Letter to Father.

Tonight I was bathing on a bit of beach by the Trade Scheme with Claire and Michael in the offing when a couple rolled up and Claire introduced me all in my old bathing trunks. It was Mr and Mrs High Commissioner, the Gutches, whom I hadn't met before. We are going to their cocktail party on Saturday. The agricultural chaps at Kukum have let me borrow their Landrover to get the hang of driving, and I hope to get a license here, where it is relatively easy, and avoid all the rigmarole in the UK. The Australian Secretary of State, or something, Mr Lambert, and HE are coming round the nursery on Thursday and I've got to be there. There has been no forestry officer there all the year and everything is overgrown. At the moment we're building a bridge. Before, the only access was by a slithery plank over the ditch I enlarged last year.

6 March

Writing report most of day.

Evening – went to Scottish dancing with the geologists at the Masonic Hall.

8 March

(next two days written by Claire). Went with Hill in the Landrover to Kukum, where we were joined by the Gutches and Lambert, and walked round the agricultural buildings and then the forest nursery. Answered Lambert's questions on 'what we were trying to find out'.

9 March

Chris typed report, talked with geologists and borrowed

equipment for trip to Gold Ridge; also went to PWD and found out about house – hope to move in tomorrow.

10 March

John de Rover sent his Landrover round to the hotel and I made two quick trips with stuff to our new house and took the family. Later in the morning I took out the last load in the geological truck driven by Philip. It is a very pleasant place by the sea and we all had a swim. Got an iron, butter, meat, bread, and a bicycle on loan from Mr Blair.

12 March

I phoned Dick from Rové police station and learnt that the Landrover was by the Agricultural office, so I bicycled there and called at the office and the Treasury. Eventually set out with three geology labourers and collected Silas, Samuel and John, who then drove, from Kukum.

We disembarked at Nalimbu River old crossing and had a long walk through tedious grass seven to eight feet high. We also ran into tacky sensitive plant, *Mimosa pudica*, which was unpleasant. After a halt and a drink from the water-bottle, we at last reached the Tinahula River at about 2.30 pm and made camp in John Grover's old site, where we had tea. I then went four fifths of a mile up river with Silas, Samuel and John, seeing some good looking stands of *Albizzia*. Sometimes we had to wade waist-deep. We started back about 5 pm, keeping pacing and compass data so as to be able to correlate with aerial photos. There were many mosquitoes.

13 March

Fine. Set off along the track through riverine jungle first of all, with some quite good timber of *Albizzia* and *Vitex cofassus*. After a short rest we emerged into grassland, then through ridge forest and out into more grassland. In the distance we could see Ombombo, or 'Grassy Knoll', but we decided not to camp there as there is no water. On through good ridge forest, finding pack-lugging very hard, until we reached Dr Stanton's old camp site on the ridge at 11.25 am and camped there. It is good taun forest (*Pometia pinnata*), in gently sloping country.

14 March

Silas sick with fever, so left John to look after him and set off with the others southward along the ridge, through magnificent close-canopied forest, tall trunks and long vistas, beautiful in morning light. When we reached Ombombo there was a grand view out to sea as far as Malaita.

15 March

Did 1,000 feet of enumeration along a branch ridge in the morning while it was fine. There were eight *Pometia pinnata* of timber size to the acre.

Lunched at camp, while it came on to rain. Packed up and left when it stopped, but heavy rain began again when we were below Grassy Hills. When we reached the old camp site there were so many mosquitoes that we tried camping on a shingle bank by the river, but found that the water was rising very rapidly; so in the end we camped on the bank and lit a fire in the tent.

16 March

The boys did not sleep much in the night, owing to mosquitoes. Fine morning, went up river and did 1,000 feet of enumeration line in lowland forest, and there were plenty of mosquitoes here, too. We turned back when continuous thunder began to roll in the hills and reached camp well before the rain. Meanwhile, two boys had stayed in camp and made a low bunk for all of them.

17 March

Mosquitoes bad in the night. Off at 8.15 am, crossing the Tinahula, now less in flood than it was. Then steadily over the grassy plain, reaching the stream next to the Nalimbu River at 11 am and having a rest there before crossing the big river about half an hour later. It was just over waist deep in places and fast, and the mosquitoes there were very bad indeed. We pushed on along the road and waited at the turning to Raimale village from 12 to 1.30 pm, but there was no sign of the Landrover, so we continued towards Tenaru until we were picked up by a private bus, and then we met the Landrover, with Claire, Joanna and Philip driving – he had thought the pick-up time was 3 pm. Then we had a joy-ride to the Tonga road-head, splaying the front wheels in a hole on the way back. Got bread and cakes at Blum's, and so to Rové, shower, shave and tea. Happy family reunion. Walk by the sea, Michael playing in the breakers on his own.

18 March

Sunday. Mr Hill called at lunch time with an order apparently that I must fly home to England without my family. Concerned over this.

19 March

The order about flying home had been misunderstood and all is OK. In the afternoon I had a good practice drive with Walter, stopping and starting on a hill.

20 March

Driving test with Mr Semple – up the ridge and out to China town. He commented that my steering was erratic and gave a demonstration run; but gave me a certificate, so I got my license at last!

Worked on Vanikoro report – economics of reafforestation, till 5.30 pm.

21 March

de Rover's Landrover picked up family and luggage for trial weighing-in at Trade Scheme – thirty-three pounds to spare.

Finished last chapter of report, started appendices.

22 March

Handed in two copies (one for Chief Secretary) of report on Vanikoro and Tevai, with map of Sundi River reafforestation area and report on Santa Cruz to Mr Hill.

Reading up Colonial Regulations I and II and Estimates for 1956 for exam next Thursday.

23 March

Hill returned copies of my reports and I gave them to Peebles.

24 March

Working on Santa Cruz map. Gave Lawrence River map to Philip to have copies done by their draftsman.

Saw Norris about leave – we get 125 days in England plus forty-four days travelling time each way.

29 March

Pidgin English exam at 8.30, by Peebles and Anderson with a Solomon Islander assistant – passed.

Colonial Regulations exam rest of morning, invigilated by Norris. Vincent also sat.

In the afternoon I paid last bill at Trade Scheme. Obtained bus timetable. Arranged about storage of stuff. Leave and Last Pay Certificate arrived. Income tax clearance certificate to Trade Scheme in last moment rush.

Platform used to fell Kauri Pine on a slope. Varikoro.

30 March

Letter to Father.

It is incredible to think that this time next week we will be in Sydney and about to embark.

We are living in a new house some way out of Honiara and about ten yards from the sea. Fine for the Easter holidays – we just stay here and life is one big picnic.

I have had a week's expedition whilst here. A company toying with the idea of moving in on Gold Ridge wanted to know if there was enough timber to make logging pay for the road.

We are looking forward to being home. We have 118 days leave in England and forty-four days travelling time each way. The new regulations entitle us to more, but unfortunately we did our first eighteen months before the new regs came into force and so get part of our leave at the old rate. Anyway it is not too bad.

Sorry you thought we were shipwrecked. Several boats have been adrift around here with fatalities.

31 March

Lunch with the Gutches at Government House. The bus left seven minutes early and we missed it – so Captain Curtis fetched us in the Landrover. The only other person present was Mr White, from Kukum. All very pleasant. Captain Curtis brought us back, then we had a swim.

1 April

Easter Sunday. Went to 7.30 sung communion service with the Peebles.

Made lid for wooden box and painted name on boxes. Got things ready for packing.

Letter to Aunt Erica.

Yesterday we had lunch with Mr and Mrs Gutch at Government House. They are very nice people indeed and I believe they have three boys at school in England. Their last job was in British Guiana, though I do not know in what capacity. They are going on a tour of Malaita on Tuesday.

The Peebles took us to church this morning. It was the Church of England or Melanesian Mission Church, and it was a sung communion with bags of popery – processions and incense swinging and bells going clang-clang, presumably to wake you up.

Another Sunday we went to church at the South Sea Evangelical Mission – the service taken in pidgin English by the Public Works foreman. Those are the only churches in Honiara apart from Roman Catholics, Seventh Day Adventists and Methodists. Brian Twomey arrived back from leave on last week's plane. He is a South African and spent his leave touring in Basutoland and Portuguese East Africa. He came to tea with us on Friday. On Tuesday he is going on the same plane as us as far as Vella Lavella in the Western District as he has some work to do there and the plane is the most convenient way of getting there.

It has been stormy tonight but I hope it is fine by then. Anyway the trip is short hops as far as Lae, where we spend the night, and after that we have four engines.

2 April

Packed.

Collected Landrover from office after lunch. Collected Claire and returned bike to Blair's. Weighed suitcases – 132 pounds – exactly our allowance. Weighed myself – ten stone – lost one and a half stone since 1953.

3 April

Got up at 5.15 am. Drove to airfield, collecting Walter at Kukum on the way. Delay of one hour owing to an oil leak. Breakfast after calling at Russell Islands. Brian left plane at Vella Lavella. Called at Bougainville, crossed New Ireland, then landed at Rabaul for refuelling. Followed coast of New Britain, then over to New Guinea. Landed at Finschhafen, then Lae. Bus to Hotel Cecil. All very tired.

4 April

(written by Claire). Left hotel 9.30 am, but had to wait at terminal a long time. Flew over New Guinea, refreshments at Port Moresby.

Took photos of barrier reef at about 4.30 pm and shore of Australia, near Mackay, when it came in sight. Waited on hand and foot all day by beautiful hostess. Michael slept most of the afternoon and evening.

Arrived at Sydney about 1.15 am (5 April) and at Hotel Metropole 2.45 am.

Returned to England by SS *Oronsay*.

* * *

Back to the Solomon Islands.

15 September

Letter to Erica and Mu.

SS Orsova. Yesterday morning we came out of a fog bank and found ourselves in blue seas again, after the steely colour of the channel and Bay of Biscay. Last night the temperature of the swimming bath was 62° and I had a swim for exercise; this morning it was 70° and I had another. I also tried Michael out with his new rubber ring, but it was still too cold for him and the shock caused breathless cries of anguish, though he had been longing to go in and afterwards continued to show great interest in the other children who were bathing.

We have a pleasant cabin, forward on the port side and with a porthole. Michael has a mattress on the floor. He could have had a cot, but it would have left so little room.

24 September

Letter to Aunt Erica.

The weather is fine and we are just in sight of South Africa, it looks like ranges of low sandhills about ten miles away. We reach Capetown tomorrow morning. Up till now it has not been very fine and there has been a cold wind most days.

At Las Palmas we went inland in a motor car to the Spanish town of Teror and saw the parched countryside and the banana groves. In the afternoon I found a bit of rocky coastline and had a lovely warm swim in the surf.

There are two other families going out to Honiara aboard, a lawyer and an entomologist, neither have been before.

25 September

Got up just as the sun was rising over the Hottentot Mountains. Went on deck to photograph Table Mountain. Went ashore after 9.0 am and got a car, drove round the Mountain via Lion's Head, Camps' Bay, Llandudno, Hout

Bay fishing harbour and back over Constantia Nek through woods of Monterey Pine. Stopped at Botanical gardens and Rhodes Memorial, photographed 'Physical Energy'. Saw Koodoo and Wildebeest in park, also secretary bird and ostrich. Picnicked in botanical gardens. Sailed again 6 pm.

12 October

Letter to Aunt Erica.

We had a lovely drive round the mountain at Capetown. It is a beautiful place. I heard a chaffinch in the pine woods and was told it was a 'Cape Canary'!

The coast near Capetown is ideal for swimming, sandy coves and rocky headlands, and above the road tower the 'Twelve Apostles' – a continuation of the plateau.

It is a country of clear dry air and blue mountains in the distance. Pity it's such a mess politically.

Yes, the lawyer, who is a New Zealander, is going to help the Attorney General in Honiara.

In Melbourne I saw Bob Ingle again at the CSIRO Forest Products Research Laboratory. Do you remember, I saw him three years ago? We had a couple of interesting talks together. He wants me to see if I can get an aromatic oil from the karamat tree – it yields it in New Guinea.

We arrive in Sydney tomorrow morning and fly out the same evening. We shall be glad to be able to unpack ourselves on dry land again. I am looking forward to work, swimming and the jungle. I only hope we have a house to ourselves in Honiara.

A funny thing – on the quay at Melbourne we met Bob Michalek, on his way from Vanikoro to Tasmania, most unexpected. He is a Czech, and used to come to our house.

13 October

We arrived in Sydney at breakfast time. Morris Middleton's agent and then Mr Small from Burns Philp came to our cabin. Went ashore and through customs. Taxi to air terminal, left baggage there. Had to re-pack, twenty-five pounds overweight (132 pounds allowed). To botanical gardens, lovely there. We watched a floral procession, met Fenemores (entomologists) and had tea. Back to air terminal and flew off at 8 pm, stopping at Brisbane 9.45. Sitting by door, no window, but ample space for Michael's cot.

14 October

Breakfast as dawn broke over banks of cloud, then came in to Port Moresby. On to Lae, where it was rather clouded. To Hotel Cecil and slept till lunch time, and afterwards gave Michael a good long swim in the paddling pool, then had a long swim with Claire. Walk to the shore with Fenemores. Beautiful evening in the garden after supper.

15 October

We were roused at 4.15 am for breakfast and off about 6.0 am. Called at Finschhafen, Rabaul, Bougainville, Vella Lavella and Yandina. It was cloudy when we arrived at Honiara at 4.25 pm. Surrendered gun, temporarily, to customs. Met by all the Trenamans in the new Forest Department Landrover and drove to their house on the ridge for tea. Rain came as we went down to the hotel for the night.

21 October

Sunday. Fine. Went to Rové with Claire and Michael and all had a pleasant bathe, swimming over coral gardens.

In the afternoon watched birds around the house: leaf-green parakeets with red breasts; bright blue parakeets with orange bills (these were seen in the morning); a parrot the size of a barn owl, head, neck and chest bright scarlet, wings purple, back light chocolate, first seen poking its head out of a tree, later flew to another tree; starlings in hordes, also a bird of starling size with buff underparts; yellow-bellied honey-eater and white collared kingfisher.

A Safari to the interior of Guadalcanal. From this point we had to start walking. Keith Trenamen is standing by the Land Rover door.

22 October

Letter to Aunt Erica.

We got here exactly a week ago. First of all we were in the hotel, which was not very comfortable, and noisy. Now we are living with the Trenamans, in a pleasant situation on the top of the ridge; but we hope to be able to move into a house by Wednesday, where we can stay until the rightful owners come back next month. I expect we shall go to Vanikoro about February. The Trenamans have three small boys, the youngest smaller than Michael, so it is a houseful. Michael's prickly heat that he had down at the hotel is a lot better now, but he seems to have chronic squitters. He is happy and had one or two lovely swims at Rové, splashing around in his tyre well out of his depth.

I am having an interesting time making tracings of my maps of Ndeni and Vanikoro with a view to preparing prints of them.

Brian Twomey and Geoff Dennis are still here just the same as usual. The two young geologists are away on leave and the senior one, John Grover, is on tour. HE is on tour in the New Hebrides.

There has been almost no rain in Honiara since we went on leave, except what came the week-end we arrived and today – so everything is pretty parched looking, but now green shoots are rapidly sprouting from the withered tufts of grass.

30 October

Set off with Keith Trenaman, Silas, Oli, Basil and Caspar in the Landrover to the Konga roadhead. Thence on foot through jungle down to the Tina river, which we descended, knee-deep, to its confluence with the Toni river. Keith, whose last job was in Uganda, remarked that you couldn't do this sort of thing in East Africa because of the danger of catching bilharzia.

We continued up the Toni river after lunch and made camp on the bank about 3 pm. Rain set in as we climbed the precipitous ridge to the north-east, finding some good *Pometia pinnata* forest, and the river was rising by the time we returned to camp.

31 October

We continued up the river and one of its tributaries, then climbed a spur to the north-east finding more good forest. Here Keith set off for home, while we went on for a mile or more, descending eastwards, then following a stream to the north-east where we found a good place to camp. After a brew of tea I went out with the gun and watched a scorpion seizing winged termites as they emerged from a tree.

1 November

Having tried some photography as the sun rose among the trees, we headed north-west up to the ridge, then south-west along it to the hill-top where we left the ridge yesterday, keeping a pacing and compass record of progress through the jungle. Near the hilltop we found a lovely stand of *Pometia pinnata.* Westwards across a watershed through medium forest and down to the camp for a much needed swim. Spent the afternoon resting with an upset tummy. Out before sunset trying to shoot sandpipers by the river and damaged the rifle slightly in attempting to extract a cartridge which had jammed.

2 November

After swimming in a clear pool we had a hard march through jungle to the Tina river and so to the Konga roadhead where the Trenamans met us at 3.15; so back to Honiara via Tenaru, Kukum and China Town.

3 November

Made five prints of Santa Cruz map and sent one to Mac. Made list of trees, previous one having been lost.

Engaged new houseboy, Camnis.

5 November

Tried to identify some Guadalcanal timbers.

In the afternoon prepared to go to bush. Borrowed surveyor's chain from geologists.

Heard news from Brian Twomey – Hungary fighting Russia; Britain destroyed Egypt's air force; England to Australia air route stopped at Beirut.

6 November

Left Konga roadhead about noon. To first camp, taking the track between the rivers through good lowland forest. Shot at a sitting duck with my .22, but missed.

7 November

An uphill grind with packs to camp 2. Boys improved shelter and made a bed.

10 November

Left camp at 7.0 am and reached Toni River at 10.15 am, having spent about an hour looking at trees on the way. Also shot at a wild turkey. Had a good swim in a large pool in the river while the boys caught, cooked and ate three fish. On to the Tina River, where I stalked a duck and shot it through the heart at twenty-five yards, but missed the mate. Rested and lunched by the river. Basil shot a green pigeon. Back to Honiara.

12 November

Public holiday. Had the duck I shot on Saturday, very good.

Got world news – situation less serious in Egypt.

18 November

Letter to Aunt Erica.

I am glad you are having a fine autumn. I miss the seasons here, but it is good to think we shall be seeing all four of them in 1958–1959.

Mr Trenaman has gone on a trip to Vanikoro with Jim Tedder, leaving me to get on with the exploration of potential forest reserves here, which I have been doing in the last three weeks. It is a great help now we have our own Landrover, and last Monday, which was a public holiday, and this Sunday, we all went to Trenches beach which is a pleasant place for a good open swim off a sandy beach. This time we took the Barwicks, whom we met on the boat.

Tomorrow we are moving house again, to a house on top of the ridge which will probably be cooler, and we will probably stay there until we go to Vanikoro about February. We have been having a house to ourselves these last few weeks, but now the former occupants are back and ready to move into it.

The last few days I have been living in a leaf shelter in the jungle about twenty-five miles away with three boys. Fortunately the leaves are pretty waterproof, because it rained a lot. Most of the distance is by road, but there is a day's march through jungle with loads and two rivers to cross, in fact we were lucky being able to get back last night –

the second river came up to my tummy and if it had been any higher we might have had to wait a few days for them to go down. A few hours after we crossed they would have been much more flooded and quite impossible owing to the rain that comes after midday. There is a daily rise and fall which you have to take into account.

There is a cocktail party at the High Commission on Friday which puts the lid on any bush trips, but I am happy to stay here for a change and give the weather a chance to improve.

(By Claire) No. I am afraid I haven't touched my recorder since we came out, partly because if Michael sees it he makes a grab at it. I am thinking of getting him a mouth organ for Christmas and then there will be a lovely noise with the two of us hard at it. I have been doing quite a bit of sewing though, for myself mainly, and I must now get on and make M some more pants as I don't expect there will be much time for that after the baby's arrival.

19 November

Packed up and moved house to No. 3 on the ridge – two Landrover trips with trailer.

25 November

Sunday. Fine, peaceful day. Read a little, Spent morning carving a boat for Michael from a bit of wood.

After tea we all went a walk down the lane – wooded valley and grassy hill above reminiscent of Encombe.

Finished reading *Edward Wilson: Nature Lover.*

Got ready for bush.

26 November

Driven to Konga by Keith with Silas and five boys. Walked to camp, having a swim in the Toni and lunch on the way. Boys made themselves a bigger shelter.

* * *

27 November

Completed old strip to twenty-seven chains, Silas identifying many new trees by native names. Did the opposite strip, a short one, and down the stream to camp.

30 November

Packed up and set off up the stream to complete the strip we left unfinished yesterday. Then continued homewards, having a meal (bully beef and tinned pears) at the Toni River, and a swim and soap down. Met a bush man and his wife on their way upstream to a potato patch. Proceeded to Tina River, brewed tea in usual spot. Reached Konga at 1.50 pm. Fine. Sketched view of interior (now a twenty-three inch by sixteen inch water colour). Keith came in Landrover at 2.50 pm. Stopped at Tenaru to inspect logs prior to loading on Muliama – or rather to watch how Silas inspects them.

1 December

Found baggage in Customs shed, but not allowed to take it as documents haven't come. Got a pair of boots out however.

4 December

Bill of lading for personal effects having arrived at Trade Scheme, I was at last able to collect our stuff and spent latter part of the morning unpacking it. Had to use a screw from sewing machine for gramophone. Bought gramophone needles from store. Played many of our records at tea and after supper.

5 December

Collected Silas, Paul and Oli from Kukum; other boys failed to turn up. To Konga after changing a flat tyre. Weather not promising – heavy rain when we reached the Toni – made a shelter to have lunch under. Rain stopped when we reached hilltop. On to camp. Enlarged house and had additional bed made. More rain.

8 December

Setting off homewards, we stopped at our first strip and went down it to look at unidentified trees. One was *Spondias dulcis*, about fourteen feet in girth.

10 December

Spent much of day studying aerial photographs and trying to work out topography of Tenaru River drainage area. Sketched hills after tea.

16 December

Letter to Aunt Erica.

*This morning we had a lovely swim at Rové (where the painting was done) with the Barwicks, and I showed David the corals and fish on the reef. After tea Claire and I planted a tree (*Pithecolobium Saman*) in the garden, with Michael helping – it is bare rocky grassland up here and every tree counts. Before supper Mac dropped in for a few minutes; and after supper I practiced 'Ave Maria' on my guitar after the record you gave me.*

My main task in the bush was finished the week before last; last week I attempted a reconnaissance in a new area, but we landed up in a hole full of mosquitoes with no way out except the way in, so we made a strategic retreat and came straight home. (There should have been a trail to get us through the mosquito belt and into the forest by nightfall, but we had no local guide and came to a river which was too deep to walk up and had nothing but tangle both sides). I am not going away any more now until the baby comes. Keith's first trip to Vanikoro wasn't a success – the engine broke down at Santa Cruz and he had to be towed back, leaving the Tedders marooned on one of the Reef Islands. Now he has been off again on the ship fetching the Tedders and should be back on Tuesday, we hope having had a successful trip.

We have played your gramophone records a lot. Les Sylphides *is one of our favourites. The gramophone has a pleasant tone, not at all tinny.*

We have a fine view from this house, on top of the ridge. Inland are high mountains (8,000 feet) and across the sea we can see the islands of Nggela and Savo, and when it is clear, the distant mass of Malaita. The sea between here and Savo is called 'Iron Bottom Sound', because of all the ships that were sunk there during the war.

(by Claire) Thank you for our own and Michael's Christmas cards. M really does enjoy his too, they have been exclaimed over and shown to us and then put into his toy box. We have been keeping the beakers you gave us for him for Christmas so he will soon have those to play with. He piles things into his engine so I think he will quickly learn how to use them, as well as putting them to every other possible use.

We are very lucky in our present house as there are lots of banana and paw-paw trees round it, and we have been having a lot of fruit from them; also a lot of fresh vegetables from the local market. I shall miss it when we go back to Vanikoro. I had a letter from Mrs Filewood from there, the other day. They are due to go on leave soon, but she said that Mr Filewood's relief was bringing his wife and two small children, so Michael and I will both have company.

18 December

Worked out an overall result for volumes per acre – 10,000 super of Pometia and 5,000 of other useful species.

Reading *Story of an Insect Garden*. Full moon – out looking for crickets. Found one quietish, slender fellow in the cypress bush, who sings by transparent moving plates on his back.

24 December

Wrapped up presents and decorated room with three balloons from church service, *Morinda citrifolia*, Hibiscus and red paper.

25 December

Michael opened stocking – contents: book (present from Laura), whistle, apple. Other presents after breakfast. Mine from Claire was *The Family of Man* which I spent much of the day looking at.

30 December

Sunday. All went for a swim at Rové, walking first to the Trenamans, then getting the Landrover.
1 pm. Claire began pre-birth symptoms. Keith brought Landrover.
2 pm. backache every ten minutes. Rang doctor.
3 pm. to hospital. I waited by beach till 3.30 when I went to be present.
3.45 pm. Baby boy born. Blue at first owing to knot in umbilical cord. Normal colour later.

Luke got supper. I bathed Michael and put him to bed.

Letter to Aunt Erica.

Claire had another baby boy this afternoon at a quarter to four in the hospital, where I took her three quarters of an hour before in the Landrover. Dr De Beau and the sister and myself were there and it all went off nice and quickly. It was interesting that there was a proper knot in the umbilical cord so that its head was bright blue when it was coming out, but it got the right colour afterwards. The doctor said he'd heard about that happening but not experienced it – it is a cause of deaths. It had evidently tied the knot itself in its wriggling! Perhaps it is a lucky sign! The sister reckons it weighs eight or nine pounds.

This morning Claire and I had had a swim at Rové and Michael too. She didn't reckon anything was happening until 1 pm. It is nice to have it all over.

I bathed and put M to bed myself tonight and have told him he has a baby brother. I'm sure it will be good for him.

* * *

Above: Michael at Rové, Honiara.

Below: Michael playing in our garden at Vanikoro.

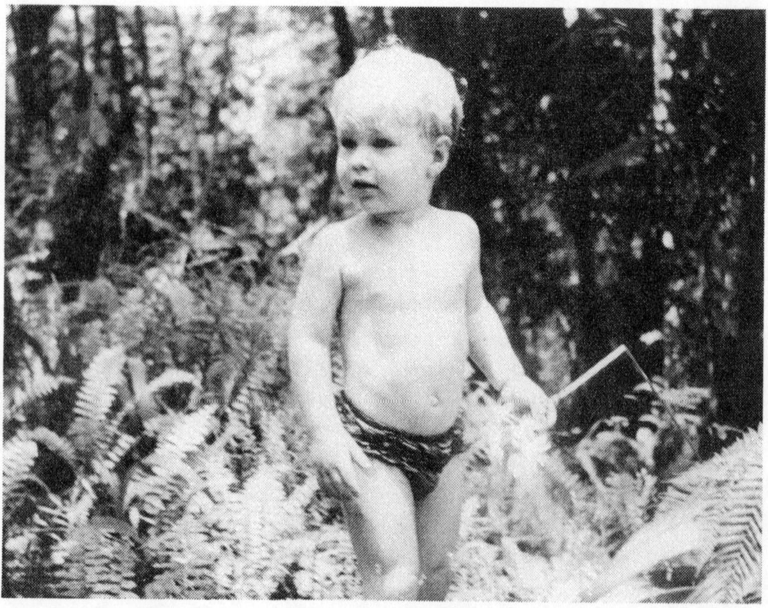

Claire with the boys in the garden at Vanikoro.

31 December

Left Michael at the Barwicks and spent the morning in the office, after sending four telegrams to England and Malta for £2.

To hospital after 2.0 pm to see Claire, stayed till 3.30 pm. Back to office then home to tea. Many fireworks audible.

* * *

1957

1 January

Out to see Claire at hospital, taking Michael. Had a play together outside before going – showed him the sensitive plant. Returned and got lunch for self and Michael.

3 January

Office all morning. In the afternoon I went out to hospital, leg seen to. Took parcel to Claire – microscope. Took it back, small but very good for £4. Looked at blood cells, pollen grains, chloroplasts in guard cells and a few hours later thronging bacteria decomposing the same leaf.

6 January

Sunday. Took Michael down to upper Rové Creek and both of us had a swim. Returned and put him to bed. Labelled Selaginellas and liverwort collected at the stream. Drew spores of *Tmesipteris* under microscope.

At 3 pm I collected Claire and the baby from hospital in Landrover.

8 January

Tried to identify Hugbolo – got as far as Rubiaceae. I continued trying to identify Bolanono and looked at Hugbolo under the microscope.

9 January

Keith looking for plantation sites near Kukum. I still working on timber identification, got one definite – *Myristica buchneriana*. Read *The Forester* by James Brown of Stirling 1871 – on draining, very good.

20 January

Sunday. Sat on step with Claire after breakfast, then went through the plants I'd collected in the bush and later Claire cut my hair.

In the afternoon I examined lycopod spores under microscope, also *Trichomanes*. Wrote to Alston (British Museum) for details of various fern species. After tea, walk with Claire and Michael to new house. Discussed names – down to James and Jonathan now.

22 January

To Mount Austin via Mataniko River with Oli. Fine, National Park looking beautiful. Saw plenty of *P.pinnata.* and *Vitex*. Reached view to other side of Lunga River. Had a swim in Mataniko pool on way back.

23 January

Took boys from Kukum to new plantation site to dig a well. Took specimen from diseased balsa tree and spent morning looking at fungus under microscope – oomycete I think. Telegram from James Tedder: there is the probability of early trip to Vanikoro. Invitation to dinner at Government House on Tuesday.

24 January

Fine. Out to Tenaru, abortive venture along tractor track –

Landrover got stuck – tried the other way by Brothers' Mission, following another false line on the way. Lunched, and swam in Tenaru River. Crossed southwards to the other river where boys caught an opossum by chasing it up a tree until it leapt from a great height into the river. I tried to buy its freedom without success, and it was bound hand and foot onto a stick and carried by two boys. The opossum was later roasted in the fire.

25 January

Took two guides and went one and a half miles north-east until we reached decent *Mangifera* forest. Wasi caught a possum with a baby and I kept the latter when the mother was killed, carrying it in the pocket of my shirt or shorts. Feeding opossum with hankie soaked in milk. Picked up at 4.30 pm by the Trenamans, and so home. Groin painful, sores on leg.

26 January

Temperature last night 100.1°, down this morning. To office, wrote reports on Poha and Tenaru River trips. Opossum feeding well on milk from eye-dropper. Took him tree climbing after tea and played with him after supper. Ron Warren came in with a young megapode.

27 January

Sunday. Possum eating *Morinda* and pawpaw flowers and *Piptadenia* leaves.

To Rové with family including opossum. All had a good swim in the new swimming pools.

28 January

Took boys to plantation valley and spent morning measuring

accurately ten *Gmelina* trees with Silas at Rove plantation. Collected some Bulunali leaves for opossum. Measured eight cedro in coronation gardens. Collected mango leaves for opossum.

29 January

Spent the morning at Kukum measuring Balsa and *Gmelina* trees with Silas, seven of the former and nine of the latter. Balsa planted 1953 now averages two and a half feet in girth and forty feet high. *Gmelina* planted 1955 now one and a half feet in girth and thirty-five to forty feet high.

In the afternoon continued measuring cedro in Coronation Gardens. They were planted in 1953, best specimen now two and a half feet girth and forty feet high.

To dinner party at Government House. Back at 11.

30 January

Collected boys and *Albizzia Lebec* seedlings to take them to plantation site. Found that the *Mary* is going to Kira Kira on Saturday, planning to go on it. On returning home Claire told me the little opossum had died, apparently of loneliness, poor little thing. Buried, it very sorry indeed.

31 January

Out to Kukum and fetched boys to plantation site. Back and annotated field books. Claire came at 10.45 am – out to Mataniko for Jock Elliott to show us our furniture, then to look at paints back at Honiara.

Now not going to Kira Kira till 16 February!

11 February

Letter to Aunt Erica.

There is really no news from here. We were to have gone to Vanikoro on the Mary *on 16 February, staying at Kira Kira for a fortnight on the way, but the* Mary *ran itself on a reef and is now up for repairs. It is a bit frustrating as I have nothing but bits and pieces to do and in this climate if you don't have some absorbing or regular work you get a feeling of stagnation, lassitude, liverishness etc. However there is now a pleasant little tidal swimming pool at Rové, made by prison labour to keep sharks out, and we had a lunch picnic there yesterday with the Fenemores and I had a romp in the water with half a dozen European children.*

We jotted down Michael's present vocabulary, it is:
Quack; Duck; Wu wu (= dog); Mooo (= cow); Moo (= moon); Tea; Daddy; Mummy; Baby; 'bye; Ni' Ni'; and 'oodleoodleoo!'

Did I tell you about our baby opossum? Last time I went to the bush I stayed the night in a native village on a hilltop and next morning they took me to see the forest nearby and one of my boys climbed up a tree and caught an opossum which had a baby in its pouch. The mother was killed and eaten and I was left holding the baby, which travelled home in the pocket of my shorts or exploring all over me with its grasping hands and prehensile tail. It had lovely fur and big brown pop-eyes. At home it slept with a hot-water bottle (dettol bottle in a sock) and we fed it milk from an eye-dropper. It was happiest climbing trees, but got lonelier and lonelier for its mother until one morning Claire came out to fetch it from its tree and there it was lying dead on the ground. We were heartbroken, but it would have been worse if it had grown up on Vanikoro where there are no possums and then pined and been lonely there. Luckily I have got a couple of good photos of it which a friend had enlarged for me.

That time in the bush my boys caught three opossums. The first one was chased up a tree and I saw it through binoculars coming out of the tippy topmost branches with a boy just underneath it and in desperation it took a flying leap out and landed in the river sixty feet below, at the feet of Silas who was waiting with a knife, but I told him not to kill it. It was the size of a cat, with unborn young. I tried to buy its freedom, but it was tied to a stick and kept alive till evening when it was killed and eaten. I felt so sorry for it. The boys are callous, but it is their natural food and they have to live.

14 February

Claire to hospital with baby, latter now eleven pounds one

and a half ounces. Registered him, James Merlin. Did some packing.

18 February

Fetched Claire at 4.0 pm. Later to library together – got our twelve books to take to Vanikoro.

20 February

Cleared up office and walked home at 11.0 pm having got liver from butcher and wood box for seedlings from Trade Scheme. Helped Claire pack and in afternoon took bulk of luggage to office to await *Kovala*. Roped up chest and trunk. One inch rope 2s. 9d. for ten yards (half a pound) – just right
amount for chest. After tea all to China town. Bought material, gramophone records.

21 February

Got a box top from Trade Scheme and six pounds of butter for Tedders. Then back to house to continue packing. Lunch with the Trenamans then to China town to get things for the Tedders. Left house at 5 pm and made two trips with Land-rover to get stuff and family aboard *Veronica*. Sailed at 8 pm.

22 February

Rough in the gap between Guadalcanal and San Cristoval. Overcast. *Veronica* rolling a lot. Claire, Michael and James all sick. Arrived Kira Kira 9 pm.

23 February

Selected a plot for *Balsa* and *Albizzia* trees by the river with Jim Tedder.

Went aboard *Veronica* at 1.30 pm and set off for Pamua, meeting there Miss Stead and two assistants. Girls' school there having trouble with the labourers and human nature! On to Pawa, left the Balsa seedlings there with Mr Saunders. Then round to an anchorage at 'Joe's' on the lee side of Ugi. Joe came aboard to see Jim.

24 February

Sunday. Set off at 1 am, off Ulawa at daybreak. Rough, rather a risky landing in the dinghy. Landed in a small cove by the village of Ahia.

Made HQ in a large house then went to the stream for a bath and shave, having had grapefruit and porridge to eat. Went to look at forest a couple of miles south-east, passed through a patch with pure stand of *Terminalia* sp.

I gave talks on forestry and mountaineering through an interpreter at a meeting after the church service.

25 February

Walked across the island by a good path, finding some patches of sizeable timber in the hills. Met pot-holes in coral with sea gurlging ten feet beneath, deep pools and ribbed sand.

26 February

Sailed about 2 am. Fairly rough. Not sleeping, took a pill, retched then felt better. In the bows at about 4.45 am watching Southern Cross, Milky Way, Jupiter, Venus and Mercury rising before the sun and crescent moon with ghost moon. At the wheel for an hour round sunrise. Breakfast at Three Sisters coconut groves – lovely lagoon.

Arrived Kira Kira for lunch. Saw to sample plots in charge of Joel Naqu, three species by river, *Balsa, Albizzia* and *Gmelina.*

Michael's second birthday party, fun and games on the lawn.

27 February

Went with Claire to the trial plots and put Joel Naqu right. Wrote report on Ulawa sitting on the verandah and typed it in the afternoon. All went to a little cove at 5 pm and had a boisterous swim.

28 February

Letter to Aunt Erica.

We got here on 22 February, coming on the small ship Veronica. *From 23 to 26 Jim Tedder and I did a trip to Ulawa so that I could look at the forests there. We stayed in a large house in a village and were very comfortable on our camp beds. It was a difficult landing in the dinghy in a heavy swell on a rocky shore, but the weather was good, the sea bright blue and we had several bathes. Claire stayed here with Margaret and the children. On Tuesday we had Michael's birthday party in the shade on the lawn. There was a cake with two candles on it and after I'd blown them out several times to show him, he at last blew them out himself. Then they had games on the lawn, the chief one being Michael running away as fast as his fat little legs would carry him and Gregory and Ian hurling themselves on top of him so that he fell down laughing.*

The Kovala *is coming for us tomorrow to take us to Vanikoro, so we are hoping it will be calm.*

We have seen all the Tedders' coloured slides of island life, some taken while they were marooned for three weeks on the Reef Islands. Then last night we showed all ours, including the one of you at Lickey, with the Scots Pine and Rosebay willowherb. I have been organizing trial plots of seedlings from Honiara and the field assistant is called Jol (or Joel?) Naqu, and is Naqu's brother. He looks and speaks like him too.

Our houseboy, Camnis, is young, intelligent and conscientious, which is pleasant for Claire.

We have called the new child James Merlin. He was nearly Jonathan, but James had always been Claire's favourite, and I hadn't a particular favourite.

* * *

1 March

Embarked on *Kovala* before noon. Set off for Star Harbour and anchored there for the night. Slept on camp beds on deck.

2 March

Left San Cristoval. Sea smooth but with heavy swell. We saw a turtle in Star Harbour. There were many fish about and as we reached the open sea dolphins came to wish me a happy birthday. Michael sick. Claire slept in the cabin. I tried it, but finished on deck.

3 March

Utupua sighted about midday.

Decided against going to Vanikoro today as uncertain of passage in the dark. Anchored in Utupua lagoon about 5 pm and all went ashore for a good swim off the beach. Rowed along to the small lagoon later – no birds.

4 March

Arrived Vanikoro about 11 am.

Met by Filewood and Jeffries. Emergency – quick unloading onto *Toby*. Chap called Webb had blown his hand to bits and went to Kira Kira to meet doctor. Lunch at Filewoods, then to house at 3 pm. Boys bringing stuff up. Got lamps in order. Good to be back. Roses out, lime tree heavy with fruit.

5 March

Took over cash from William. Boys bringing boxes and furniture up, then clearing round the grounds.

Mosquitoes very bad indeed.

7 March

Left boys to repair mosquito netting and make chicken enclosure. Up tractor track with William, Mala, Paul and Camnis. Paul and I put in quarter mile posts for Ambi River survey. Boys burning vegetation near house, later put the ash on raised beds.

9 March

Went to see the boys' house and gardens – fairly tidy, but mosquitoes *terrible*. William says mosquitoes bad since September. Had my two boys working on the chicken wire and made a door for the run myself. Hung it in the afternoon.

James eleven pounds fifteen ounces.

10 March

Sunday. Quiet morning. In the afternoon made a chair for Michael out of mangrove wood and *Commersonia Bartramia*, finishing it just as it got dark.

13 March

One cock and three hens (white) were brought up and started calmly scratching away in the hen run.

14 March

Went down to the store with Claire. Paid £5 for our cock and three hens. William and boys making a shutter for Michael's room.

15 March

Took Mala and two boys to sample plot two and began

measuring the trees. Mala digging the base-line ditches.

In the afternoon, Mala carried on. I continued plotting map.

17 March

Letter to Aunt Erica.

The trading boat Bouro *came in this morning and brought your letter of 20 February.*

We have been on Vanikoro since 4 February and are properly settled in now. When we arrived there had been an accident – one of the Australians had blown half his hand off and the Kovala *had to return immediately to Kira Kira with him. Three ex-hospital patients who were to have gone back to Santa Cruz were thus marooned on Vanikoro, so I employed them myself as gardeners and we now have several beds of beans coming up and, between the house and the stream, a chicken run with three white hens and one white cock. We brought fifty yards of chicken wire with us from Honiara.*

Last Sunday I made a little arm chair for Michael out of mangrove poles and planks from bush timber. Claire then made a little red cushion for it and it is a success.

Recently we have had two pigeons from the bush, one of which I shot myself when out surveying, and yesterday John brought in another he had shot with my gun. They are very tasty.

Also I have now got a fishing rod, from the bush, with a reel and eyes that I brought out from England. I tried it out for the first time this morning – no luck though!

There was a very high tide here some weeks ago, as a consequence of which there is a lot more sand at Peou which makes it pleasanter bathing. Claire, Michael and I had a good time there this morning. There are still some of the old lot in the bush, and many new ones who seem decent chaps. The new manager taking over from Mr Filewood while he goes on leave is Mr Jeffries. He has a wife and two small boys.

We have heard that Mr Trenaman is coming from 29 March to 11 April, so he will be staying with us.

It has been raining a lot and is raining now. The chickens have a little house with a corrugated iron roof and leaf walls. Now they are all fast asleep on their perches.

19 March

Left for the bush in the tug at 9.30 am, then walked up to the first of the lines and beat about the bush. Found kauris growing up fast in the lines, repressed elsewhere. After lunch went further up the road and found the same story. Came out on another hilltop. Returned in time for tea.

20 March

Set off for Lawrence River camp at 3.0, arriving 4.30, with Paul and Alfred carrying my things.

21 March

Left labour roofing hut and set off up the Horseshoe with Mala and Paul. Investigated a site for sample plot at first ridge junction. Then did a circuit of secondary ridges. Came back down the strip at point 4000 feet and the far arm of the Horseshoe, seeing another possible sample plot area. Back to camp at 2.0 pm.

22 March

Rainy. Left the labour to take stuff down. Set off across country with Mala. Passed through a likely sample plot area near camp and then some patches of advanced regeneration. Got to the old profile diagram plot for lunch. Then on, across two rivers and two more regeneration ridges, striking the road below the big tree. Mala caught one baby pig. Home about 3.0 pm. After supper had gramophone on, danced to *Les Sylphides*.

27 March

Off to the bush about 9 am, reached camp about 10.30 am. Had early lunch then up ridge behind camp. Took girths for possible sample plot. Explored a hilltop on the map and found its connection with the main ridge – not marked on map.

28 March

With Michael and John Cula did a walk round the ridges to the north and east of camp. Returned after noon, then home.

30 March

Paid boys and brought office work up to date. Keith Trenaman and the Tedders arrived in *Kovala* about 2 pm, out to see them, then all back to house for tea and supper. Had records on. Keith staying in our house.

31 March

Sunday. Tedders came and all went a picnic up the river, Greg and Ian walking and Michael and James being carried. Built a shelter with pen-knives! Keith and I fished with worms and caught a three inch fish! Returned for tea. A good day.

1 April

In spite of rain did a tour of two lines to the Ambi River, looking at regeneration with Keith, who shot a pigeon which we had for supper. Bishop Hill had arrived in the *Baddely*, so I went down as Immigration Officer. The Bishop came up to the house and christened James Merlin, wearing his full regalia, then sailed again at 6 pm.

2 April

Weather promising in early morning. Set off for Lawrence River camp with Keith, accompanied by heavy rain. Had lunch and then continued up the ridge behind camp and reached the top near the road. Came down part of the way along the side of the ridge, looking for areas for pre-exploitation experiments.

3 April

Set off up the Horseshoe – sample plot area looking very lovely in the sunlight. Found masses of regeneration, including many saplings. Looked at the open forest area at 4,000 feet. Up above the timber line to a look-out in a *Syzigium* tree.

4 April

Went up to Sundi River with Keith in the tug but had trouble getting over the bar. Investigated William's intermediate lines and an area of good regeneration in old undergrowth further up. Concluded poisonings desirable to assist regeneration of kauri in all undergrowth areas, but lines useful in newly felled areas of *Macaranga* growth.

7 April

Off at 8.0 with Keith, Filewood and Jeffries up Lawrence River to camp, thence round Horseshoe. Lunch back at camp, then up Long Ridge to point 1600 and through thick secondary growth to the road. They think that the area can easily be worked by haulers and tractors. Down the track, home at dusk.

8 April

Paul and boys failed to get to Sundi River and all did erosion control instead. Went round the near regeneration areas, Home plot and Home plantation with Keith.

9 April

Letter to Aunt Erica.

The Tedders have been on their Far Eastern Tour, calling here on their way out and are now here on their way back, and Claire had Gregory and Ian today when we were all up at the bush, including Margaret. They have been to Ticopia and beyond, to Anuda. They brought Keith Trenaman with them and he has been here about ten days. We have been out in the bush every single day, including Sunday, when we walked nine miles in the jungle with the manager and deputy manager. So Keith can really feel he's seen about all there is to see, and I've got a lot of interesting work to do on growth rates and regeneration experiments. The Sunday before last we all went up to the picnic place on the river, including four children, and had a good time swimming and Keith fishing with the new rod I've made, though we only caught one little fish about four inches long!

James was christened by Bishop Hill on 1 April in our sitting room. He put on his mitre and shell inlaid staff. He's rather a jolly old boy. He'd just done 6,000 miles of touring in a small boat and 400 miles or so on foot, in New Caledonia and the New Hebrides.

We've now got a hen run, three white hens and a grey cock. They are all very healthy and happy, but refuse to lay eggs. Well, they'd better improve their ideas by Christmas, or else!

Now we are doing scientific work within the areas I mapped last time it is more coherent and getting interesting as it enters the next stage.

We have now got two house boys and they are both jolly good – intelligent and willing and one of them has been a house boy for many years before.

Michael looks at all our books now and anything *with pictures, however grown up. I am wondering if we should have one of the old annuals of mine –* Pip and Squeak *or something – sent out, what do you think? He gets through his own books in no time and then it is so much the worse for ours – though he is improving a lot and will take a book sometimes to his little table and sits in his little chair to look at it.*

10 April

All the Tedders to lunch, and they and Keith left in the *Kovala* about 5.0 pm.

13 April

Studied sections of root sheath of kauri with microscope. Also found *Rhizopus* (a common fungus) on sole of shoe and a *Rotaria* in the gully.

James weighed thirteen pounds six ounces.

22 April

Trying to identify weeds with Merrill round the house. Drew a threadworm from Michael under the microscope.

27 April

Tagging and measuring seedlings and saplings in Home plot. Painted gall damage on Kauri leaf; put leaves in jar to obtain insect. Out by starlight on the lawn together.

James weighed fourteen pounds two ounces.

4 May

Letter to Aunt Erica.

Thank you for your letters of 4 and 17 April which have just come on the Milos.

I'm sorry you didn't get a letter for a month, but now we are away from Honiara we are very lucky indeed if we get a ship a month.

Michael now seems to have a word for most things that he comes across regularly – though all his words begin with either B or D – ie. 'dore' = sore and 'boon' = spoon. I took him out in the canoe this morning as it was calm and we paddled over to an island of sand in the river mouth. He is very interested in 'boe' (=boats).

We have got two posts and a cross bar on the lawn now that we use for tenniquoits, which is fun.

Our launch has arrived at Honiara and Mr Trenaman is using it for a tour of the West before sending it on to us on the next big boat.

James is OK. There doesn't seem to be much news so I'll stop.

7 May

Heavy rain and prolonged thunder in night. Southeaster blowing strong am. Boys around house and nursery – 390 Hoop pine (*Araucaria Cunninghamii*) seed sown.

To home plot in the afternoon with Mala, Paul, Alfred, John, where we started poisoning trees.

8 May

Mala and company got on with poisoning trees in home plot. I with two boys laid out regeneration sample plot off tractor track.

Later I completed dominance classification in home plot.

13 May

Showery still. Got ready for bush and left about 11.30. Turned out fine. Had lunch and then went to sample plot with Mala to measure trees.

14 May

Heavy rain in night. To a branch of Horseshoe Ridge, started plot for pre-exploitation experiment. Several false starts on wrong bearing, not having studied map properly first.

15 May

To plot as yesterday. Laid out corner trenches and Paul started digging them. Returned about 3.0.

16 May

A lovely fine day. Up at 6.0 or soon after. Finished laying out the first pre-exploitation plot.

Lemon tree outside tent two foot seven inches tall. Removed Karamati sapling from over it.

17 May

Paul and company got on with trenches in pre-exploitation area. I with Mala, Cula and William surveyed base-line for next pre-exploitation area, then measured the remaining trees in sample plot Horseshoe SW. Lunch at camp then back home.

22 May

Finer at last. Sent Paul to re-do trees on bush sample plot and Mala to collect kauri seed. I went to Home sample plot and took eight photographs.

Over tea discussed with Claire idea of buying a cabin cruiser in England instead of going to another colony.

Found three eggs in box in the hen house, our first – at last!

23 May

Moth appeared from kauri leaves in which caterpillars had been reared. Killed it by ether, sketched it and packed it for CSIRO.

Spent morning tagging young saplings up the tractor track.

26 May

Letter to Aunt Erica.

There are a couple of boats going to Honiara in the next few days so now is the time to write.

It's been raining quite a lot last week and we've been getting on with the sample plot work that can be done from here. The week before was finer and we had a profitable time at the Lawrence River camp.

I am expecting our new launch on the next timber boat and want to get as much done here as possible so that the boys can work further afield when we have our own transport.

The other day we found three eggs in the nest-box! They were the first. We were all looking forward to nice fried eggs for breakfast and then when the moment came, the boys, having fried the eggs, hashed them up into little bits and put that on the plate.

We'd have had them boiled only there weren't any egg cups. It is wonderful that they are laying at last – we'd begun to feel that the hens weren't earning the coconuts we have brought up for them. There are two new calves now and so there is more than enough fresh milk for everyone. At first it used to go solid almost immediately, after being brought to the boil, but now it seems better. Our beans are producing very well and there are usually some over to give away.

It is perhaps early to think of Christmas, but when you do I would like any of those new Hobbit books we have been discussing. I have been reading the early history of North Wales in my book Snowdonia *in the New Naturalist series and find it very interesting. I didn't realise the close connection between Snowdon and King Arthur and the crag of Dinas Emrys the home of Merlin. It will make an added interest when I go back there.*

I noticed pustular galls on leaves of young kauri trees and found tiny white caterpillars in them. I kept some leaves in a jar with a gauze top for three weeks and at last got a beautiful little moth a quarter of an inch long with crimson eyes and chestnut wings with black edgings and white stripes. Quite possibly a new species, anyway I'm sending it to Australia to be identified and also rearing more specimens for the British Museum. I am packing it with cotton wool in a .22 cartridge case and sealing it with sticking plaster after drying over silica gel.

The family are all flourishing and send their love.

27 May

Four new boys. Saw Assistant Medical Practitioner Francis about ear. Boys on sample plot up tractor track.

Attended to the outward mail. None for us on *Marjery*.

Read. Still very wet.

28 May

Brigantine *Yankee* arrived first thing.

I entertained four boys from the *Yankee* and Dr N. Alice Strahan, with whom I had a walk round about.

See 23 May 1954 for the previous visit of the *Yankee*. They were sailing westward around the world and Dr Strahan asked if I had any suggestion as to where they might stop in the Solomons. I said that Jim Tedder, the DC Eastern, had been 'marooned' on one of the Reef Islands for some months to do a survey and no doubt he would be glad to see them.

'Good idea,' they said, 'let's go there.' They found Jim with acute appendicitis, gave him penicillin injections and took him to Honiara hospital where he made a full recovery. On the island he had been reading *The Power of the Mind* by Alexander, and trying to use such power to get help in his predicament.

30 May

Stayed at home copying in data because *Marjery* expected, but when it came it was off again before we had taken our mail down!

James weighs fifteen pounds six ounces.

2 June

It is Camnis' holiday, so we are doing washing up etc. A pair of medium sized birds with strong, tern-like flight swept up to me and then veered quickly downhill, disappearing over the pasture in the direction of the river. Body white, wings pointed, black. Black collar, long, trailing, reddish legs. Afterwards described it to Mala who knows it. He says it lays its eggs on the big blocks of coral on top of the reef, not making a nest, and in a high tide sometimes the eggs are swept away. The eggs are white with black spots. This must be the White-headed Stilt. According to Mayr, 1945, its distribution is 'from the Philippines to Australia and the Papuan region. In the south-west Pacific recorded only from

New Britain, where it seems to be an irregular winter visitor from Australia.' So it would seem to be a new record for Vanikoro, if not for the Solomons.

3 June

Gale from south of east. Boys repairing nursery house and canoe house. Also sowed 360 hoop pine seed. Finished monthly report.

pm. up to plot, plotting position of young trees.

Very windy, got dark early. Returned 4.30.

4 June

A bit promising early, then set in wet. Abandoned plan to go to bush.

At 2.30 pm on hearing purple gallinules calling from several directions, I took the .22 and went out. Shot one emerging from the side of the track. Later on down to pasture. Saw four there altogether from the end of the track. Shot at them in turn, killing one at forty-five yards. Claire and I had one for supper, a very tasty stew. Weight – one and a half pounds. Plucked and ready for pot – one and a quarter pounds. Purple round neck, greeny blue-turquoise patch on leading edge of wing. White scut. Red frontal patch and beak.

6 June

Heavy rain in night, slept very soundly. Off to work in the morning, gave up almost immediately because of heavy rain. Dashed downhill to camp. Read Lawrence.

In the afternoon, up again, carried on in gloom and drip, returned in heavy rain. Finished *The Essential T. E. Lawrence* having enjoyed reading it very much. Nine inches of rain were recorded in this twenty-four hours.

7 June

Awoke at 1.0 am – river risen, ground shaking with pounding of boulders in river bed. Got up – river on level with camp and pouring into boys' house. Mainstream a mighty jet the speed of an express train. Soon subsided. The morning promised another wet day, so set off for home. Measured rise of river – eight feet rise in bed, fourteen feet rise at corner by the cliff. River bed bearing marks of violence, scoured banks, shattered trees.

10 June

Rain stopped at last, but terribly humid and enervating. Landslides along tractor track and erosion barriers destroyed.

13 June

Really fine at last. Mala says it's the Queen's birthday holiday, so a holiday it was. Up the tractor track with Claire and Michael, bathed in pools. Fine and cool fresh trade wind. Later on down through pasture (new cattle fence) and swamp to river, thence to river mouth. There was a low spring tide with much sand. Saw two stilts – body and head white, wing dark green, paler on forward edge. Fine dark bar on shoulder, long pink legs. One slightly taller and not so pure white about the head as the other. Both standing on one leg and occasionally swivelling round a few degrees, perhaps to face the wind. Saw male golden whistler by the river bank.

Later, in the evening I shot at flying foxes which were attacking the kapok tree.

17 June

Fine. Organized nursery and in the afternoon set off for camp with all the boys except Paul and Alfred.

* * *

18 June

Wet day. To SP with Mala, started measuring trees – defeated by rain. Retreat to home. Boys on erosion barriers.

19 June

Samuel brought us some pork, having shot the sow which was causing trouble in their gardens.

2 July

Rather overcast, with some rain in morning. Sent boys up to bush to get on with pre-exploitation area nonetheless.

Wrote report for June.

2.0 pm set off for bush myself.

3 July

To SP No. 8 with all boys. Paul and company painting trees, did nineteen in all. Mala and I laid out base line, bearing 320 degrees. Then to pre-exploitation area, completed demarcation and started enumeration. Back to camp at 2.30 pm.

9 July

Fine morning. Sail sighted! Auxiliary ketch *Arthur Rogers*. Went aboard with Peter and there were five English aboard, traders.

Later – off to bush.

11 July

Wet, but fine enough to lure us up to pre-exploitation area – got wet – returned home. Went on ahead myself and did the trip in about one hour five minutes. Wet afternoon.

Bob and Diana Hepworth from the *Arthur Rogers* came up for bath, after visiting bush. Dinner aboard, followed by drinks at Jeffries.

15 July

To camp by dusk.

18 July

Fine. Completed layout of plot. Did half the enumeration. Back about 2.30 pm. Rested after lunch, till it was time to get supper. Found rats had eaten all the candles! So had a chat in the boys' house by the light of kauri gum.

19 July

Completed enumerations of the plot. Returned home to find Claire in midst of preparations for cocktail party for Rear Admiral Toulouse-Lautrec commanding French forces in the Pacific.

20 July

Frigate *Francis Garnier* sighted from lookout 11.0 am, arrived about 11.45. Out to meet her in *Toby*, went aboard, delivered message to admiral, lunch with him, captain and senior medical officer. The admiral asked me if I knew the history of the French interest in Vanikoro and when I said that I didn't, he told me:

'In 1785 King Louis XVI sent La Pérouse to make a voyage of discovery, and he was never heard of again until many years later, after the Napoleonic wars were over, when a British ship reached the island of Ticopia, 140 miles east of here, and the king of the island presented the captain with a sword hilt, taken from Vanikoro, which he recognized as having belonged to La Pérouse. It turned out that his two ships, *La Boussole* and *L'Astrolabe*, reaching Vanikoro at dusk had run aground on the barrier reef. Approached by fleets of canoes in the morning, one ship had opened fire with cannons and consequently had been massacred to a man; but La Pérouse held his fire and parleyed with the natives, with the result that some of them survived for years on the island and may have bred with the natives; but none of the survivors were found.'

In the evening there was a cocktail party at our house.

21 July

Sunday. Fine, but a few showers later. Went aboard with Claire, Michael and the Jeffries at 9.45 am. M was medically inspected including X-ray. All saw over the ship, took colour photos, returned for lunch in the garden (cheese from ship!)

It was in the ward-room of the *Francis Garnier* that I first came across the Tintin books (Objectif Lune etc), which I liked so much that I got some sent out from home.

22 July

Saw Mala, who was in bed with fever. I was feeling very tired after the week-end. Sent off the admiral's message. Boys working around house. Copied and added up pre-exploitation plots data.

5 August

Letter to Father and Aunt Erica.

I am duplicating this to save saying everything twice in different words, and will send you both a short letter as well. The island has been out of air letter forms for months and that and the lack of ships going in the right direction has resulted in a lack of inclination to write letters.

At the end of May we had the Yankee *again (brigantine from America going round the world). It is Commander and Mrs Johnson's last time round and it was nice to see them again. We had some of the crew up to our house. Then we all went out in the* Toby, *including Michael, to see it off, and what a sight it was, coming across the lagoon towards us with the boys and girls letting out one after another of eleven sails!*

In June we had thirty-four inches of rain at the coast and more inland. One week we had two periods of twenty-four hours with nine inches each. On the first of these occasions the boys and I were in the Lawrence River camp when at 1 am one night we were awakened by alarming reverberations and emerged to find the river transformed into a jet of high velocity and already beginning to pour into the boys' house eight feet above the normal water level. Fortunately the rain had already eased off and the water soon began to subside. Downstream at a corner the level had risen fourteen feet. The reverberations of course were caused by boulders being rolled downstream. One consequence of the flood was that lots of sand was brought down and deposited outside the river mouth, making an excellent weekend playground for Claire, Michael and me – it's so clean and open.

On the early morning of 9 July a lusty cry announced the sighting of yet another unexpected sail. This time it was the auxiliary ketch Arthur Rogers *a Brixham trawler owned by Bob and Diana Hepworth who had sailed her out from England some ten years ago and are seriously contemplating trading in these islands. They came from the New Hebrides. They are pleasant people and came up here for tea and two lots of hot baths. We have had dinner aboard. it is a comfortable and clean ship. It has a tiller but no wheel. Bob was a photographer before the war and Diana a fashion model. Last night they gave a show of coloured slides (projected) and you can tell how good they were when I say we had over two hundred and were still interested. They were of the trip from Panama, with the Galapagos, Marquesas, Tahiti, New Caledonia and New Zealand – some beautiful scenery and not at all like the Solomons.*

While they were away at Santa Cruz and Reef Islands we had a different interlude. One Friday night I came down from the bush and found Claire working hard at preparations for an official cocktail party next day. There had been a flood of telegrams from the Acting High Commissioner to say that a French Warship was going to visit Vanikoro, containing one French Rear Admiral, and I had to present HE's message to him and have a party for all and sundry, which went according to plan. They were a pleasant crowd. I had lunch aboard with Admiral Toulouse-Lautrec, the Captain and the MO, and he went to great trouble to explain all about La Perouse's ill-fated expedition to Vanikoro in 1785. The French keep a cross on the reef.

We saw quite a bit of them that weekend, and they even gave Michael a free medical examination including a chest X-ray. They showed us over the ship, too – the Francis Garnier

The Milos *is due on 20 August, and the Jeffries, who have been replacing Mr Filewood while he was on leave, are going out. They gave a farewell party the other night for all, including the twelve Australians from the bush, us and the* Arthur Rogers *people. Michael is as mischievous as ever and 'wee Jamie' is sitting up and taking notice and even beginning to crawl, so soon I expect we shall be coping with two chimps instead of one, though I hope they will to some extent cope with each other.*

Letter to Aunt Erica.

Thank you for your letters. I will send the stamps you ask for when I write an air letter, if they aren't needed on this one. Thank you for sending the books, which I expect will arrive this mail. Incidentally, we already have Peter Rabbit *and* Tailor of Goucester. *Claire and I know most of the former by heart 'but round the end of a cucumber frame, who should appear but Mr MacGregor!'*

We have put burnt shell down for the hens and also a dummy egg in the nest box. We got a boy to make this but unfortunately he made it rather square. It was duly painted white and put in the nest box and next morning, would you believe it, the hen had laid a square egg! But apart from that one we haven't had any, except for a dozen or so we had a few months ago, which were jolly good.

James has been having rather a noisy chest and I hope he isn't going to have my old trouble. It's better now, anyway.

Matthias has now got his wife and three piccanins here, and they all live together in the little house we built for Selwyn – rather crowded, I imagine. The piccanins are all smallish; the youngest, Veronica, is a sweet little baby usually seen in a calico over its mother's back.

We are growing some fine China cabbages now, but we certainly couldn't spare one to try on the hens!

The Hepworths have two dogs and the most gi-normous black cat you ever saw. One of the dogs has a strong strain of English sheepdog, but the other, although its daughter, looks more like a fox terrier. The pseudo-sheepdog's mother came with them from England – real sea-dog types!

6 August

Saw off the *Arthur Rogers* – C and I in *Toby* with others, out beyond reef.

11 August

Letter to Aunt Erica.

It was raining hard earlier this morning and now has eased off to a steady drizzle.

The Milos *is expected tomorrow, I think, and we are hoping that my eighteen foot motor-launch will be aboard.*

*Thank you very much for sending the books for Michael. Actually we had already got the two new ones (*Pets and Playmates *and* Peter Rabbit*), so we are going to put them away and keep them for James. He likes the* Pip and Squeak *annual.*

Almost all the mango trees have been flowering recently, so we are hoping to have a lovely crop of mangoes around Christmas. We had one or two early ones just now and Michael loves them – so do we. The hens aren't laying, the beans are over and the island's out of fresh meat and vegetables, so we're down to tins and vitamin pills again. A worse crisis was when the Company ran out of beer a few days ago. The Australians drink from two to four dozen bottles a week each owing to the strenuous nature of the work. Fortunately the trader's boat Endeavour *came in the other day with a quantity to tide us over until the big ship.*

Claire and I have been to a couple of parties with them recently in the evenings. They are a pleasant crowd.

We are having some success with China cabbage, which is very good indeed.

Michael grew one inch in the last two months. His height is now two feet eleven inches. Blackie has produced two tabby kittens, she reared them in the jungle and brought them in when they were able to run around. Their grandmother, Pippa, is still here. One of the kittens is going to Ling, the storeman, whose cat was killed by the sheepdog from the Arthur Rogers.

Our big white cock is very uppish – comes into the house and attacks the cats. Claire thinks that if we put him in the pot the hens might lay more eggs – having less to think about.

James is now learning about standing on all fours. He can already crawl enough to fall off the bed when you leave him in the middle of it for a few minutes.

12 August

Milos came in and promptly went on the reef, where it stayed all day. Non-arrival of launch – poor show.

13 August

Milos still aground. Sent Mala, Paul and four boys to Lawrence River camp to carry on with experimental poisonings. I went up to 4a and finished positioning seedlings there, then started 4b. Took pedometer – one and a quarter miles to 4a. Morning's work amounts to five miles.

15 August

Finished surveying positions of trees. Collected a *Lycopodium phlegmaria* and a shrub with scented flowers, also some diseased Kauri leaves.

Mr and Mrs Trevenna, 'shipwrecked' passengers from the *Milos*, came to stay.

16 August

USS *Virgo*, 10,000 tons, off reef at dawn to help *Milos*. Spent morning plotting seedlings. *Milos* got off reef at last, just before dark.

Letter from Claire to Aunt Erica.

I feel it is a very long time since I have written, please forgive me. The books you sent for Michael have arrived, also the adorable sun-suit for James. I am putting it away for the time being but it won't be for long. He weighs seventeen pounds thirteen ounces now, and is just getting his top front teeth, they are giving him rather a lot of trouble. The bottom ones are already through. Although he has become quite mobile when on a bed, getting up on all fours and then slipping down again, he does not like being left on the floor on his tummy for long. I am in the process of making a mattress for the cot; the boys have been picking coconut fibre for me, and I've made a case from ticking bought at the store. We have also fitted the cot with casters so that it can be moved easily onto the verandah for Jamie during the day. He and Michael sleep in the same room at night. Mickie is a true little boy now, and always seems to be in the wars; a fortnight ago he fell off the verandah and bit his lip – a very nasty cut. I thought it would be sure to leave a scar but there is very little sign of it now. The real danger is from knives as he is always taking either the boys' bush knives or ones from the kitchen. He imitates them in cutting sticks, saying he is making a boat, which is his passion at the moment – understandable seeing how many we have had recently.

The Milos *arrived early this morning to load timber. The captain was in such a hurry to get in and started that he ignored the pilot boat guiding him in and is now stuck on the reef. He did this at high tide so will have to wait until this evening before trying to get off. In the meantime the cargo for here is being taken off, other cargo shifted and brass ballast thrown overboard in an effort to lighten her. Luckily it is a fine day, although it looks as if a bit of a wind is getting up now.*

17th. Yesterday an American naval ship came down and managed to pull it off in the evening. All the passengers have been living ashore for the last two days. We have had a couple with us.

17 August

Down after lunch to see the Jeffries off in the *Melanesian*.

The MV *Melanesian* was on its maiden voyage. It was the latest acquisition of the Government fleet, bigger and better than anything we'd had before. When it was time to sail the captain, a young European, had disappeared. At last, however, he was found in a house near the sea, where he had been drinking with the Australians. We could see that he was not too steady on his feet as he was helped aboard.

'If that ship is still afloat in six months' time' Lionel remarked, 'I'll eat my hat!' Tragically, he never had to eat it.

1 September

Sunday. Wet morning. Claire down to help stock taking in store. Michael and I went to bear-pool, later down to collect Claire. In the afternoon Claire went again to the store. I went out in canoe exploring edge of mangroves. Afterwards Luke showed me mysterious bit of metal from Tuo. Lit copper and all had baths.

1 October

Whole family left for bush in tug. Weather not too good. Walked up to camp. Paul and Luke making floor to tent. Later I walked up to workings.

4 October

All walked down to river, saw Jim Creber with his truck off the road. Michael was towed back in the canoe.

5 October

Working on September report. *Mary* came with mail and met. officer Afflic – later collected £300 cash from him.

7 October

Paul started nursery beds. Then Mala told me it was a public holiday.

Soviet space satellite seen over Australia 7.40 pm.

8 October

Paul sowed six beds with about 120 *Pinus caribbea* seed each after mixing with mycorrhiza inoculated soil. Also five beds of *Araucaria Cunninghamii.* Mala and four boys to camp at Sundi River. Paul sick in afternoon.

Down with Claire to pay rations bill. Satellite much in the news still.

14 October

Cula in hospital with belly-ache and vomiting. Down five times during day. Suspected arsenic poisoning, gave ferric hydroxide in case it was, but realize it might be something quite different.

We had been poisoning trees since May, but only received a list of precautions, symptoms and treatment on the last visit of the *Mary*, and immediately several people, of whom Cula was the worst, began to feel ill. Fortunately it was a temporary 'epidemic' and soon abated.

15 October

Cula a bit better after a good night's sleep, and tummy ache gone. Worked out vote position and sent telegram for more for Research.

3.30 pm Cula's temperature 103 degrees, headache, chest pains. Talked to SMO Honiara on radio. Prescribed nivaquine and penicillin.

16 October

Down with Claire to see Cula – better.

23 October

Found golden plover wounded by bird of prey, which died in my hand. Skinned it and ate it.

Letter from Claire to Aunt Erica.

You must not get worried if suddenly there is a long gap between letters as it simply means there has been no ship or possibly no warning that one was coming, so no time to write. After all the excitement of the Milos *things have been very quiet. We were only able to put up those people because we happened to have a spare camp bed (now up in Chris's camp for when I go up again) and a divan thing we brought from Honiara.*

The mattress is a great success and I have also made some seat cushions for a wooden settle-type seat we have in the sitting room – much more comfortable now. Yesterday I tried my hand at making mango chutney. Not too bad but a bit gingery, although the recipe said one and a half ounces ginger and garlic to one pound mangoes and chillies. I would try bottling some if only we had the bottles. I did try doing some 'five corners' (carambola) in a coffee jar and they seem to be all right still, but I had no more jars complete with metal top and rubber ring.

I can hardly believe it is so near to Christmas, I wonder what it will be like this year. I must get busy making things for the children. I thought I would make a golliwog for M out of some old black socks of Chris's, and a duck for J as I have some yellow towelling. For Matthias's children I think I will try and make some clothes, probably the most popular thing. M has great fun with them, although they rather let him have his own way too much.

Thank you for starting on pullovers for us. I think I would like a deep sky blue, or warm pinky red, or coral, any of those would go with most neutral skirts (I have my grey one). Tiggie is going to get some warm dress material, I don't know what colour – perhaps to match it.

For my birthday, although you shouldn't bother about such things, here are a couple of ideas – only ideas. One and a half yards chiffon – forty-four inches wide for a blouse and buttons. I've seen rather a pretty pattern in a Woman's Own *– they give a diagram for cutting. Colour soft rose red or pink to go with snippet enclosed. Another idea – Helena Rubinstein, Silk Minute Make Up – colour opalescent rose, a combined powder and foundation. I find this type of make up suits me better than separated powder and cream and I'd love to try hers some time. The colour I've quoted may be too pale for here.*

21 November

Letter to Aunt Erica.

The Milos *is due in tomorrow with Mr Trenaman and, we hope, my launch. Keith will presumably stay with us until the DC comes, about 26th*

We've been having some good fine weather recently and I've been up at camp three days this week. It is pleasant there, only five minutes from the road and our two tents are a score yards or so from the boys' house through the trees. We have camp beds, a floor of wooden poles laid horizontally, a separate leaf kitchen, and tables made of bamboo lashed tightly together. On two occasions so far all the family have been up, and we hope to do it more often with the launch, which will make it much more convenient.

I am making Michael a wooden cart for Christmas, with wheels of wood and washers of flattened-out beer bottle tops. James crawls everywhere and clutches everything. There is no sport he likes better than to give you a sharp nip with his two little teeth and then beam with silent laughter as you cry out. He is now at the stage of maximum all round menace, as he can get around and do things but has no discrimination – at least I expect he *thinks he has, but his idea of discrimination isn't ours.*

Michael has been told 'Big ship come bimeby' and was all expectant this afternoon, but I told him 'Time sun he come up big ship come' – I don't know whether he understood or not. Whenever there is a yell of 'Sail-ho!' down below Michael dashes out and joins in. In fact I was a mile up the track working in the bush last week when a Chinese boat came and I first heard the big yell and then Michael's shrill voice joining in.

Addition from Claire. *I'll just append a brief note as there is the usual rush before the ship goes. The DC arrived earlier than expected and yesterday we all went with him on the* Mary *round the island. He had to pay a visit to Buma, the village on Tevai, and Chris and Keith took the opportunity of having a look at the kauri forest nearby. That end of the island is quite spectacular and Chris took a couple of colour photos, the mountains fall fairly sheer to the sea in places. I and the children stayed on board.*

I am sending a little something for Christmas, for the house really, but it will have to come by surface mail. The Milos *has been considerably delayed this time so there is no hope of it reaching you in time.*

'Nausicaa', Our launch, in the Lawrence river.

22 November

Fine. *Milos* arrived after breakfast. Down with Claire and M. Launch arrived! Saw Keith aboard, then all came ashore.

DC (Mr Pearson) arrived in *Mary*. Up to lunch and later to dinner. No Mail!

Trip round the *Milos* in new launch with Keith and Claire – goes well.

23 November

Down to *Mary* and all sailed round Vanikoro. Fine, but swell in exposed part beyond Tevai. Stopped at Buma, then Keith, Mala and I ashore lower down and reached kauri forest on E – W ridge at 600 feet, down to col at 420, back to salt water, bathed, embarked.

24 November

Sunday. Wrote letters and took mail down, but only just in

time as it happened, *Milos* going early.

In the afternoon we had tea outside. The *Baddeley* came with Vaughan and the Hunts – all had tea in garden.

25 November

To Sundi River in our launch with Keith, Mala and four boys. Walked up to operations area – showed Keith, also inspected poisoners at work. Lunch at camp, then down and back in the launch.

27 November

Letter from Claire to Aunt Erica and Aunt Mu.

Have decided to send this little gift by Air Mail after all, I hope it doesn't arrive too late. If these covers don't fit the egg cosies you will have to take them to the next jumble sale you hear of. I have had great fun doing them and Michael enjoyed watching the oodle-oodle-oo growing. I wish our own would produce a few more eggs! They sometimes lay about two a week for a few weeks and then stop.

Keith Trenaman has been down and is probably going tomorrow. We have enjoyed his visit very much and I think it has given Chris fresh encouragement (not that he needs it) but it is good to feel that your work is appreciated. The new DC Eastern has also called in, he is only temporary until the Tedders come back from leave. The latter are hoping to come back to this district for at least part of their next tour so we will be see them again.

We have just heard that there is a possibility of us going down to Australia on the Milos *in August and then flying home. They are keen that officers should not lose so much time in travelling and I believe it will soon be compulsory to fly one way. Of course this time for us it will probably mean we have more time before departing for Oxford.*

We continue to love the life out here although we look forward to coming home. The new launch should add to our activities and outings.

9 December

Jamie trying to stand by himself. Michael trying hard to swim in pool.

Paul started poisoning trial plots. Anti-frog fence made for nursery.

Got ready for bush.

10 December

Tired after bad night. To Sundi River by launch with Lionel and boys. Had a swim trying to dislodge whaler [a small open boat] aground on a rock. Sank whaler, towed drums in. To works with Lionel in the red international truck. Damaged left shin. Returned to camp in truck.

11 December

Slept well. Feeling a bit low all the same, and ulcer on right knee. Watched the boys at work most of the day, with a long break at midday, reading Don Quixote.

Got down to river by evening, and finished strip.

12 December

Bathed ulcer with hot water and lemon. Feeling weak. Watched boys at work then returned to camp to rest and eat.

Note from Claire about message from DC. I returned by launch, catching up the messengers, Vila and Nati, half-way.

13 December

Did office work. *Mary* came – sent mail including watches to Angus and Coote. Took mail out myself in launch. Watched *Mary*'s departure from nursery.

Poison put out for crabs in nursery (spoiling seedlings).

16 December

Up at 6.0 am, off at 7.0 am in launch with four boys to Sundi River. Took Michael for the ride. Caught a fish on the way back. Dip in pool.

In the afternoon painted the name *'Nausicaa'* on the launch.

18 December

12.50 am Michael woke us up shouting and five minutes later there was a vicious earthquake. Some crockery was broken and we all got out of the house. There were slight shocks until dawn. Tired after disturbed night.

Sent telegram about earthquake to Honiara.

19 December

Plotted maps.

In the afternoon by launch to Sundi River – got lift to camp in Creber's truck. Got supper, read *Grapes of Wrath*.

20 December

Up early. Surveyed to river with Cula and Nioni.

Walked down, caught a barracuda on the way back, then the fishing line caught on the prop. shaft and took half an hour to undo.

21 December

Out to reef with Mala and the boys, Claire and Michael coming too. We had a swim and then left them at the Saboe Bay end of the reef and went home. Vila fetched me from the house at about 1.30 pm – water up – binoculars showed boys marooned on big rock, canoe returning. Dashed out in launch – dicey rescue on reef in nasty cross-swell – all's well that ends well. Got some forty fish into freezer.

Evening – painted Michael's Christmas cart – red, wheels primrose.

25 December

Christmas Day. Presents for all including house boy's family by Christmas tree on verandah.

Lunch at Filewoods with bush-boys, Michael and James too.

Filewoods and Chaperlin up for supper, then all the bush-boys – ended up with songs and guitar. Party finished about 1.0 am.

27 December

Letter to Aunt Erica and Aunt Mu.

Thank you so much for The Fellowship of the Ring. *It is a lovely book to have and I am already well into it. I am sure I shall read it many times. I re-read* The Hobbit *some weeks ago and have lent it to a missionary, Mr Vaughan.*

We have had the first proper Christmas since we've been married, being together and in our own house. The week before, on Saturday, I took the boys out to the reef and fetched them back in the afternoon, they having speared about forty fish, which were then kept in the deep freeze for their Christmas feast.

We decorated the house with all sorts of leaves and purple and red berries from the forest, and had a young kauri pine six feet high as a Christmas tree.

In the morning we all had our presents including Matthias, Miriam, Hilda, John Mark, Veronica, Camnis, Alan Mala and Paul. For lunch we all went to the Filewoods, where they had all the Europeans from the bush, and the Filewoods and Mr Chaperlin came to supper with us and the rest to a party after supper for drinking, dancing and singing. We were about sixteen in all. There was dancing to the gramophone on the verandah and then singing with the guitar. They went home about 1.0 am, which for Vanikoro is quite late.

Yesterday I was ill with an upset tummy, but to-day I am better.

The Filewoods are giving their New Year party on Saturday instead of next week, while the boys are still around. Some of the boys have gone to Utupua for two days for a change.

It has been raining over Christmas, after a prolonged spell of fine weather.

Michael is delighted with the xylophone – he is a bit heavy handed with it at present but does enjoy it. James is very pleased with the rubber bear.

Addition from Claire.

Just a note as the Baddeley *is in and we mustn't miss the mail. Thank you for my lovely soap. I started using it straight away and am keeping it strictly for myself. We have had a very enjoyable Christmas and the children were very good out on Christmas day but Jamie wouldn't go to sleep that night – teeth trouble as well as excitement I think.*

It was the first time we have had all the Europeans up here and I think the party was quite successful.

28 December

Rainy. Claire getting ready for fancy dress. *Baddeley* came, Vaughan to tea and later with Bishop Hill for bath.

To party as an Arab Merchant, Claire the merchandise. Back about 11.30.

31 December

Kovala sighted. C and I out in launch – brought Mr Sykes ashore, also new charge hand, Robert. Sykes staying with us.

1958

1 January

Riotous noise in night – some of our bananas cut down. I doing monthly accounts – 9s. 9d. out, inexplicably.

Interesting talking with Sykes. Thinking hard about future and wrote Keith indicating I am not keen on returning here next tour.

4 January

I listed ferns and club-mosses of Santa Cruz Islands and described them as far as possible.

Put old cartridge case on kitten's hurt paw – secured with elastic band and bandage to make splint.

5 January

Fine. To beach with family. Low spring tide 9.30. Jamie enjoyed himself in the shallows. Arranged to all go to Sundi River early tomorrow for the week.

6 January

Up at 5.40 am. Off in launch with family and boys at 7.15 am. By truck to camp and then to workings. Claire and I walked round bush, collected some epiphytic ferns.

7 January

Losing quite a bit of blood from suspected hookworm –

rather demoralizing (later, in England, this was found to be due to a polyp, which was removed surgically).

8 January

Feeling better than yesterday, also children behaving better, especially James.

9 January

Boys getting on with poisoning. I put in five new control line posts with Alfred in westerly direction.

In the afternoon inspected past work with Paul.

In the evening, we watched scores of rats in the tent.

10 January

Cut and surveyed the last line to the east at the road bend. Back at sundown. Had hot baths, all glad to be back.

11 January

Claire and I to hospital to look for medicine for hookworm. Found some capsules 'to be taken as directed by a veterinary surgeon.'

After tea sorted out ferns for British Museum.

12 January

Found .22 rifle with wasps' nest inside barrel. It was lucky I happened to look along the barrel before putting in a round to shoot a flying-fox.

16 January

Michael out all morning fishing with Camnis in canoe – not back till after lunch. Claire reports that Michael can actually swim!

21 January

With family in *Nausicaa* to Saboe Bay, there met *Toby* coming back and followed it back to Peou, having received £500 from Firth, who spent the rest of the morning looking at my books.

Letter to Aunt Erica and Aunt Mu.

Thank you for both your letters.

I have had quite a correspondence with David Walford, whom you mentioned, about an automatic pistol which I succeeded in illegitimately importing into the Protectorate! So we know each other, you might say, though the relationship is *somewhat that of the law and the criminal! (The English police had asked my father to hand in his Colt .32, which he had had in Africa in the 1930s; so he sent it out to me, for protection against crocodiles at close quarters. I did not realize that I would not be allowed to import it.)*

This time there were no air letter forms on the island until the ship came, so the rush is even more chaotic than usual.

Forest Department operations at the moment are on the increase and I now have four staff and eleven labour, with a prospect of William and his family and four more labour descending on me at any moment. So what with our two houseboys, and Miriam, Hilda, John Mark and Veronica, we are getting to be quite a community!

Some new collapsible aluminium huts were to have arrived with the new labour, but haven't, but that is so typical of the Solomon Islands. After waiting two and a half years for my launch, my eyebrows or whatever it is, just fail to react.

*Michael often goes out for whole mornings at a time (*and *late for lunch) with Camnis, the houseboy, in a canoe fishing (*and *catching fish!). And last Saturday Claire, M, J and I all piled in the canoe and paddled up river to our old picnic place and fried sausages on the beach.*

Jamie had a wonderful time, scampering round at the water's edge laughing, only it sounded like drowning noises when we were trying to doze, and then throwing quantities of sand in our face when we weren't expecting it.

23 January

Doing plotting.

Potting of seedlings going on in nursery, also preparation of trial plots. Worked out trigonometrical method of putting in posts. Claire cut Michael's and my hair after tea.

24 January

Sent Mala and two boys to upper trial plot area to start clearing. I took *Nausicaa* round to jetty, using oars.

With Michael, Camnis, Matthias and John Mark to fetch the boys from Sundi River. Back 5.0 pm, after very pleasant trip. Malay apple fruiting, and we had some for supper.

30 January

Up to virgin kauri forest outlier to reconnoitre possible Nature Reserve. Found plenty of kauri including two clumps of big trees, also several saplings and some regeneration of both kauri and *Dacrydium*. Typical slope-type forest, easy to walk through.

At sunset took *Nausicaa* round to other side of wharf. Spoke to Nati. Mala cooking a crocodile he'd caught.

31 January

Off alone in *Nausicaa*. Ahead of Lionel, so stopped engine and drifted over reef near Sundi River. Saw a turtle hiding under a rock, fish and coral etc.

Michael out all morning fishing in canoe with Camnis and John Mark – caught fish which they ate on return with potatoes they dug up.

8 February

Tinkered with *Nausicaa* with Mala. Started writing an account of our stay on Vanikoro. After tea we all went down and visited the old steam engines by the workshops. (photo p. 206).

20 February

Telegram from Honiara about flying home.

22 February

Gave 200 cigarettes to boys to celebrate one hundredth acre poisoned. Laid out trial plots with Cula and Alfred.

27 February

Michael's birthday tea – tin lorry and soldiers for present. Then all out in launch to Kombe Bay and back at sunset.

1 March

Paid boys. Silas, Cula, Alfred and Nati de-blocking sewer. Midday temperature 90.5 degrees F – humid.

In the afternoon, family dip in pool then I to reef near jetty in launch for a goggled swim – got some measure of confidence.

2 March

All went down to beach, fine, rising tide. I waded to sandbank and stalked six grey waders which later came within eight or ten feet of me as I lay behind a fallen tree. Had a good view. Later a dozen or so waders of different species landed on the sandbank.

17 March

Condominium (of New Hebrides) vessel *Don Quijote* arrived with French Resident Commissioner and party. Went aboard to say hello. French boat out to reef – aqualunging.

18 March

Lancaster bomber with French markings came and circled reef from about 8 to 9 am.

Claire and I went out to reef in launch – at length tied up to raft over the shoal in False Passage. Dived with the rest of them, who were also dynamiting. Found: bits of wood, lead sheeting, incised lead ingots, pig iron, lumps of graphite, and an enormous anchor. Two more anchors were discovered later, one beneath a huge niggerhead of coral. Claire swam too, and saw the anchor.

The party included the Resident Commissioner, Madame Maj, another French couple, the captain, and divers including a New Zealander. Back late for lunch, both quite burnt.

21 March

Michael sick with fever.

Disc mollusc collected in jungle at 300 feet above sea level.

23 March

Very humid. Michael still feverish.

At 8.30 pm Claire discovered Michael having convulsions, which became rigour. These went on for about two hours, when he was put to sleep with a barbiturate (Nembutal) tablet obtained from Lionel. Meanwhile hot and cold water treatments were tried. Both of us desperately worried; but in the end he slept peacefully by our bed for the rest of the night.

24 March

Michael normal, drank a glass of milk. Sent telegram asking for interview with Doctor. Both very tired.

Talked to SMO on radio at 4.30 pm – gave M two cc of penicillin as a result. Nivaquin already given (one and a half) considered enough. Michael weak and miserable, to bed.

25 March

Down to talk to SMO, but not on the air in the morning.

Prepared swing for children and fixed it after lunch under the flamboyant tree. Spoke to SMO (Dr Roberts) at 4.30 pm. Tea in garden, then gave Michael repeat injection.

26 March

Waited for SMO am and pm, but not there.

29 March

Paid everyone. Took Michael down to sandbeach for swim at low tide before tea. After tea he enjoyed a swing.

30 March

Letter to Aunt Erica.

We have been rather a long time without any mail at all, but the DC is expected next week and then possibly Keith, and HE, and then the Milos.

Michael has been rather sick and had some alarming convulsions at one stage, but is now very much better and was down to the sand beach for a swim yesterday afternoon.

This morning I had all the boys up (dressed in their Sunday best) and took a group photograph of the lot, being twenty or so, also some of Matthias's family. If I sell them post-card enlargements at 6d. each I should make a bit of pocket money out of it, if enough buy them, that is!

Recently we've had several trees cut down round the house, mainly medium sized mango trees of which there were too many. It has let a lot of light in, opened the view up and let the breeze in. Also I think possibly there are fewer mosquitoes, but just as many flies unfortunately.

I have just fixed a swing under the flamboyant tree and everyone seems to enjoy it very much. James was very quick to go on it, but Michael hung back at first as he was convalescent. Yesterday however he got started with it and seemed to find it very funny.

We've been having a few premature April showers during these

Forest Dept. Vanikoro.
Left to right: William Piaito, ?, Paul (behind), Matthias, Miriam with Veronica, John Mark, and Hilda, with Silas standing behind them, ?, John Cula, the three right hand people not known, and right in front is Michael.

last few days and the south east trade seems to have set in in earnest at last. Before we'd been having a period of calms at the end of the north west season.

We had a lovely holiday when the French underwater expedition came. We went out to the raft on the reef and tied up the launch, and Claire and I swam about with masks and watched the goings on. The water was only ten or a dozen feet deep and beautifully clear. Now we are thinking of our journey home and it will be very good to see you again.

Michael was rather frightened when a French Lancaster bomber flew over to photograph the reef, but now he understands that we are all going in a big plane 'bimeby' and is quite looking forward to it. We've got a whole lot of records of 'Uncle Mac's Nursery Rhymes' and Christopher Robin ones and Michael loves them and dances all over the place. James frisks about too and gives more cause for amusement, as M tries to imitate his rapid waddle, which is very funny. Hope you are all well.

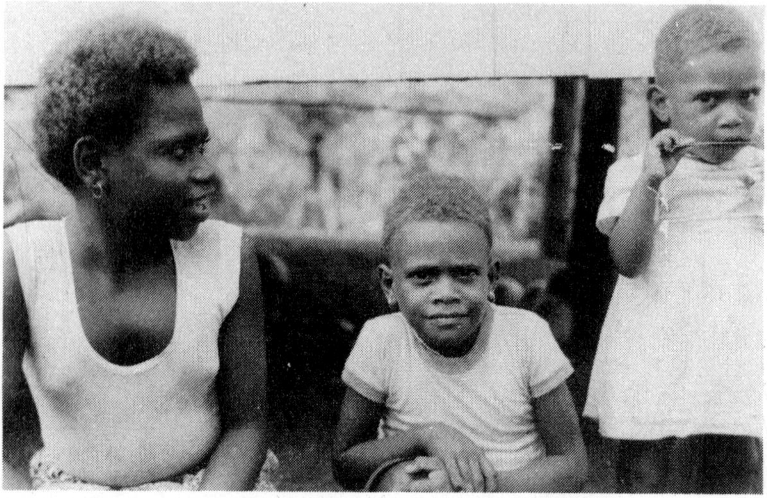

Hilda, John Mark, Veronica.

1 April

Walkabout in trial plots – *Pinus caribbea* and Balsa getting away now. Acacia wants light, so does balsa. Rest OK. Copied out Nggela and Reef Islands vocabulary.

2 April

Endeavour came, towed by *Toby*, with lots of mail. Had an exciting time opening it – birthday presents – harmonica for me from Daddy, *Lord of the Rings* from Aunt Erica, toys.

4 April

Letter to Aunt Erica.

At long last the mail has come, with all our birthday presents too! Thank you so much for The Two Towers. *I enjoyed reading the first book very much and now feel I have it all to look forward to over again! Also for Michael's present,* Benjamin Bunny, *which is one of the nicest I think. And for your two letters.*

Pineapples are like this (sketch). The leaves are rather swordlike, with toothed margins and thick like a cactus. It is related to the aloes. The fruit grows in the centre of the rosette, and has a top knot rather like a miniature plant, which when cut off and planted will eventually produce a pineapple itself, though a quicker way is to plant the suckers, plants that grow out of the side and will produce a fruit in about nine months.

I am so looking forward to an English winter again, strange as it may seem! I am very much inclined now to stay in England for keeps. I do not like being away from you and the family for such a long time. But there are all sorts of considerations to make it a difficult thing to decide. One thing, places like the Solomons are getting nearer to England in travelling time every year.

Michael was thrilled this morning at a dead rat of Pippa's on the verandah and led me by the hand to see the 'mouse' as he called it. Later, when Pippa started eating it, he called out 'No hand, no hand' and 'Poon, poon' meaning she was eating it with her hands and shouldn't she be given a spoon to eat it with!

Michael is completely better now from his illness.

HE's ship is nearly due now and I must end.

5 April

Long wait below at office. *Betua* came at last with rain. HE, Mrs Gutch and Captain Curtis came ashore. Had tea at Filewoods. M and J both very good. Jim up to lunch and to stay. Talked news and developments all afternoon and non-physical healing in evening. Steady rain.

10 April

Got ten gallon drum ready and later filled with water and taken to launch. Fixed awning frame. Got ready to go bush.

* * *

Arrival of mail. Vanikoro.
With 'missionary cooking pot' Alan Mala and Silan Ronoe.

Ray Angel, Jim Greber, Phil Haebeck (?)
Australians in the Bush. Vanikoro.

11 April

Stuff carried down to launch at jetty. Considerable trouble starting engine and then failure a quarter of a mile from jetty. Towed back by *Endeavour* – replaced carburettor screws. Off again and went steadily and without incident, except for retrieving Jamie's hat, all the way to Nanua, where we stopped for lunch, and were then unable to start – salt water in the cylinder – workshop job. So unloaded boat and pitched camp by the beach. Fish for supper. Many ants but harmless. Lovely white sand and clear water. Supper by the stars.

12 April

Rowed over to Lavaka Reef and dropped a messenger to go to Buma and summon the Council. Rest of morning spent going round island and then goggle fishing etc in pool on other side of island, Michael too. Jamie asleep.

In the afternoon all rested on fly-sheet spread out under trees. Then two canoes arrived, Ben and others. They went to Lavaka for the night, with Camnis. Fish baked in leaves for supper.

13 April

Sunday. Fixed clothes line for Claire. Then Jim and I did a pacing and compass circuit of the island. Then all had a lovely swim in Michael's pool near the tent.

Photographed the arrival of the council in two canoes and sat in on the council meeting.

Sighted *Mary* from other side of island. She came quickly, packed up and left. Manning and Keith arrived. Keith staying with us.

Birds on Nanua: many reef herons; little mangrove heron – small and hunched, yellow legs, seems unable to fly (or might be young reef heron); sandpiper (glimpsed); white headed petrel (flew past); pigeon.

17 April

Letter to Aunt Erica.

We have now had Jim Tedder's and Keith Trenaman's visit, and quite an assortment of ships, with the Milos *still to come.*

When Jim was here he had work to do on the other side of Vanikoro, including surveying, which I was going to help with, and taking a native doctor and two assistants who were part of the 'Yaws camapign' – giving everyone an injection against yaws to stamp the disease out of the Protectorate. We were going to spend the first night at Buma, on Tevai and the second one on Nanua, the dream island we'd never yet managed to visit. But on the way out we stopped at Nanua for lunch and then the launch's engine wouldn't start again, having salt water inside from a bust gasket – so we spent two nights on Nanua instead of one and were only too sorry to be rescued! The second day we rowed across to the mainland of Vanikoro and sent a boy by canoe to Buma and later two canoes came from Buma with the native council, and Jim had his council meeting on Nanua, with Claire and me present. The money that the natives get from the Government for the use of their forests is paid into the council, and Jim was helping them decide how to spend it. They are going to pay for a schoolteacher (salary £18 a year increasing to £36) – a schoolhouse, a council house, and pig-wire to keep out pigs from an enclosed area of allotments to be let out in plots at a rent of sixpence or one shilling per year to individual natives; also a selection of useful tools for communal use.

Nanua was glorious after Vanikoro – sandy beaches, clear water – millions of ants, but they didn't bite and one just let them swarm over one. We sent our house-boy away and camped by ourselves. We are arranging to break our journey at Calcutta coming home and hope to see something of the Himalayas by going up to Darjeeling for a few days, though it will be in the monsoon still. I am trying to get help from the Indian Forest Service and have visions of a Forest Department rest house in the foothills of the Himalayas with a view of Kanchenjunga and Everest (some hope!).

We feel it is too good an opportunity to miss and the difficulty is there are so many ways you can fly round the world that you don't know which to take and where to stop!

Most of all though we are looking forward to coming home to England and seeing you soon.

18 April

Caught extra cat and took it down, at length delivered it to the *Don Quijote* – wanted for rat island.

Letter from Claire to Aunt Erica.

Thank you so much for the blouse material, it is just the sort of thing I was wanting and I hope I am able to make it up nicely. Now that all our visitors have gone I must get on with some sewing for us all; time is so short now. Actually I believe we may have another visitor some time next month as Mr Trenaman wants to get the best authority on forests in Australia to come down and assess how much royalty the Timber Company should pay on wood they export. At the moment they pay a very low sum. The man who will be coming is, I think, the brother of Chris's tutor at Oxford.

Chris has told you all the news so I can only repeat how much we all loved Nanua, it was a wonderful break. The French ship Don Quijote *has been up again – this time to collect some New Hebridean Native Council members who have been doing a tour of the Solomons and are being transferred from one of our Government boats to a Condominium vessel. They were in the care of one French and one English DC, who we had up to lunch yesterday. They are all due to leave this afternoon. Mrs Filewood is going down to the New Hebrides with them as she has not been well lately and will fly to Australia from there. She could possibly have gone out on the timber ship which is calling next week, but they have had no reply to their query about a passage for her on it. Also she is quite keen to get the chance to see some more of the islands. I hope we are able to do our trip as we plan and that it is a success and does not prove too difficult with the children.*

Jamie has grown a lot in the last couple of months and has also got some more teeth, we were beginning to wonder just when he would get some more bottom teeth.

23 April

Spring tides. Had *Nausicaa* beached, scraped and painted. Did the copper anti-fouling paint myself and anti-fouled myself in the process. Back late to lunch, cleaned up and slept solidly from two until four. Office work after tea.

24 April

Mary arrived in the morning with Jim aboard. *Delos* came in towards noon. Jim and I went aboard and had lunch with Professor Elbert who is a philologist investigating the local language. Each village speaks a different language. The professor is interviewing Alfred.

25 April

Got two Pileni boys for Professor – one from Company.

Letter to Aunt Erica.

It is all the same as usual here, and rather muggy and enervating at present. I'm going round to my camp at Sundi River later today, but there's a missionary boat due in today and therefore a chance to send a letter.

The road is on the other side of the island now and there is a bridge over the Willi Willi, which flows north. It is pretty there, very good kauri forest and very steep country, the road with hairpin bends and steep drops to the river. Where the ground is exposed it is all red.

There are lots and lots of mangoes now, and Michael's face has got a sort of yellow look around the chin from being perpetually soaked in juice. He always dashes out at dawn to get the night's windfalls. We've also been having pawpaw, pineapple, bananas and a few oranges, but there are masses of pineapples just getting ready. We have never had so much fruit here.

3 May

Took three carbon tetrachloride capsules for hookworm, followed by magnesium sulphate, followed by breakfast, at approximately one hour intervals. Paid boys.

4 May

Sleepless night.

Alan Nielen, Michael, Claire, and Jamie at the corner of Uniport hut.

5 May

Claire and I off early with boys to Sundi River, lift in truck, taking two Uniport huts. Weather cleared a little. Got up the walls of one hut. After lunch and a rest at camp we started back at 4.0 pm with the launch to ourselves.

6 May

Off again with Claire and family. Steady rain all morning, but got one hut completed by afternoon and another half completed. Lunch in tent.

22 May

Overslept till 8.0 am, hasty breakfast, then to see boys at work. Later caught truck to workings, then inspected lines. Back in launch at dark – lost rudder coming in over sandbank.

23 May

Boys out looking for rudder and gudgeon. I went down later. Looked at seedlings in nursery and planned plots.

In the afternoon I went along mangroves at low tide looking for rudder.

Michael sick – sore eyes – suspected measles.

Thinking about collecting birds for British Museum.

24 May

On Claire's instigation moved three sick boys to police lines, to be waited on by convalescents.

Silas out to collect small birds for British Museum.

26 May

Public holiday. Beached launch and fitted new gudgeons – cannibalizing Company's Simplex at Lionel's suggestion. Finished by tea-time – some improvization with an old eye-bolt found on the scrap-heap.

28 May

Michael at last developed measles spots.

29 May

Michael with heavy rash, but insisted on being up all day.

1 June

Henry brought in a male Golden Whistler he'd shot with bow and arrow. Painted it and put it in spirit for British Museum. Hoping to make a bit of a collection for Macdonald.

3 June

Henry brought up a white rumped swiftlet that he'd caught alive, for British Museum. Killed it, spent afternoon painting it and put it in spirit.

James with measles rash, but full of beans all the same.

8 June

Letter to Aunt Erica.

It's been very wet recently, but yesterday was a beautiful day from beginning to end, sunshine, a pleasant breeze and the air as clear as crystal. Even the flies and mosquitoes were on holiday and we spent the afternoon out under the trees. Today, however, the usual humidity is back.

Measles has been through this side of the island and is now at the native village of Buma on the other side. Michael and James have both had it now. Michael was pretty miserable for a day or two, but Jamie just ran around as usual all the time, though he had plenty of spots.

Both house boys had it at the same time, so we had an opportunity to get in training for England with the house-work.

We're expecting a visit shortly – the Kovala, *with a naval officer and a member of the Advisory Council; also Professor Elbert, who is being picked up from the Reef Islands where he has been staying a couple of months. He's a philologist from the University of Hawaii and stayed with us on the way out – very nice chap indeed.*

I think it rather unlikely we shall break our journey in India, unless we get a very favourable letter from the forestry chap I've written to in Calcutta. I'm not keen on mucking around in foreign places with the children and would prefer the extra time in England. If we come direct we should leave Honiara at 8 am on 26 August (that is fixed anyway), spend two days in Sydney and arrive at London airport at 12.45 pm on 2 September (Monday). We'll probably come on a Britannia, stopping at Darwin, Jakarta, Singapore, Calcutta, Karachi, Beirut and Zurich. It's got to be fixed fairly soon now. I don't suppose we shall see much on the way, but I'm quite looking forward to it anyway. If we stop in India we'd probably arrive in England on 13 September (Saturday).

Now it gets to thinking about packing up I feel sorry to be leaving

Vanikoro – it has been our home for so long and though like anywhere else it has its disadvantages, you can live fairly close to Nature and without too much fuss. I expect we shall come back to the Solomons – there is an empty house waiting for us on Isabel, in the West – same old story!

11 June

Discussed stopover or not – *not*!

Painted rufous fronted fantail – pleased with it.

12 June

Public holiday – but with Alfred to SP number one – measured trees and looked at plantings. Tried to catch small birds with .22 without success. Got wet going back. After tea planted a Syzigium tree.

14 June

In the morning I did bird census in Home plantation and in the afternoon, sketched a prepared kingfisher.

15 June

Sunday. Completed kingfisher with much help from Claire, then cat got it and ate the head – very mad indeed.

Painted pigeon.

16 June

Took Cula and company to Ambi area experimental poisoning and left them to get on with it. Stalked a flock of small birds, shot a male broadbill. In the afternoon painted it quite successfully, put it in spirit.

18 June

Did some leaf tracings. Preparing to go to bush (Kombe River). Set off about 4 pm with Silas and party, they having returned from camp earlier. Moored boat safely up river and walked to camp.

19 June

Overcast. Surveyed from Kombe River to point reached last time, then started on other side of river. Knocked off at 11.15 am in time to avoid downpour. Off again at 3 pm, but soon retreated in rain. Rain all night.

20 June

Sent Henry to take *Nausicaa* down river. Rain stopped at 11 am so we completed survey of cut line towards Saboe – some kauri forest there. Returning we met Henry who said launch was full of water and rudder missing! Much anguish. Struck camp and set off down – I diverted my footsteps and miraculously found rudder in mangroves by river immediately!! Engine out, however because of a wet magneto. Favourable wind, but it was near gale force so we tried to sail home. Boat difficult to control in wind. Everyone was manning the sweeps – tending to go broadside on – steep seas and breakers, reef to leeward, but managed to round the point and got into sheltered waters. So home. Much relief. Sticks of tobacco all round.

23 June

Laid out trial plots with Silas and Afred.

In the afternoon worked on launch – dug out Company's magneto – good spark. Not starting yet though.

* * *

24 June

Removed half a gallon of water from sump. Worked on engine all day without getting it to start. Made new gasket for carburettor.

26 June

Milos came in at dawn. Down with Claire and Michael to get mail. Silas also had an unsuccessful try on the engine.

Letter to Aunt Erica.

It is with mixed feelings that we are getting ready to leave this place for good. It has been our home for so long that I do not know how we shall feel in a strange house at Oxford. It will be worst for Michael I should think – I can remember how helplessly furious I was when we moved out of Oakfield. Of course Michael has had a bit of moving around in the early days so he may be more conditioned to it than I was.

A new engineer and a Polish secretary have come on the ship, also three Australians for the bush, one of them is a German from Danzig. We have met the latter and he seems a nice chap. He has two very expensive cameras and is a professional photographer (or was). I have told him to watch out for the damp and fungus that attacks cameras – he didn't know about it, either.

Last week I was camping up the Kombe River in very wet weather and the launch got filled up with water where it was moored down on the river. We rowed it back with a gale behind us, heavy seas and a reef to leeward – much *too exciting. We got back OK, but I've spent the last three days solid working on the engine and it still won't start!*

28 June

Down with Claire, collected cash from office (£500), paid boys. Silas produced a slaty flycatcher, which I painted in the afternoon.

9 July

Up early and after a wait, off in *Missawen* to Sundi River with Alf, Camnis and Mesoi. Lift up in Jim's chassis – dangerous! Arrived at hauler. I was taking a photograph from down below when the heavy steel cable smacked down and struck me a glancing blow on the leg – a lucky escape – skin just broken. It also took the viewfinder off the camera which I was holding.

16 July

Rumour the *Melanesian* is lost!! [See entry for 17 August 1957.]

18 July

Melanesian now thought to be lost with all hands – six Europeans and about thirty Solomons Islanders – a terrible and mysterious disaster – planes searching the seas.

19 July

Wreckage of *Melanesian* starting to be found.

Screwing together parts of open crate for chest for our packing.

26 July

Preparing for party, which started at 7.30 pm and went on till 1.30 am. There was singing and dancing, and flash photography by Gideon and me; and we were given a present of £25. Bed at 2.0 am.

27 July

Wrote six new verses of the 'Vanikoro Bush Song'.

29 July

Walked up to new Uniport camp on hilltop on old ridge. Put in posts down ridge with Alf on base line bearing 310 degrees. Discovered gross inaccuracy in map.

31 July

Down to see launch. To Sundi River in launch with Alfred – going like the wind – with the wind. Carried pack up to camp. Slept under leaf shelter.

1 August

Inspected poisonings with Robert, including complete treated area. Showed boys exhibition patch done last September.

2 August

Paid boys. Claire had a sale, made £16.

Ben Tua and his small sons, Albert and Tumoto came – tea together on lawn.

5 August

Rain in night – water in taps at last.

Concern at non-arrival of *Toby*.

7 August

Saw Silas about party.

Finished crate for chest.

* * *

8 August

Silas fetching boys from bush, Robert and company walked.

We all went down to the party at Pattisons – a feast of pig and fish. Took flash colour pictures, and Claire made a speech. Boys danced afterwards.

11 August

Toby arrived at last. Down with Claire to see it arrive; also saw Silas.

12 August

Down and saw Lionel – says *Mary* not leaving Kira Kira as native crew refuse to go out of sight of land, being afraid because of the *Melanesian* disaster.

Finding it difficult to settle down to anything now – wandered round trial plots. Packing etc. in the afternoon.

16 August

Telegram – *Kovala* coming for us next week! Some doubt as to which plane we'll catch.

Re-measured kauris by manager's house.

18 August

Off early with Alfred and Silas to Lawrence River camp. Walked round the pre-exploitation plots giving instructions. Lunched in a fine stand of kauri at number two; also identified some trees that hadn't succumbed to poison. Returned to camp via other side, swam in the river, then back home.

* * *

19 August

Did a demonstration preparation of ferric hydroxide (antidote for arsenic) for benefit of Silas and George.

Final clearance before packing suitcases.

20 August

Cases carried down to store. Pre-pack of air luggage and a pre-weigh – 164 pounds – twelve pounds to spare.

21 August

More or less finished packing. Boys painting launch and digging a hole in trial plots.

After dark *Kovala* came in, with mail.

22 August

American yacht *Utopia* came in.

Went aboard *Kovala* about 10.0 am and left before noon.

Met Captain Wild (the crews of the government boats would not now put to sea unless they had a European skipper). Set course for Santa Anna. Lunch before we got outside the reef. Took a pill. Heavy rolling set in.

23 August

Claire not feeling too good. Camnis sick. Spent morning on the forehatch. Bread, cheese and beer for lunch. Sighted Santa Anna before sunset. 'Set' of twenty-five miles (due to faulty compass?). Heavy rolling in night.

24 August

Sunday. Arrived Kira Kira about 1.40 am. Went ashore 7.0 am. Rehabilitated passion-fruit cuttings with Jim.

Breakfast – grapefruit, porridge, egg, lemon marmalade! Michael and James having grand time with Gregory and Ian. Saw new house, and balsa plot – eighteen inch girth after seventeen months, some more! Away again 10.0 am.

Easy going till we got to the end of Makira, then got very rough – confused seas coming up to Marau sound.

25 August

Berthed at Honiara 5 am – new quay. Breakfast aboard, all very pleasant. Phoned Keith – heavy baggage to PWD, then got Land-rover and down to work – bank, passports, hospital all done. Lunch at Trenamans. Weighing in at Trade Scheme.

26 August

With Keith to river – thence to airport and off to Lae. Weather a bit mirky. Hotel Cecil as usual.

27 August

Off in skymaster. Weather fine at Moresby. Photographed barrier reef and coast near Mackay. Formalities at Brisbane and supper. Arrived Sydney about 11.30 pm.

28 August

Walked over to the Domain. Things to do in George Street. Fun in David Jones' toy department. Back via botanical gardens and had tea there. Children having soup in bedroom.

29 August

Packed up and took luggage by taxi to air terminal. Then to

botanical gardens and eventually met Helen Filewood for lunch – a koala bear each for the kids.

After we got to the terminal, Claire found she had forgotten her watch – dashed back to the hotel in a taxi to get it and found I had also left my camera on top of a cupboard – then out to Mascot – Hungarian dinner. Off at 9.0 pm to Darwin, in a Britannia.

30 August

Cloud seas over Indonesia, photos at dawn. Saw Java well. Stop at Jakarta. On to Singapore – into monsoon. Shower and refreshments there; also at Calcutta, where we bought a shawl. On towards Karachi as darkness fell. Claire stayed aboard at Karachi, while I talked to an Indian at the refreshment place. Left for Beirut about midnight.

31 August

Reached Beirut after about seven hours' flight. Clocks back three hours. Dark as we arrived. Coffee at airport, then on over the Mediterranean. Snap of Cyprus and cloud sea at dawn.

Up Italy and over the Alps to Zurich, then on to London airport where Daddy met us and drove us home – tea at 'The Kettle' on the edge of the New Forest. Fine, lovely to be back.

As a closing piece, two letters that we received after we left the Solomon Islands are included here. One is from Geoff Dennis, the other from the Tedders.

BRITISH SOLOMON ISLANDS PROTECTORATE

Per Airmail FORESTRY DEPARTMENT,
GPO BOX 6,
Honiara,
Guadalcanal.
June, 1959.

* * *

C.J. Hadley Esq.,
c/o Imperial Forestry Institute,
South Parks Road,
OXFORD
England.

Dear Chris,

I do hope you, Clare and the infants are well and enjoying the change of climate and environment in UK.

Keith T. has asked me to send you the records of Sample Plot No. 1 (Vanikoro – Home SP) and, as the enclosures are all that I could find among the litter of records in the office which might be what you require, I am sending them accordingly. Would you please return them, in due course?

As you are probably aware, Keith departed for UK after I had been only a week in the department, so I didn't have much time to learn what's what. I've been tied down to the desk most of the time since, but manage a trip out occasionally to visit the plots at Tenaru, Rove and Mt. Austen, and spent three interesting weeks recently examining Pometia *forest areas behind Rere,* Campnosperma *and* Terminalia brassii *areas at Allardyce Harbour (Sta. Ysabel), and* Dillenia *forest on Vangunu accompanied by two timber experts from Australia, who are interested in forming a big company to develop the natural timber resources in British Solomon Islands. Both Rere and Vangunu offer the best possibilities at present – difficulties of access from the coast and lack of building sites, road making material etc. preclude Allardyce for the time being – and something worthwhile might develop if only Government will speed up its Companies Registration and Forestry legislation. I look forward to Keith's return, when I hope to go bush more frequently.*

I keep fit – haven't suffered an attack of malaria yet, in spite of almost thirteen years of residence here, and must have some natural immunity to fever and some other local diseases. Honiara continues to grow – unfortunately still topheavy with Government servants – and we now have big ships berthing alongside the new wharves at Pt. Cruz.

The Duke's visit was a huge success, as you probably have heard, and even Graciosa Bay was honoured by his presence. The forestry personnel from Vanikoro managed to secure passage to Santa Cruz to see him. The Duke deflated the ego of some of the VIP at the Government House reception by requesting all the gentlemen to attend without coats, and set the example himself!

Please let me know if I can do anything for you from this end, Chris. Best wishes to you and yours.

Sincerely, Geoff D. [Dennis]

Kira Kira
San Cristoval
22 May 1959

Dear Claire and Chris,
At last the photos – such as they are, after our enlarging! Anyway, hope they bring back happy memories!

Have just returned from two and a half months in Santa Cruz and Reef Islands, to hear that we really are leaving Kira Kira at the end of June. Needless to say it hurts tremendously to leave our garden, but on the other hand it is time our boys were made to toe the line by other European children.
1 June. This letter got away to a good start but then I slipped up, couldn't get it ready in time for the ship so it was left.

Besides the dreadful news of leaving Eastern our main items are Prince Philip's visit to Graciosa Bay and me climbing Tinakula.

Perhaps you have seen the television film of the Prince's visit? It was on recently in the UK and according to a letter from Phil Pudsey Dawson the Graciosa Bay section was most thrilling though my 'bony knees obscured half the screen at times'. The day was most informal. Rather than tell you the whole programme a copy of the Eastern News *is en route sea mail with a ball to ball description of the day written by the Press Officer (for the day) Mike Russell who next day became Agricultural Officer Eastern. You should have seen the ships arriving from Reefs. On one trip* Mary *had 150 passengers, luckily the weather was kind by then, after a small hurricane had blown the day after we reached the Bay. We crossed in a rolly sea but no wind. At 4.0 in the morning I went on deck and Prince Philip said the usual – 'Can't see land yet', in fact it was blowing from the north-west with squalls of rain and considering the moon was but the size of a rind of cheese one was lucky to see the sea. At dawn land was sighted fifteen miles to the north – wrong side of Santa Cruz – so it was 8.30 before we reached calm waters. After we unloaded and not before, the wind and rain started and continued for four days. From then on the weather was the usual pleasant Graciosa Bay with the big day just perfect. Prince Philip was easy, charming and pleased when the programme allowed him two hours of private sailing in his* Fairy Fox. *Told Margie to 'grab a fork and tuck in' during lunch, which was held above the green pool. Later the official party led by HE (while Philip was sailing) invaded our leaf hut, stole our bananas, asked Harry when tea would be ready, then swam with Margie and the children from the beach.*

The Davenports, I think we told you that Bill and Pearl are American anthropologists now living at Graciosa Bay, were absent on the day. Bill was taken seriously ill in February and all but died. The Southern Cross *called in luckily and took him to Kira Kira. It was thought he had cerebral malaria but the malariologist in New Guinea has since told him it was probably a typhus – like your sickness Chris.*

We spent a fortnight or more in the Reefs after nearly six weeks at Graciosa Bay, then of course I had a tour of the outer islands including Vanikoro where Mary *sat on a reef at 5.0 one evening off Saboe. This delayed us twenty four hours then rain in the legendary Vanikoro style delayed us and finally stopped us from leaving for Ticopia for days. I was frightened I wouldn't find Ticopia and quite convinced Vanikoro couldn't be found with such rain. Forestry Lodge is much the same. I have obtained a hydraulic ram and hope to instal it this October. It will pump water from the swimming stream into a tank. Found white ants in the bathroom but you are probably not worried about that detail.*

On the way from Reefs Headman Joseph Hool, another Santa Cruzian and self landed by canoe on a steep boulder beach on the north-east side of Tinakula. From the sea the only obvious route seemed to lie up one spur which had vegetation almost to the summit on the north-east side. On the beach we found an old leaf shelter and a pool with two pints of fresh water. Before dark I went around the coast and climbed up into the pandanus forest. Great gullies twenty to thirty feet deep and less than twenty feet wide with steep crumbling sides occur every few hundred yards. These converge until near the summit they are separated by inches wide ridges or even join. After a quick climb Joseph had managed to get half way up the hill by walking in a gully.

Next morning at 6.0 we set off – not up the obvious gully – to a ridge and up through 300 or more feet of pandanus and coconuts, then one hundred feet of coconuts, then six feet high kunai grass, tree ferns and millions of tiny ants. Birds in dozens, pigeons within feet of us. Within 400 feet of the summit our ridge was six inches of crumbling scoria with a drop three sides of us, so we retreated 500 feet and crossed a gully onto another ridge. This also stopped in a knife edge, so we joined a gully and climbed up it. Loose scoria rock, a slide of fifty degrees one hundred yards long, cut out of lava and polished by the water was the most difficult piece. Large falls of rock we carefully avoided, though under one we found drips of water and stayed a while to collect some. Joseph and Patterson decided it was high enough for them, their feet were also sore. I went on, vegetation now being inch-high moss on the stones. Within fifty feet of the summit ridge, clouds came down and I retreated. It was a 'nark', but immediately on the other side of the summit ridge the ground is but a cliff face so had I reached the ridge I might have a) gone right over, or b) found the gullies cutting back into the ridge made progress along it impossible. Still you would have enjoyed it and I was sorry you were not there with your climbing experience. We should have somehow made time years ago to do the climb. We reached the bottom exhausted and dry and covered in black scoria dust by 2.30. The ship came in at 4.0 and it was home via Graciosa Bay. The mountain is still quiet; no rumblings while we were there and just a little steam near the top.

But tell us how the rest of your course went and what you feel about going to Nyasaland. Wouldn't you prefer to return here now?

Did Keith tell you of interest in the forests near Rere, Guadalcanal, as well as Isabel and Vangunu. On tonight's news one of the timber men said 'When the forests are cleared it might be good agricultural land for cash crops'. On this depressing note – love from us all,

Margie and Jim.

POSTSCRIPT

After we left the Solomons we had a postgraduate year at Oxford, where our daughter Sally was born and I finished my work on the growth rate of kauri pine and worked on the ferns and club-mosses of the Santa Cruz Islands.

In 1959 we went to Tanganyika (soon to become Tanzania), first to Tabora, where Deborah was born, and I did enumerations in the dry deciduous 'miombo' woodland, and then to head office in Dar es Salaam. At this stage the boys started going to boarding school in England (or rather Michael did, Jamie later on) and we returned in 1964. I was a forestry consultant in Somerset, Devon and Dorset for a couple of years, then became Nature Conservancy Warden Naturalist of Upper Teesdale National Nature Reserve. Then in 1971 we moved to Lewes and I became Nature Conservancy Council Assistant Regional Officer for Surrey.

In 1977 Claire and I separated and in 1983 I retired to live in Swanage. Claire has re-married and the children are thriving in their various occupations. Michael works for Lloyd Northover in London and promotes corporate images; Jamie has given up being a yacht skipper and now manages property in Mallorca; Sally is a team senior in social work in London; and Deborah is art mistress at Hornsey school for girls, and also acting coordinator for environmental studies.

EXPLANATORY NOTES FOR SOME OF THE TERMS USED.

Survey

Chain and compass survey is usually done by a team of three men, one at each end of the chain and one with the note-book, compass and Abney level. The chain may be sixty-six, or one hundred feet long and measures the distance from point to point. Direction is measured by prismatic compass and the slope of the ground by Abney level. The distance measured up or down a slope will always be longer than the distance on the map and the map distance is found by multiplying the ground distance by the cosine of the angle. A page from a field note-book (see figure) illustrates this. The example also shows heights above sea level (measured by aneroid barometer), streams, cliffs and form lines, which are rough contours showing the shape of the land.

The data are plotted on a sheet of cartridge paper using a box-wood scale, protractor, dividers and a sharp pencil. The survey usually goes in a loop, joining up with the starting point or another point of the survey, and when plotted on paper there is usually a closing error, which has to be adjusted.

Enumeration

Recording of trees by girth class and species was usually done in chain-wide strips every ten chains (a chain is sixty-six feet) at right angles to the survey lines which ran along the crests of the ridges, taking a ten per cent sample. Timber heights of a proportion of the trees were measured by means of a simple but ingenious device called a Christen hypsometer, which works by the principle of similar triangles. A form factor for use in calculating the volume of tapering trees from a measurement of girth at breast height was obtained by measurement of felled logs.

On Guadalcanal, where the terrain was less rugged and aerial photographs were available, it was possible to use partly randomized strips so that a reliable minimum estimate could be obtained by statistical analysis.

Silviculture

After logging, the naturally occurring regeneration of kauri seedlings is usually swamped by invading secondary species such as *Macaranga.* The first approach to this problem was to cut lines through the secondary growth at intervals. letting the light in. A development of this method was to frill-girdle the invading trees with a knife and pour a dilute solution of sodium arsenite into the frill with a fine-spouted watering can.

Sample Plots

Groups of kauri at different stages were chosen for regular measurement to obtain growth data. The trees were marked with a ring of paint where measurement was made with a steel tape, and the plots were demarcated by trenches in the ground at the sides and corners. Plots of kauri seedlings were measured for height growth.

Trial Plots

Small plots were cleared and planted with quick-growing exotic species as an experiment.

Profile Diagrams

When in the forest all you can usually see is a mass of small trees and the lower part of a large tree a few yards away. The structure of the forest may be studied in the following way: a narrow strip about two hundred feet long is marked out and all the small trees up to a certain size are felled, identified if possible and measured. The height, height to first branch, width and depth of crown of the larger trees are then measured, and the position of all the trees, large and small is plotted. A diagram can then be drawn to scale, showing the structure of the forest.

Trochus shells

These are a marine gastropod with a pearly flattish-based conical shell. They are found on the reef and traded. It is illegal to collect those under two and a half inches in diameter.

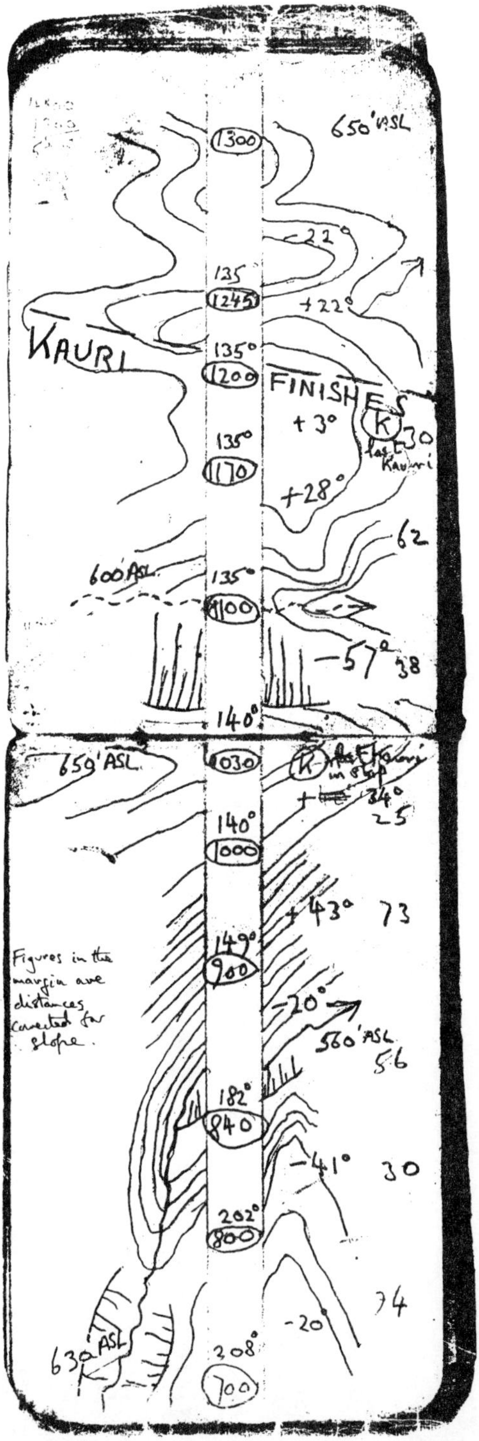

A page from a field note-book.

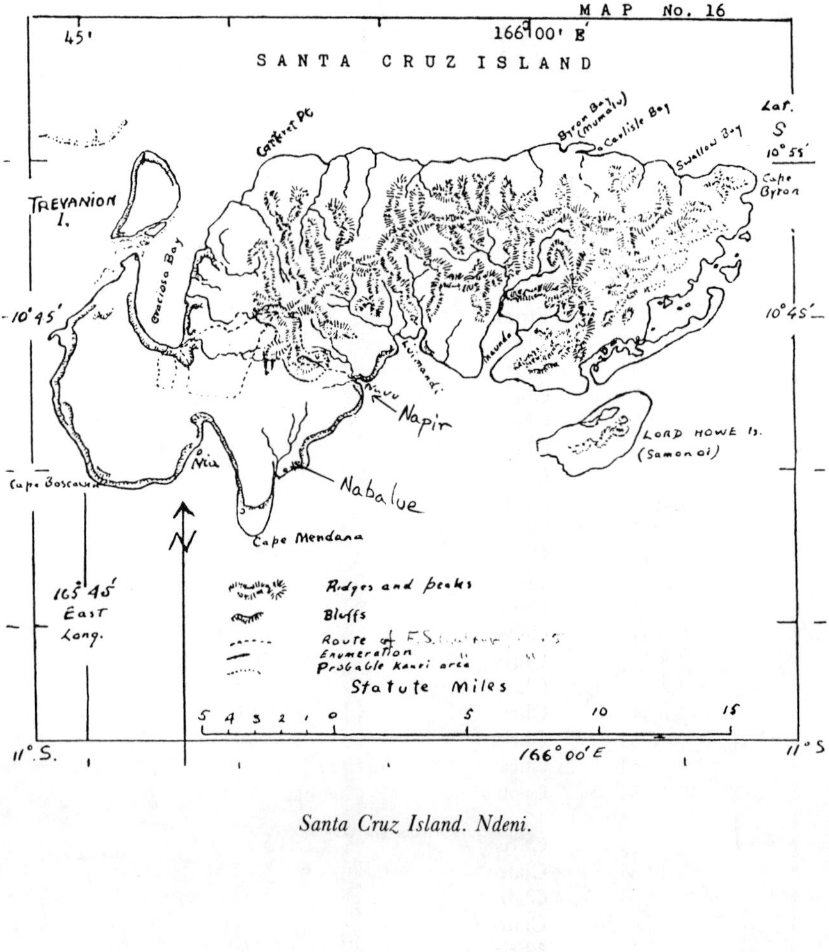

Santa Cruz Island. Ndeni.

APPENDIX 1

LIST OF LETTERS USED IN TEXT

Abbreviations. A.E.: Aunti Erica. D.&T.: Daddy and Tiggie.

Date	From	To	Page	Notes
10.11.53	Chris	A.E.	11	
19.11.53	Chris	A.E.	12	
5.12.53	Chris	A.E.	12	
11.12.53	Chris	A.E.	13	
13.12.53	Claire	Erica and Mu	14	
4.1.54	Chris	A.E.	19	
11.2.54	Chris	D.&T.	40	
25.3.54	Chris	D.&T.	50	
28.3.54	Chris	Aunt Muriel	52	
10.4.54	Chris	Aunt Phyl	57	
12.5.54	Chris	D.&T.	65	
20.6.54	Chris	D.&T.	79	
4.8.54	Chris	Aunt Phyl	85	
4.8.54	Chris	A.E.	86	
15.8.54	Chris	D.&T.	87	
29.10.54	Chris	D.&T.	111	
30.10.54	Chris	A.E.	111	
17.11.54	Geoff Dennis	Chris and Claire	114	
3.12.54	Chris	A.E.	117	
12.12.54	Claire	A.E.	120	
19.12.54	Claire	Tiggie	121	
13.1.55	Claire	A.E.	127	
10.2.55	Chris	D.&T.	134 135	
12.2.55	Claire	Tiggie	136	
11.2.55	Chris	A.E.	135	
27.2.55	Chris	A.E.	138	
28.2.55	Chris	D.&T.	139	
2.3.55	Chris	D.&T.	140	
26.3.55	Chris	Aunt Muriel	142	
28.3.55	Chris	D.&T.	143	
7.4.55	Chris	A.E.	145	
19.4.55	Chris	A.E.	147 148	2 entries
5.5.55	Chris	A.E.	152	

Date	From	To	Page	Notes
29.6.55	Chris	D.&T.	156	
1.7.55	Chris	A.E.	156	
2.7.55	Claire	A.E.	157 & 158	2 dates
7.9.55	Chris	D.&T.	166	
26.9.55	Claire	Erica & Mu	168	
26.9.55	Chris	A.E.	169	
21.10.55	Chris	D.&T.	173	
23.20.55	Chris	A.E.	174	
12.11.55	Chris	A.E.	179	
24.11.55	Claire	Chris	184	
9.12.55	Claire	Erica & Mu	187	
9.12.55	Claire	Chris	188	
24.12.55	Claire	Chris	191	
28.12.55	Claire	Chris	192	
12.12.55	Chris	D.&T.	192	
21.12.55	Claire	D.&T.	192	
28.1.56	Chris	A.E.	200	
29.1.56	Chris	D.&T.	201	
26.2.56	Claire	Tiggie	205	
5.3.56	Chris	A.E.	207	
5.3.56	Chris	D.&T.	208	
30.3.56	Chris	D.&T.	213	
1.4.56	Chris	A.E.	214	
15.9.56	Chris	Erica & Mu	216	
24.9.56	Chris	A.E.	216	
12.10.56	Chris	A.E.	217	
22.10.56	Chris	A.E.	219	
18.11.56	Chris and Claire	A.E.	222	
16.12.56	Chris and Claire	A.E.	225	
30.12.56	Chris	A.E.	227	
11.2.57	Chris	A.E.	233	
28.2.57	Chris	A.E.	237	
17.3.57	Chris	A.E.	240	
9.4.57	Chris	A.E.	244	
4.5.57	Chris	A.E.	245	
26.5.57	Chris	A.E.	247	
5.8.57	Chris	A.E., D.&T.	254	
5.8.57	Chris	A.E.	256	
11.8.57	Chris	A.E.	257	
12.8.57	Claire	A.E.	259	
23.10.57	Claire	A.E.	262	
21.11.57	Chris and Claire	A.E.	263	
27.11.57	Claire	Erica & Mu	265	

Date	From	To	Page	Notes
27.12.57	Chris and Claire	Erica & Mu	268	
21.1.58	Chris	Erica & Mu	272	
30.3.58	Chris	A.E.	276	
4.4.58	Chris	A.E.	278	
17.4.58	Chris	A.E.	282	
18.4.58	Claire	A.E.	283	
No date	Chris	A.E.	284	
8.6.58	Chris	A.E.	287	
26.6.58	Chris	A.E.	290	

APPENDIX 2

The Vanikoro Bush Song
(Some of the more printable verses)
Tune: Old Trinidad

In Vanikoro, or so I hear,
The situation is mighty queer,
All night long, work overtime,
All day in hot sun, skivin' time.

Drinkin' chai and coco-cola,
Drinkin' chai and coco-cola,
Both before and after dinner,
Skivin' for the Company dollar.

Bill Powell the foreman's a bit of a card,
And he's there to see that you all work hard,
And at the moment, as a matter of fact,
It's a bit of a wonder you all ain't sacked.

Drinkin' etc.

I've often heard the manager pray
People not to shoot cows in the family way.
Now Nielen with the Texas boots is back
The prospects of the herd ain't quite so black.

Drinkin' etc.

The forest officer comes now and then,
But now he ain't goin' to come again,
'Cos he says he's used up all his luck
A hangin' on like grim death to Jim Moore's truck.

Drinkin' etc.

LIST OF ILLUSTRATIONS AND MAPS

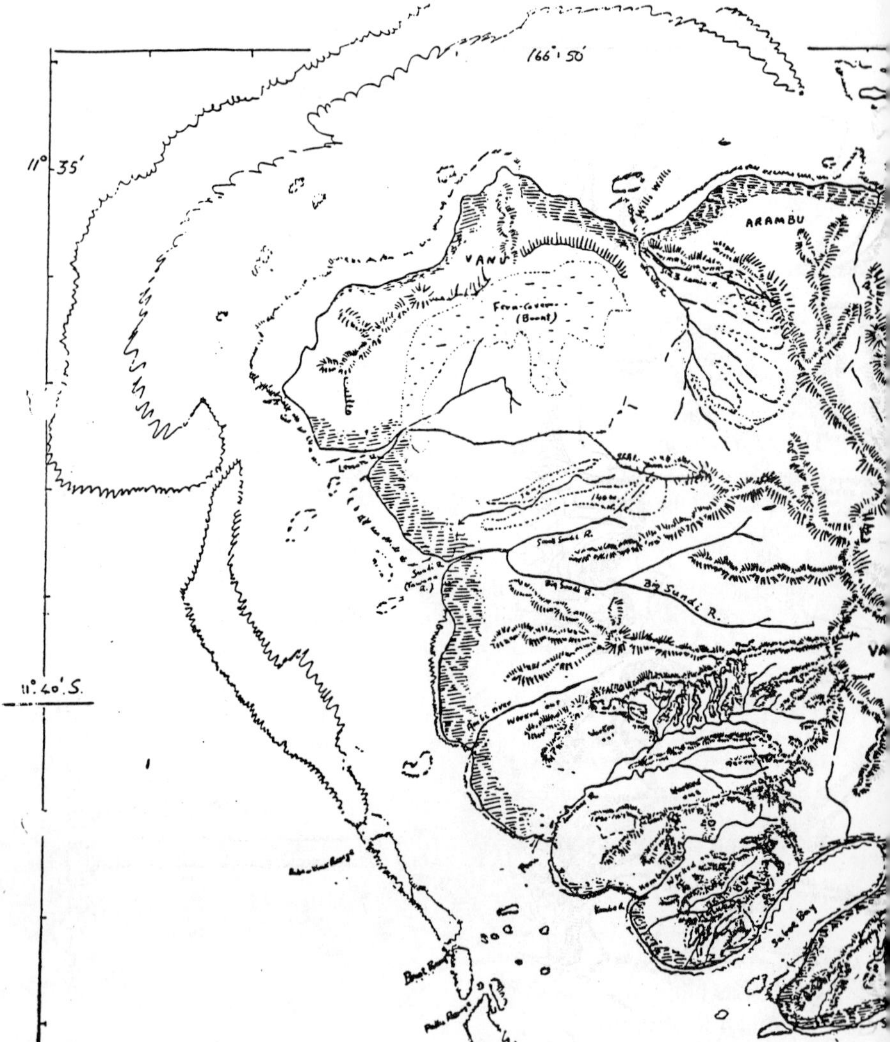

Crown Copyright. Reproduction based on Admiralty Chart 986 with the permission of the Controller of Her Majesty's Stationery Office.

VANIKORO ISLANDS
PART OF THE
SANTA CRUZ GROUP